Environment and the Arts

79.95

Less   20%

63.96

Purchased by:

D0205064

ENVIRONMENT AND THE ARTS

Environment and the Arts

Perspectives on environmental aesthetics

Edited by

ARNOLD BERLEANT
Long Island University, USA

Ashgate

Published by
Ashgate Publishing Limited
Gower Houe
Croft Road
Aldershot
Hants GU11 3HR
England

Ashgate Publishing Company
131 Main Street
Burlington, VT 05401-5600 USA

Ashgate website: http://www.ashgate.com

British Library Cataloguing in Publication Data
Environment and the arts : perspectives on environmental
   aesthetics
   1.Environment (Art) 2.Environment (Aesthetics)
   3.Architecture – Environmental aspects
   I.Berleant, Arnold, 1932-
   701.1'7

Library of Congress Cataloging-in-Publication Data
Environment and the arts : perspectives on environmental aesthetics /
edited by Arnold Berleant.
      p. cm.
   ISBN 0-7546-0543-4
   1. Nature (Aesthetics) I. Berleant, Arnold, 1932-

   BH301.N3 E58 2002
   111'.85–dc21

                                                             2001046127

ISBN 0 7546 0543 4

Typeset by Manton Typesetters, Louth, Lincolnshire, UK and printed and bound in Great Britain by MPG Books Ltd, Bodmin, Cornwall.

Contents

Notes on Contributors   vii

Acknowledgments   xi

Chapter 1   Introduction: Art, Environment and the Shaping of
             Experience   1
             Arnold Berleant

Chapter 2   Data and Theory in Aesthetics: Philosophical
             Understanding and Misunderstanding   23
             Ronald W. Hepburn

Chapter 3   The Two Aesthetic Cultures: The Great Analogy of Art
             and the Environment   39
             Yrjö Sepänmaa

Chapter 4   Art and Nature: The Interplay of Works of Art and
             Natural Phenomena   47
             Arto Haapala

Chapter 5   Nature Appreciation and the Question of Aesthetic
             Relevance   61
             Allen Carlson

Chapter 6   Embodied Metaphors   75
             Kaia Lehari

Chapter 7   Urban Richness and the Art of Building   89
             Pauline von Bonsdorff

Chapter 8   Front Yards   103
             Kevin Melchionne

Chapter 9   Aesthetics, Ethics and the Natural Environment   113
             Emily Brady

Chapter 10   From Beauty to Duty: Aesthetics of Nature and
              Environmental Ethics   127
              Holmes Rolston, III

Chapter 11   Embodied Music   143
              Arnold Berleant

Chapter 12   Dot.com Dot.edu: Technology and Environmental
              Aesthetics in Japan   157
              Barbara Sandrisser

Chapter 13   Environmental Directions for Aesthetics and the Arts   171
              Yuriko Saito

Index   187

Notes on Contributors

Arnold Berleant is Professor of Philosophy (Emeritus) at Long Island University. In four books (*The Aesthetic Field, A Phenomenology of Aesthetic Experience* (1970), *Art and Engagement* (1991), *The Aesthetics of Environment* (1992) and *Living in the Landscape: Toward an Aesthetics of Environment* (1997)) and numerous papers he has elaborated a field theory of aesthetics in which the main factors of creation, appreciation, performance, and object are interdependent and inseparable, bound up in an active process of aesthetic engagement. He has also written on particular arts, ethics and social philosophy. Berleant is Past President of the International Association for Aesthetics and has also served as its Secretary-General. He has also been Secretary-Treasurer of the American Society for Aesthetics and President of the International Advisory Committee of the Finland-based International Institute of Applied Aesthetics. He has lectured widely and his work has been translated into many languages.

Pauline von Bonsdorff studied at the University of Helsinki, where she took her doctoral degree in aesthetics in 1998. She has worked as a journalist and taught courses at the University of Helsinki in aesthetics, comparative literature and Swedish literature since 1987. In 1994 she was appointed assistant professor of aesthetics and from 1999–2001 she worked as an acting full professor of aesthetics. She has been active in the Finnish and Nordic Societies for Aesthetics and in the International Institute for Applied Aesthetics. A large part of von Bonsdorff's research is in environmental aesthetics with a focus on questions related to habitation and the relations between culture and nature. Her research interests also include the philosophy of mind and body, emotions, aesthetic experience, aesthetic value, contemporary art and feminist aesthetics. Her recent book-length publications in English are *The Human Habitat. Aesthetic and Axiological Perspectives* (1998) and *Aesthetics in the Human Environment*, ed. with Arto Haapala (1999).

Emily Brady is lecturer in Philosophy at Lancaster University and Docent in Aesthetics at the University of Helsinki. Her interests include environmental aesthetics and environmental philosopy, philosophy of mind (especially theories of imagination) and Kant's philosophy. She has published articles in the *Journal of Aesthetics and Art Criticism* and *Environmental Values*, and recently co-edited a festschrift on Frank Sibley's aesthetics. Her research in environmental aesthetics has been applied in a practical context through three research projects: 'Aesthetics and Environmental Management', with Finnish partners; 'Humans in the Land: The Ethics and Aesthetics of Cultural Landscapes,' with Norwegian partners; and 'Aesthetic Value in UK Environmental Conservation.' She is currently writing a book on aesthetics of the natural environment.

Allen Carlson is Professor of Philosophy at the University of Alberta, Edmonton, Canada. His teaching and research interests include aesthetics, environmental philosophy, and especially environmental and landscape aesthetics. He is co-editor of two collections of essays in this latter area and has published articles on the aesthetics of nature, on landscape appreciation, and on environmental assessment and evaluation. His research has appeared in various anthologies and in journals such as *The British Journal of Aesthetics, The Canadian Journal of Philosophy, Environmental Ethics, The Journal of Aesthetics and Art Criticism, Landscape Journal* and *Landscape Planning*. He recently published *Aesthetics and the Environment: The Appreciation of Nature, Art and Architecture* (2000).

Arto Haapala received his PhD at the University of London in 1988. In 1992 he was a Humboldt scholar in Bochum (Germany) and was appointed Professor of Aesthetics at the University of Helsinki in 1995. He was Visiting Professor at the Philosophy Department of Lancaster University (UK) in 1999–2000 and Fulbright Scholar and Affiliated Professor at the Philosophy Department of Temple University (Philadelphia) in 2001. His publications include *What is a Work of Literature?* (1989), *City as a Cultural Metaphor* (edited, 1998), *Aesthetics in the Human Environment* (edited with Pauline von Bonsdorff, 1999), and *Interpretation and Its Boundaries* (edited with Ossi Naukkarinen, 1999), as well as articles on different problems in aesthetics, particularly on ontology and interpretation. He has also done research in Martin Heidegger's philosophy and is currently working on a book on existential aesthetics.

Ronald W. Hepburn was born and educated in Aberdeen, Scotland, and spent the greatest part of his academic career in the Philosophy Department of the University of Edinburgh. There, from 1964, his teaching centered for some years on philosophy and literature, aesthetics more broadly, and philosophy of religion. From 1975 to his retirement in 1996, he held the Chair of Moral Philosophy. His research and writing have persistently explored topics on the borderlands of religion, morality and aesthetic experience: experience of art, but even more of nature, a neglected area in mid-twentieth-century analytical philosophy. Opposing inner forces and modes of thought have motivated and sustained his thinking: on the one side, openness to elemental experience, to the sublime, the numinous; and on the other an equally persistent scepticism, an extreme wariness over ambitious speculative claims. His earliest book was *Christianity and Paradox* (1958); and his two subsequent books, *'Wonder' and Other Essays* (1958) and *The Reach of the Aesthetic* (2001), are collections of papers on interrelated topics.

Kaia Lehari studied history of art at Leningrad State University, St Peterburg and received her PhD in Philosophy from the State University of Moscow with a dissertation on *Space in Architecture as an Aesthetic Problem*. She also studied at the Hochschule für die Industrielle Formgestaltung Burg Gebiechenstein, Halle and at Oxford University. Since 1976 she has lectured on the history and theory of architecture, industrial design and aesthetics as Assistant Professor at the Academy of Arts, Tallinn. For the past 15 years she has been interested in the problems of environmental aesthetics and has contributed to numerous conferences. She published her monograph, *Space. Environment. Place,* in 1997 (in Estonian) and was co-editor of the book, *Place and Location*. She has also published numerous articles and papers on environmental aesthetics in Estonian, Polish and English, including "The Metaphorical Landscape" and "The Road that Takes and Points," *Place and Location*. Tallinn : EKA, 2000; and "The Concept of Comfort and Its Aesthetical Meaning," *Proceedings of the 13th International Congress of Aesthetics*, **3**, Lahti, Helsinki, 1997.

Kevin Melchionne received his PhD from the Department of Philosophy of the State University of New York at Stony Brook, where he wrote on the aesthetics of everyday life. He is Director of Exhibitions at the Tyler School of Art, Temple University and Affiliated Faculty with Temple's Department of Philosophy. He is the curator of *Place of Memory: An Archaeology of Site-Specificity, 1969–1999; Lost Tribes and Aesthetic Adventures: the Picture Stories of Ben Katchor; Utopiaries: Fictions for Cultivated Space*; and *Soft Cell: The Bounds of Comfort*. Melchionne is a 2001 Pennsylvania Humanities Council Fellow for Arts Commentary and a former Renwick Fellow at the National Museum of American Art, Smithsonian Institution. He has written for the *Journal of Aesthetics and Art Criticism, Art Criticism, Philosophy and Literature*, and *American Ceramics*.

Holmes Rolston, III, University Distinguished Professor and Professor of Philosophy at Colorado State University, is often called 'the father of environmental ethics' as an academic discipline. He was recently featured in 'Fifty Key Thinkers on the Environment' (ed. Joy A. Palmer, 2001). Rolston has written seven books, including *Philosophy Gone Wild, Environmental Ethics, Science and Religion: A Critical Survey, Conserving Natural Value*, and most recently, *Genes, Genesis and God* (Cambridge University Press). He gave the Gifford Lectures, University of Edinburgh, 1997–98. Advocating environmental ethics, he has lectured on all seven continents and is Past President of the International Society for Environmental Ethics.

Yuriko Saito, born and raised in Japan, received her PhD in philosophy from the University of Wisconsin-Madison, and is Professor of Philosophy at the Rhode Island School of Design. Her writings on environmental aesthetics, environmental ethics, and Japanese aesthetics have appeared in *The Journal of Aesthetics and Art Criticism, Environmental Ethics, The Journal of Aesthetic Education, The British Journal of Aesthetics* and *Landscape*, as well as in the *Encyclopedia of Aesthetics*.

Barbara Sandrisser writes and lectures on Japanese aesthetic ideas, the aesthetics of environment, comparative aesthetics, and the aesthetics of architecture, vernacular architecture and landscape. For 12 years, she and two partners ran a mid-sized architectural and environmental design firm in New York City, The Paul Partnership. She has experience in conceptual, architectural and site design and in cultural and historical resources studies. Her interdisciplinary approach emphasizes cultural context, and balancing functional analysis with aesthetic perception. Her design projects range from rehabilitation and reuse of old neighborhoods and buildings to landscape concepts, master plans and contemporary structures. Her work appears in numerous books and journals, including *Architecture, Landscape, The Journal of Aesthetics* and *Art Criticism, The Journal of Value Inquiry*, and the Japanese journal, *Landscape Design*.

Yrjö Sepänmaa is Professor of Literature at the University of Joensuu, Finland and is currently on leave, having been awarded an Academy Professorship in environmental aesthetics by the Academy of Finland for a five-year period. He is the author of *The Beauty of Environment – A general model for environmental aesthetics* (1986, 1993, in Korean 2000). He has written extensively on environmental aesthetics, mostly in Finnish. Other topics that interest him are the future of art and the philosophy of literature. His ongoing research project, entitled *The Theory and Practice of Applied Environmental Aesthetics*, deals with questions related to the application of aesthetics to real world problem-solving situations in environmental culture.

Acknowledgments

R.W. Hepburn, 'Data and Theory in Aesthetics: Philosophical Understanding and Misunderstanding', has appeared in an earlier version in A. O'Hear (ed.) *Verstehen & Humane Understanding*, Royal Institute of Philosophy, Supplement 41. Permission has been obtained from the director, Cambridge University Press. It will also appear in R.W. Hepburn, *The Reach of the Aesthetic*, Ashgate, forthcoming.

Holmes Rolston, III, 'From Beauty to Duty: Aesthetics of Nature and Environmental Ethics' is also to be published in Diane P. Michelfelder and William H. Wilcox, Jr. (eds), *The Beauty Around Us: Environmental Aesthetics in the Scenic Landscape and Beyond*, Albany, NY: State University of New York (SUNY) Press, forthcoming.

Acknowledgements

Chapter 1

Introduction: Art, Environment and the Shaping of Experience

Arnold Berleant

At the culmination of two centuries of development the arts have achieved an honored place in Western culture.[1] Throughout the world great temples – we call them cultural centers – have been erected to the glory of the arts. News comes regularly of the construction of magnificent new art museums, concert halls and opera houses that are themselves architectural monuments. The summer season is replete with art and music festivals. The arts have become a major international industry.

At the same time as the arts acquired this status, they diverged from the other great institutions of contemporary society: from science by being normative and therefore not quantifiable; from religion by dwelling on the tangible, the bodily and the sensuous; from ethics by centering on intrinsic value and immediate satisfaction instead of rules and consequences; from politics and the established order by their subversive recognition of present pain and living injustice.

Our aesthetic engagement with the arts leads us to experiences of inherent value. Yet the arts are not the only place we have such important and deep experiences. The awareness of the intrinsic worth of human beings lies at the core of ethics. Our sense of the sacred and the blessed is a religious feeling of a richly present value. The perception of community rests on both of these but adds to them an aesthetic element in the inherent satisfactions of fulfilling human relationships.

Such experiences of intrinsic worth thus occur in many settings. What, then, is the unique gift of the arts? Perhaps we can say that it lies in their ability to focus on a quality of experience we call aesthetic. Yet the question of what makes something aesthetic has intrigued philosophers and art critics since the arts began to be discussed philosophically. This book hopes to contribute to our understanding of this fascinating but elusive issue. Such a contribution, however, is only part of its intent.

Throughout the century that has just ended, the arts have not only flourished in their customary forms as painting, sculpture, architecture, music, theater, literature and dance. They have pressed with growing insistence beyond their traditional boundaries. In Dada and the many innovative movements that followed, painting has incorporated taboo materials and subject matters,

1

employed texts in conjunction with images, broken out of the canvas and extended beyond the frame. Sculptures have enlarged their size and form so that we can walk on, through, and into them, and they have expanded into environments, both enclosed and out-of-doors. Architecture has gone beyond monumental edifices, challenging conventional shapes and structures and merging with the site. Music has employed new modes and ranges of tone production, both in the synthesizer and in the use of noise and other traditionally nonmusical sounds, and has explored different performance venues, as in environmental music. Poetry has relinquished rhyme and meter, while fiction has transformed the novel and other traditional forms. Dance has not only developed into different styles of modern dance but has broken away from conventional standards of gesture, lightness and grace. Theater, along with other arts, has developed forms that require active audience participation. Indeed, interactive art has become a common feature of the current scene. These apostasies of the modern arts not only pose a challenge to customary ways of appreciating art; they also challenge conventional ways of explaining them. Criticism has had to revise its classical standards and the theory of the arts to reconsider its age-old axioms.

One of the ways in which the arts have expanded has been to reach out into the larger environment: the natural environment, the urban environment and the cultural environment. The interrelations, indeed the fusion of art and environment, have become increasingly pronounced. This is more than an enlargement of the scope of art; it has become a challenge to its very core. The collaborative interplay between art and environment places traditional aesthetic theory in question, for it focuses many of the theoretical issues that the changes in the modern arts have raised. Indeed, it can be said that in aesthetic theory, as in the arts themselves, no belief or explanation has remained untouched.

Everything, then, is open to discussion and redefinition. The essays in this book contribute to such a reconsideration in ways that not only help clarify our ideas about theoretical issues but offer substantive insights of their own for particular arts and environments. Although their authors represent many different approaches and interests, this collection reflects the breadth with which they see the aesthetic in human life. They not only consider the general question of the bearing that environment and art have on each other but also examine specific arts, such as literature, architecture and music. And they deal with a variety of issues, such as whether aesthetic appreciation is similar or different in the arts and environments, how the aesthetic appears in the urban setting, the interplay of ethical factors with aesthetic ones, and the implications for aesthetic values of the cultural environment, from scientific technology to the conditions of everyday life, on art and environment.

Yet central to all of them is the value we call aesthetic. The aesthetic as we know it is a human experience of value. How, then, do things merit our respect for their intrinsic worth and how does the aesthetic contribute to their value? In probing this and related questions, the authors of these essays explore the many faces and places of this kind of experience, both in the arts and in environment. This last, which has come to be known as environmental aesthetics, is gaining ever greater attention and importance as the arts move beyond the frames by which custom has honored and protected them.

Let me introduce these studies by exploring several different matters. I want to say something about the leading ideas and main concerns of this new field of environmental aesthetics, about what environmental aesthetics is and what kinds of issues it is concerned with. It would be hard to discuss such questions without including the bearing that our understanding of the arts has on them, so the interrelations of environmental aesthetics and the arts, the theme of this collection, will be a frequent motif here. And because extending aesthetic ideas to environment expands its traditional scope, matters other than artistic and aesthetic ones, in particular ethical interests, become implicated in the discussion. Mentioning some of them will foreshadow the essays later in this book that develop those issues. All these concerns may lead us in curious and unexpected ways.[2]

The Arts and Environment

The philosophical study of the arts has traditionally been considered part of the field of aesthetics. Indeed, with some important exceptions, aesthetics has been preoccupied with the arts almost to the exclusion of nature, despite the fact that the founder of modern aesthetic theory, Immanuel Kant, developed his views at the close of the eighteenth century almost entirely with reference to nature. Nonetheless, as aesthetics emerged as an independent discipline, its application was primarily to the arts, and its hallmark has been the distinctiveness of its concepts and the independence of art from the rest of intellectual culture. Art was held to be a unique creation. Its objects were different from other things and enjoyed a special ontological status. And appreciating them required the beholder to adopt a unique attitude of disinterested contemplation.[3] Art thus gained its independence and importance, but at the price of isolation.

It is ironic that the theory Kant developed with reference to the aesthetic enjoyment of nature has been so powerful a force in the theory of the arts. It is equally ironic that the renewed interest in natural beauty has encouraged ideas that often run quite contrary to the Kantian aesthetic. What the essays in this collection show, in different ways and to different degrees, is how thoroughly the traditional distinction between art and nature has been breached. In fact, a concern with environment is one prominent direction among many that modern aesthetics has taken in pursuing interests that cross the boundary that has kept art and aesthetic appreciation distinct and separate from the other objects and experiences of human life. Moreover, pursuing aesthetics in environment involves many other fields of inquiry, fields that had been deliberately and steadfastly excluded from aesthetic theory, such as ethics, psychology, theory of culture, art theory, epistemology, criticism and even metaphysics. Work in environmental aesthetics is even being done that combines aesthetic interests with anthropology, social theory and political science, and still other literature in the field links it with biology and with the history of ideas. As with art itself, aesthetic theory has vastly expanded.

Still, a central focus remains. While the boundaries of environmental aesthetics may merge with other disciplines, its center is recognizable in its very name: the application of aesthetic concerns to environment. This, however, does not say enough, for how should we proceed? Empirically? Conceptually? Metaphysically? And on what sources should we draw? Criticism, artists' statements, the arts themselves, the philosophical tradition, or more recent intellectual movements? In exploring this rich yet unruly field of inquiry, the essays that follow will make use of all these.

Environmental Aesthetics

Interest in environmental aesthetics is relatively recent. It goes back only twenty or thirty years, although people have sung about the beauties of nature since ancient times. Even though environmental aesthetics is concerned with appreciating nature, it goes well beyond appreciation, as we shall see. While environmental aesthetics has received the most sustained attention from philosophers, the area has attracted scholars from many other disciplines, including art history, architecture, city and regional planning, and psychology. These fields bring different perspectives to bear on our understanding of environment, for environment is a prime example of a field of study that cannot be adequately understood from a single vantage point, not unlike environment itself. Environmental aesthetics bears on the creative arts, as well. Not only has the environment become the locus and subject matter for many artists in recent years, but how we grasp environment has implications for the practice of a number of different arts. Further, it has theoretical significance for our understanding of the more traditional arts of painting, sculpture and architecture. And finally, environmental aesthetics identifies important values in ecological thinking, ethics and other branches of the philosophical tree, values that are often overlooked.

It will help in locating environmental aesthetics to inquire further into what we understand by aesthetics and how we can interpret the idea of environment. Then I want to consider how environmental aesthetics has emerged both as an interest for artists and as a subject of aesthetic inquiry.

Changing Art and Changing Aesthetics

Aesthetics is the area of philosophic inquiry customarily concerned with understanding the arts and with beauty in nature. Traditional aesthetics has shaped our understanding of the so-called 'fine arts', and those arts have seemed to confirm the claims of that theory. Central among these claims are the assertions that art is a unique and special cultural institution, that it is self-sufficient and autonomous, that it requires a special mode of attention called disinterested contemplation, and that the art object must be isolated from its cultural context and from any utilitarian purposes to be properly appreciated. These claims seem admirably suited to the fine arts, and they appear to characterize the way we approach painting, sculpture, music, theater, dance and literature. Museums, theaters, concert halls and libraries all offer special places for their enjoyment, places where we step outside the normal run of experience and adopt an attitude of attending to those arts for their own sake alone. Aesthetics and the arts thus seem to complement each other: aesthetic theory guides our appreciation of the arts, while the fine arts exemplify the precepts of aesthetics.

Yet we have just concluded a century of enormous changes in the arts, changes that continue without rest and that are often difficult to accept. Since early in that century, artists have been challenging conventions, using uncustomary materials and techniques, and breaking out of traditional patterns of work, objects and audience. How can we grasp these changes, both with our eyes and with our minds? This is where aesthetics, as the theory of the arts, should help us.

Unfortunately, traditional aesthetic theory is remarkably inflexible here, insisting that these developments in the arts be forced into conformity with the principles that have already been formulated. Yet this richness in the range of the arts is important for aesthetic theory. The modern arts bring us back to experience, in all its specificity, its unevenness and its ephemerality. And the expansion of art leads us beyond the widened and enriched range of objects conventionally regarded as art to things and situations that cannot be easily circumscribed and cataloged. Video art and the use of electronic media, for example, have generated a domain of virtual reality that art has entered. Environmental artists such as Christo and Smithson have revised and reshaped portions of the earth's surface. And we have stepped outside the arts themselves into our environment, and have discovered its aesthetic character.

With the changing, expanding arts and the enlargement of aesthetic appreciation, we need to rethink the conventional explanations that aesthetics has offered. Such developments lead us far beyond distinct and separate objects and into situations in which the appreciator works along with the artist, and sometimes *becomes* the artist, all three joining in an aesthetic context of which they become constituent parts. Art, moreover, is no longer content with its special spaces and discrete forms but intrudes on building walls, subway stations and city streets. Our appreciation of art has also broken out of conventional patterns and perceptual modalities. We now engage actively with much of our art, at times entering into its space, as in environmental sculpture and environments, contributing to its process, as in interactive theater, bringing it into our work environments and, in general, integrating artistic and aesthetic activities into our everyday life. In one way or another, art has become environmental, and aesthetics must develop ideas that can encompass these developments. What we need is a theoretical account that describes and explains how we actively participate in the realm of art.

An Enlarged Sense of Environment

As our conception of art has enlarged, so too has our understanding of environment. Everyone is involved with environment, but what is it? The usual answer that environment is our natural surroundings obviously will not do, for this overlooks the fact that most people's lives are far removed from any kind of natural setting. Indeed, such a setting is even difficult to identify, since nature, in the sense of a landscape unaffected by human agency, has long since disappeared in nearly every region of the world.[4]

Yet the question of what environment denotes merely begins the process. For even if we expand the concept to encompass the reshaped landscapes and built structures in which an increasing proportion of the world's population now lives, this does not settle the question. In fact, to think of environment in the usual sense as surroundings suggests that it lies outside the person, that it is a container within which people pursue their private purposes. Environmental researchers seem to assume that there is some *thing*, 'the environment', and that this environment is constituted by our physical surroundings. Philosophers tend to agree, sometimes including the cultural and spiritual setting. Although custom and etymology may lead us to think of environment as surroundings, the idea remains complex and elusive.[5]

It may already be apparent that I do not ordinarily speak of 'the' environment. While this is the usual locution, it embodies a hidden meaning that is the source of much of our difficulty. 'The' environment circumscribes environment and turns it into a bounded object like any other, including art objects, an object that we can think of and deal with as if it were outside and independent of ourselves.[6] Yet one of the features of the natural world that many have noted, especially in discussions of the sublime, is its boundlessness. There are also different traditions sometimes brought into discussions of the aesthetics of nature, such as Native American, Buddhist and mystical traditions, that claim a unity of the human being with the natural world. In any case, it would beg the aesthetic question to assume that environment is separate from human involvement. Any such separation must be postulated or constructed, for where can we locate 'the' environment?

Where is 'outside' in this case? Is it the landscape that surrounds me where I stand? Is it the world beyond my window? Outside the walls of my room and house? On the other side of the clothes I wear? Is environment the air I breathe? The food I eat?

Yet the food metabolizes to become my body, the air swells my lungs and enters my bloodstream, my clothes are not only the outermost layer of my skin but complete and identify my style, my personality, my sense of self. My room, apartment or home define my personal space and world. And the landscape in which I move as I walk, drive or fly is my world, as well, ordered by my understanding, defined by my movements, and molding my muscles, my reflexes, my experience, my consciousness at the same time as I attempt to impose my will over it. Indeed, many of us spend much of our lives in the electronic space of television and computer networks, space that is entirely a human construction. 'The' environment is one of the last survivors of the mind–body dualism, a place beyond, which we think to contemplate from a distance. Such a purportedly outside environment dissolves into a complex network of relationships, connections and continuities of those physical, social and cultural conditions that circumscribe my actions, my responses, my awareness, and that give shape and content to the very life that is mine. For there is no outside world. There is no outside nor is there an inner sanctum in which I can take refuge from inimical external forces. The perceiver (mind) is an aspect of the perceived (body). In like manner, person and environment are continuous. Thus both aesthetics and environment must be thought of in a new, expanded sense. In both art and environment, we can no longer stand apart but join in as active participants.

Experiencing Environment

Let me turn now to the question of environmental experience. Aesthetic perception has usually been identified with surface qualities. After all, tradition tells us, this is what our senses bring us: a direct grasp of the sights and sounds of the world, an immediate apprehension of its tastes and smells, of the textures and resistance of things. Furthermore, the convenient handful of senses that common sense distinguishes is often grouped into two separate categories, the distance receptors and the contact receptors. Of the first, the visual sense allows us to discern light, color, shape, pattern, movement and distance, with its corresponding abstraction, space. Through hearing we grasp sounds as noise or pitch, the latter qualified by timbre, order, sequence, rhythm and other patterns. Philosophic custom has identified sight and hearing as the aesthetic senses, since they allow a kind of unperturbed reflection so long associated with ideal beauty.

To introduce the other senses into aesthetic perception we must overcome established tradition, for relying on the close involvement of the body disrupts the lofty contemplation considered essential for aesthetic pleasure.

This is an unfortunate division of the senses, especially for the perception of environment, from which we can never distance ourselves. The contact receptors are part of the human sensorium and are actively involved in environmental experience. The olfactory sense is intimately present in our awareness of place and time. Even the sense of taste can contribute to that consciousness, as Proust's madeleine eloquently testifies. Tactile experience, moreover, is not simple, as we so often think. It belongs to the haptic sensory system, which encompasses both tactual and subcutaneous perception of surface texture, contour, pressure, temperature, humidity, pain and visceral sensation. It also includes other sensory channels, usually overlooked or confounded with touch, that are different in important respects. The kinesthetic sense involves muscular awareness and skeletal or joint sensation by which we perceive position and solidity through the degrees of resistance of surfaces: hard, soft, sharp, blunt, firm, yielding. And we grasp body movement indirectly through the vestibular system: the awareness of climbing and descending, of turning and twisting, obstruction and free passage.[7]

Equally important with discriminating the sensory range of environmental perception is recognizing synaesthesia, one of whose meanings is the fusion of the sense modalities. For these different perceptual courses are distinguishable only on reflection, in analysis and under experimental conditions, not in experience. More forcefully than in any other situation, environmental perception engages the entire human sensorium through which we become part of environment in an interpenetration of body and place. Thus we not only *see* our living world: we move with it and act upon and in response to it. We grasp places not just through color, texture and shape, but with the breath, by smell, with our skin, through our muscular action and skeletal position, in the sounds of wind, water and traffic. The major dimensions of environment – space, mass, volume and depth – are encountered not primarily by the eye but with the body in our movements and actions.

Powerful as the sensory dimension is in perception, it alone does not constitute environmental experience. Factors other than those directly sensed join to shape and bend our experience. For sensation is not just sensory and not only physiological; it fuses with cultural influences. This is, in fact, the only way cultural organisms like humans can experience. The separation of sensation and meaning is another of those subtle divisions that actual experience does not support, for as social beings we perceive through the modalities of our culture.[8] The perception of snow, of rain, of distance, of weight, of confusion and order – all these are discriminated and identified according to the paradigms and categories embedded in cultural practices, never by retinal or tactile stimulation alone. The same can be said about noise level, the qualities of smell and taste, and the level of light.

The perceptual world in which we move is, then, wide and rich. Thoroughly and inseparably sensory and cultural, it is a complex experiential continuum.

In addition to the sensory modalities we have been discussing, the multidimensional context of human experience includes such things as shapes and lines, the timbral and wave patterns of sound, light and shadow, pattern and texture, temperature, muscular tension, directional motion and lines of force, volume and depth. And, of course, all perception occurs within the framework of the fundamental metaphysical dimensions of space, time and movement.[9]

The human environment is, in the final account, a perceptual system and, as such, an order of experience. Grasped from an aesthetic standpoint, it has sensory richness, directness and immediacy, together with cultural patterns and meanings that perception carries, and these give environment its thick texture. Environment, then, is a complex idea, the more so when we consider it aesthetically. We have already rejected many of its common definitions: as an entity – 'the' environment; as a container within which we carry on our activities; as our physical surroundings; as the world external to our thoughts, feelings and desires. In place of these self-congratulatory concepts we begin to understand environment as the physical–cultural realm in which people engage in all the activities and responses that compose the weave of human life in its many historical and social patterns. When the aesthetic factor is recognized, perceptual directness, with its strong focus on immediacy and presence, becomes preeminent.

We come to recognize, then, that aesthetic perception is never purely physical sensation and never discrete and timeless. It is always contextual, mediated by the variety of conditions and influences that shape all experience. And because we live as part of a cultural environment, our aesthetic perception and judgment are inevitably cultural. This is not just an abstract statement; it denotes the unending variety of cultural perception. Each society at every historical period has its distinctive manner of perceiving aesthetically. This, indeed, is what may be meant when we speak of knowing a different culture, acquiring its mind-set, its feel of the world. In the arts it provides the cultural adventure we find in reading world literature, engaging with exotic art objects and viewing international cinema. It is one of the great incentives to travel. And since environment is cultural, any discussion of environmental aesthetics must, by that fact, involve what we may call a cultural aesthetic.[10]

Appreciating Environment

The idea of appreciating environment is a relatively new concept and one that enlarges the meaning of environment. It means rejecting the view that sees environment as an objective space occupied by external objects that interest us only in so far as they can be used for our own purposes. In the West it is only since the eighteenth century that landscape has been recognized as having significant aesthetic value. Since then there has been a gradual process of recognizing and preserving scenic views and areas whose importance lies apart from any industrial or commercial value they might possess. Nearly every nation and region has now set aside parks and other areas for their aesthetic value, usually in combination with historical, cultural and recreational values.

Yet this attitude toward the aesthetic value of environment resembles the traditional attitude toward art. It has tended to mean identifying places that have aesthetic value and setting them apart from the rest of our environment, much as we place art objects in museums. However, the deliberate quarantining of the aesthetic is no universal idea or practice. In fact, it is an exception to the way in which many other cultural traditions incorporate the aesthetic into social life. Much can be learned of cultural integration from the traditional civilizations of China and Japan, from the cultures of Bali and native North America, from the various indigenous populations of Oceanic, Africa and the Americas. Vestiges of the aesthetic in environment survive in the West outside the conventional sites for art in the rituals of religious worship, in fine dining, in gardening and in outdoor activities not subverted by the telic obsession with competition, such as strolling, hiking, camping, recreational swimming and canoeing.

Appreciating environment, then, is not a matter of looking at an external landscape. In fact, it is not just a matter of looking at all. Sometimes writers attempt to associate environment with our physical surroundings and landscape, with our visual perception of a scene and the ideas and attitudes through which we interpret it.[11] Yet, as we have seen, considering human beings apart from their environment is both philosophically unfounded and scientifically false. Furthermore, it leads to disastrous practical consequences, as the ecological movement has demonstrated. Similarly, our understanding of experience has expanded greatly to involve all the bodily senses and not just the eye. We now recognize that the conscious body does not observe the world contemplatively but participates actively in the experiential process.[12]

All this bears intimately on environmental aesthetics, for the appreciation of perceptual values inherent in environment involves physical engagement. Environmental appreciation is not just looking approvingly at lovely scenery. It occurs in activities like driving down a winding country road, tramping along a hiking trail, paddling the course of a stream, all these with acute attention to the sounds, the smells, the feel of wind and sun, and the nuances of color, shape and pattern. It is also found in the deep awareness, so rare in the modern world, of living in a house and a place to which we belong intimately, both in present experience and in memory. And it arises in the kinesthetic sense of the masses and spaces that incorporate us. *Incorporate* is a good word here, for it means literally to bring into the body, in this case to bring our bodies into environment, and this engagement in a whole is what the aesthetic experience of environment involves.

Environmental aesthetics moves the notion of appreciation toward a more inclusive and engaged experience than we usually ascribe to the arts. What

Walter Benjamin said about the impossibility of contemplation in filmic experience holds equally with the other arts in the present day and even more insistently with environment. It is not only the fact of motion that makes contemplation impossible in film; it is the insistence with which film engages the viewer, transforming one at the very least into an intent voyeur and, more likely, into a silent witness or an involved onlooker in the manner of a Greek chorus.[13]

At the same time, and as part of this embodied experience, we carry our knowledge, beliefs and attitudes with us, for these participate in the process of experience and enable us to structure and interpret it. Such influences of thought and attitude also point up a crucial fact about aesthetic experience of both art and of environment. It is that aesthetic valuation is not a purely personal experience, 'subjective', as it is often mistakenly called, but a social one. In engaging aesthetically with environment as with art, the knowledge, beliefs, opinions and attitudes we have that are an inseparable part of the experience are largely social, cultural and historical in origin. These direct our attention; they open or close us to what is happening and prepare or impede our participation. Here, as elsewhere, the personal is infused with the social. We are not pure sense perceptors and experience is not solely sensation. Social forms and cultural patterns equip us with the means for ordering and grasping the occasions in which we are involved through myths, theories and other explanations. In experiencing environment aesthetically, therefore, we are engaged in a social activity, not a purely personal one, and frequently on a public occasion. Our sociality is inherent in our aesthetic experience, whether of art or of environment.

This understanding of environmental experience carries interesting and important implications for appreciation. It is helpful here to think of what it means to appreciate art. Appreciating the arts requires developing a sensibility to perceptual qualities. It is naive to identify individual arts with particular senses, such as painting with sight and music with hearing. We have noted how all the senses are involved in all experience, usually directly but also imaginatively, to some degree. However, what varies is the relative prominence of the different sense modalities. Thus the visual sensory dimension does predominate in certain arts, the auditory in others, while all along engaging the other sensory channels. Yet more than physical perception, what every art requires is a developed sensibility, an acute and discriminating perceptual awareness. In painting, for instance, this includes a sharpened awareness of color qualities and interrelationships, a sense of the balance of masses and of composition, in general, a feel for the movement of line, for the degree and contrast of light and shadow, and a sensitivity to detail as well as to larger forms. In music it is an ability to listen *into* the sound, to hear the movement of inner voices, to discern different simultaneous rhythms, to notice the qualities and differences of timbres and the nuances within a single timbre, to feel the compelling force of movement and the subtle elasticities within the overall metric. We can identify the same kind of perceptual discernment in the other arts, in dance and architecture, for example, each of which has its own complex of sensibility.

This applies to environment in much the same way. Environmental appreciation employs our sensory capacities with a range and complexity that likely exceeds the other arts, making it difficult to limit or circumscribe. We experience the perceptual discrimination of textures as well as colors, the somatic consciousness of masses and volumes, the depth and directionality of sounds, the feel of wind, sun and moisture on the skin, the kinesthetic awareness of the different surfaces under our feet and of our movement as we ascend, descend or move unevenly along a relatively level surface, curving, turning or traveling in an approximately straight direction. We must recognize in environmental appreciation the importance of somatic sensibility: the bodily awareness of the force of mass, the pull of empty space, the kinesthetic contribution in physical movement, along with the visual, auditory, tactile, olfactory and gustatory qualities that suffuse all experience. Environment, more than Wagner's music dramas, may be the true *Gesamtkunstwerk*, the total, all-encompassing work of art.

People working in the environmental arts, such as architecture, landscape design, garden design and urban planning, make full use of these perceptual capacities, sometimes deliberately, but often without conscious awareness that they are engaged in the process of shaping environmental experience. What has been lacking is a theoretical articulation of that sensibility and a more explicit account of environmental appreciation, although a beginning has been made in this direction.[14]

In spite of the readiness with which environmental appreciation has often been distinguished from the appreciation of art, their dissimilarity may not be so obvious. Is the aesthetic appreciation of nature or environment different from the appreciation of art? This question has, in fact, been answered both ways. If a difference should be maintained, we may then ask whether there are any respects in which appreciation in both cases has a generic resemblance. And if it does, what implications does this have for traditional aesthetics?[15]

My own view is that these are fundamentally similar forms of aesthetic engagement that work in particular ways on the specific occasions in which we come to individual arts and environments. Appreciating both individual arts and particular environments is an intimate involvement that draws at once on the fusion of our multiple sensory capacities, on our knowledge of the objects involved, on our memories of past encounters and on our enlargement of these experiences in imagination. We employ these capacities, all of which can be cultivated and extended, whenever we appreciate something aesthetically. At the very least, we cannot be content with uncritical assumptions about aesthetic appreciation. Environmental aesthetics, in raising this question, forces us to at least consider alternatives to the traditional view.

There is another side to environmental appreciation that we should not overlook, for experiencing aesthetic values includes more than having an acute sensitivity to the delights of landscape. As noise is more insistent than music, commercial signs than paintings and a factory than a grove of trees, dominant environmental experience does not always assume a positive form. The aesthetics of environment must also recognize landscapes that damage us in various ways: by destroying the identity of place and our affection for places, by disrupting architectural coherence, by imposing sounds and smells that may injure as well as repel, or by making our living environment hostile and even uninhabitable from air, water or noise pollution. Part of their criticism is aesthetic: an offense to our perceptual sensibilities and an immediate encounter with negative value. The significance of environmental appreciation thus becomes greater at the same time as its scope increases. No longer confined to the safe precincts of gardens and parks, the boundaries of the aesthetic must be redefined to encompass all of nature, city as well as countryside, factory as well as museum, desert wastes and urban wastelands as well as mountain-rimmed fjords.

The Aesthetics of Environment

How, finally, can we explain environmental aesthetics? As the aesthetics of poetry or painting is the study of the aesthetic character and values in these arts, which includes our appreciative encounter with them, so environmental aesthetics examines aesthetic experience and value in environment. Our understanding of the experience of aesthetic value in the arts forms the bases for the different verbal judgments that can be made of them: critical, interpretive, philosophical, and the like. Similarly, environmental aesthetics requires a grasp of what environment is, of what environmental experience is, of its aesthetic dimension, and of the kind of values that develop there.

'It is something,' Thoreau once wrote, 'to be able to paint a particular picture, or to carve a statue and so to make a few objects beautiful; but it is far more glorious to carve and paint the very atmosphere and medium through which we look, which morally we can do. To affect the quality of the day, that is the highest of arts.'[16] The aesthetic environment is everyone's medium; the art of environment, the art of human living. For the perceptual world is the human world; our capacities and limitations affect the possibilities and the boundaries of that world.

To take the world fully, to employ the entire range of perception, is to magnify our experience, our human world, our lives. The goal, then, is an expanded but discriminating awareness as part of a totally engaged organic, social life. This requires alertness, intelligence and active involvement in the full scope of experience. The aesthetic sense of environment is a central aspect of such a life.

This enlargement of the scope, boundaries and objects of aesthetics raises a host of issues. Moreover, there is certainly no unanimity among scholars concerned with such questions, as the essays in this book testify. That

makes the debates all the more fascinating, for not only do the many dis-
agreements cry out for resolution but their consequences reach well beyond
the arts and even beyond environmental concerns. Let me mention just a few
of these issues, many of which will reappear in the essays that follow.

Some Current Issues

Environmental Aesthetics and the Aesthetics of Nature

It is useful to distinguish environmental aesthetics from the aesthetics of
nature. Nature has long been the object of aesthetic interest, and we can
trace expressions of it back to ancient myths and to the beginnings of
philosophical thought. Yet environmental aesthetics is different from the
aesthetics of nature. 'Environment' is the more inclusive term, for it
encompasses places and objects other than those in the so-called 'natural
world', such as design, architecture and the city. Furthermore, different
writers regard environment in distinctly different ways, at times objectifying
it as panoramic scenery, at other times including surroundings close and
personal, and even sometimes, as I prefer to do, considering environment
the contextual setting that embraces the aesthetic perceiver as a contributing
factor. To render the matter still more complex, environment may refer to
specific types and instances, such as a particular wilderness area, marine
environment or shopping mall, or it may be treated as a general category.

Indeed, whether or not there is a difference between nature and
environment, and what that difference is, are significant questions for
aesthetics. Are these terms at bottom largely synonymous or do they imply
distinct and different regions of inquiry? The meaning and relation between
the aesthetics of nature and environmental aesthetics is fertile ground for
inquiry, along with their bearing on the aesthetics of the arts.

Further, in spite of the readiness with which environmental appreciation
has often been distinguished from the appreciation of art, their obvious
dissimilarity may not be so obvious. Is the aesthetic appreciation of nature
or environment clearly different from the appreciation of art? This question
has, in fact, been answered both ways in the literature. If a difference should
be maintained, we may then ask whether there are any respects in which
appreciation in both cases has generic resemblances? And if it does, what
implications does this have for traditional aesthetics?

Environmental Aesthetics and Applied Aesthetics

The engaged character of environmental appreciation presents a challenge
to another tenet of traditional theory, the concept of aesthetic disinterestedness.
The idea of disinterestedness emerged in the eighteenth century out of
discussions first about ethics and later about art. It attempted to define a

clear domain for aesthetic appreciation based on valuing something for its own inherent qualities, unsullied by any practical interest or use. Practical concerns, it was held, confuse and adulterate the aesthetic qualities we have learned to appreciate in the arts.

The belief in the autonomy of art, however, finds little refuge in environment, where appreciation is so often inseparable from matters of practical interest, whether in the siting of a building, the design of a road or garden, or simply a trek along a woodland path. Kant's classical formulation, '[T]aste in the beautiful is alone a disinterested and free satisfaction; for no interest, either of sense or of reason, here forces our assent,' may suit the arts, on some counts, but it is hard to reconcile with many instances of the enjoyment of natural beauty.[17]

Can we retain the notion of disinterestedness in some fashion? The claim that aesthetics can be applied to situations and objects of utility forces us either to assert levels of aesthetic purity, to devise two alternative theories of aesthetic value, or somehow to reconcile the many forms of aesthetic appreciation in a single inclusive account. Indeed, environmental aesthetics can be seen as a bridge between traditional forms of aesthetic appreciation and the recognition of significant aesthetic value in other domains conventionally excluded from the fine arts, such as ceramics and other crafts, design, urban and regional planning, the circumstances of daily life, the folk and popular arts, and many of the other activities that form the life of every human culture. It also confronts us with the problems connected with environmental assessment, where practical considerations involving historic buildings, landscape preservation, and resource protection and use are closely bound up with aesthetic ones.

Environmental Aesthetics and Environmental Ethics

While the call for the autonomy of art has a noble and romantic ring and may encourage support as a way of protecting the arts from political or social interference, maintaining such isolation becomes difficult, even implausible, in so practical a domain as environment. The closer and more intimate our relation to environment becomes, the more we are enmeshed in a network of consequences, rights, interests and goals of many sorts. Often, indeed, aesthetic and ethical values seem to be in direct opposition in environment even more strikingly than in art. This appears in conflicts between the desire to preserve historic structures and districts and the need to supply sufficient, adequate housing, or to maintain scenic views while accommodating the need for commercial construction, power transmission or fast roads.

On the other hand, ethical and aesthetic values can be mutually supportive. Perhaps, indeed, an aesthetic interest in environment can help achieve moral ends. Surely increasing aesthetic value is part of what we mean by improving the quality of life. Moreover, a growing body of evidence suggests that an environment rich in positive aesthetic value not only increases feelings of well-being but reduces the incidence of physical and mental illness and of social ills, such as vandalism and crime. Here is an important area for further study.

Furthermore, since aesthetic value is a good in itself, even if not always an exclusive and isolated good, it is worthy of support for its own sake, and so can itself become a moral end. Environment as a social as well as a personal value is an important locus of aesthetic interest; but recognizing intrinsic aesthetic value in environment does not require that it stand apart from uses and purposes that are not aesthetic. In some of the most interesting cases, in fact, environmental use and beauty are inseparable, as in a scenic highway or a well-disposed farming landscape. Programs for the purchase of development rights in order to preserve agricultural landscapes, and zoning ordinances that protect scenic views express moral commitment and political will in the service of an aesthetic end.

The relation between environmental ethics and aesthetics is rich in possibilities for elaboration. Do aesthetic values play a part in the overall structure of an ethics of environment as one of the factors to be sought out and safeguarded? This could give aesthetic concerns a secondary place in environmental ethics. Yet, because of its traditional focus on intrinsic value, aesthetic value may provide a foundation of intrinsic value for the ethical values in environment, as some have argued. If this be so, then these ethical values can be said to derive from aesthetic ones. Such an elevation of aesthetic value has implications for ethical theory that lie over and beyond its application to environment. The relation between ethics and aesthetics has great significance and is gaining increasing importance. Some of the essays that follow offer fresh and fruitful insights on the issue.[18]

Art and Environment

The arts have joined environment in many ways and to many degrees. Sculpture, for example, is often exhibited in outdoor settings that may range from a lawn or garden to a 'borrowed landscape' of fields and rolling hills. Environmental sculptures may use a wide variety of natural objects, materials and settings. Music may incorporate environmental features by placing musicians or speakers in different parts of the hall or by using outdoor sounds and settings. Theater's venerable history of open air performances in Greek and Roman amphitheaters continues today in street theater. And dance has been performed using a variety of natural settings, including the seashore.

The interrelations between the aesthetics of the arts and environment raise still more challenging and complex issues. Recognizing various environmental domains, such as natural, wilderness, rural, agricultural, marine, urban and architectural environments, poses its own questions. Are the differences among such diverse types of environment comparable to those in traditional aesthetics among poetry, painting, music and dance? If they are, what then is the relation of these various environmental domains with each other in discussions of aesthetic value, appreciation and judgment? The issues concerning appreciation in the arts and in environment that I spoke of earlier recur here in somewhat different form. For example, does appreciating a natural landscape resemble or differ from appreciating an urban one? If it differs, what other aesthetic criteria are needed in critically judging them? Furthermore, how do these differing modes of appreciation relate to the appreciation of art? What, again, do our answers to these questions imply for traditional accounts of appreciation as disinterested and contemplative? Do these different environmental domains raise new problems for an inclusive aesthetic theory or do they simply embody dissimilar values?

The questions I have raised not only multiply the more we consider them but they also have great significance for the discipline of aesthetics. Whether the difference between the aesthetics of environment and the aesthetics of art is so basic that they demand two different theoretical explanations or whether a single theory can accommodate both has momentous consequences for aesthetic theory. If the aesthetics of nature, environment and art can be joined in the same theory, we must somehow develop a structure open enough to accommodate both domains in ways that honor their distinctive characteristics.

This book does not hope to resolve the issues raised here. Its contributors have different views on these subjects. Yet how they are answered has profound implications for the discipline of aesthetics.

The Broader Scene

Before turning to the reflections in the essays that follow on the questions I have raised here, let me conclude this introduction by suggesting a larger context for the normative issues that join environment and the arts. Values, and the theories that institutionalize them, have not fared well in the twentieth century. The hegemony of the sciences has exercised theoretical as well as economic and political power over intellectual culture. Philosophers have been no less vulnerable than others, and many of the philosophical movements that have flourished in the last two centuries have modeled themselves, in one way or another, on the approach, scope and methodology of the sciences. Many philosophers have accepted only quantitative and factual data as cognitively significant and have restricted their commentary to reflections, distinctions and formulations on and about them. As a consequence of this, values have been relegated to inconsequence or dismissed as non-cognitive, subjective, emotive or entirely irrational. Yet the pressing practical need to confront normative issues has begun to force philosophical thought out of such a cul-de-sac and made it necessary for both intellectuals and activists to develop ways of dealing with the multitude of conflicts that grow more and more insistent in the present day.

Environmental issues have been in the forefront here, joined by economic and political ones. Although controversies in these areas cannot always be resolved by quantitative methods, they cannot therefore be dismissed as merely arbitrary and subjective. The end of the twentieth century is a bloody banner to such conflicts of values: ethnic wars that have spread across most regions of the earth, global economic institutions and policies that threaten societies everywhere, and cultural conflicts, not unrelated to these, that breed on exclusiveness and intolerance. If we cannot find reasonable means of dealing with these conflicts, we clear the ground for impulse, irrationality and the exercise of bald power. What can the aesthetics of environment and the arts contribute here?

The issues around environmental values force us to see that these values are not purely personal, arbitrary or irrational, but lie at the heart of human life. Human well-being is not a subjective matter. It rests on the political, social and economic conditions in which we live: the governments we live under, the food we eat, the air we breathe, the relationships that form the fabric of our societies. These conditions are hard and real, and they are largely shaped by our institutions and practices. Thus our ideas about environment and art, embedded in our cultural institutions, are important beyond themselves, for they focus attention on the lived quality of our experience and on the central place this must have in any account of human welfare.

If human values are basic in practice, so may they be in theory, as well. It might prove useful to turn philosophical logic on its head and consider normative philosophy as basic philosophy. Positive experience would then become the touchstone for judgments of value. Yet what defines positive experience? Experience, one might answer, that is intrinsically satisfying and fulfilling and that, at the same time, does not diminish the satisfaction and fulfillment of others. Aesthetic appreciation can stand as a model for such experience, for its fulfillment usually does not abuse or casually impair the well-being of other living things. Environmental values enter here, for these include respecting the earth and its features – values that are as much aesthetic as ethical. Recognizing these values does not commit us to inaction or to the inviolability of environments but rather to restraint, prudence and considered judgment.

Our aesthetic experience of things, both in art and in nature, lies, then, in recognizing their qualitative values. While such experience is primarily perceptual, it is at the same time an embodied sign of the worth that such things as works of art, places and even people possess in themselves, a sign of their moral value. Because something is valued aesthetically for its own sake, we recognize the value it has in itself that makes it worthy of respect. The experience of aesthetic value helps us learn such respect and instructs us in recognizing and appreciating it. In the reverence of aesthetic appreciation, we can gain reverence and respect for the earth.

Here may lie the fundamental coalescence of aesthetics and ethics. However, the occasions and content of normative experience are affected by historical cultures, including customs, traditions, social structure and dynamics, and education. That is why they are not absolute but variable. We have finally begun to realize that the Archimedean point for which Descartes longed cannot be found in our world of process and change. This means that there cannot be any firm and unmoving foundation for values or for philosophy in general. However, this is no unhappy fate, for we discover in the variety and mutability of environment and in the ceaseless searching of the arts in the realms of perception both the exemplar of that mutability and a model for living as part of it.

Not all the essays that follow accept the characterizations of environment that I have offered here. Yet in their different approaches and in their different ways of dealing with similar issues, they stand as important and eloquent statements and exhibit the rich variety of possible responses. What distinguishes this collection is its pursuit of these questions along the twin tracks of art and environment, tracks that often run parallel, cross and sometimes converge into a single aesthetic course. Original, imaginative, and challenging in their inquiries, these essays demonstrate how the interplay of environment and the arts can illuminate both domains, two vital and experiential intellectual centers of our time.

Notes

1   Earlier versions of some passages in this essay have appeared in A. Berleant (1992), *The Aesthetics of Environment*, Philadelphia: Temple University Press;* the Introduction to A. Berleant and A. Carlson (eds) (1998), *The Journal of Aesthetics and Art Criticism*, **56** (2), a special issue on environmental aesthetics; and A. Berleant (1997), *Living in the Landscape: Toward an Aesthetics of Environment*, Lawrence, KS: University Press of Kansas. I am happy to acknowledge with thanks the permission of *The Journal of Aesthetics and Art Criticism*, Temple University Press and the University Press of Kansas for permission to use this material. *© 1992 by Temple University. All Rights Reserved.

2   I have explored many of the issues examined here more fully in other writings. In addition to the works cited above, see A. Berleant (1997), 'Aesthetics and community', *Living in the Landscape*, pp. 135–55. References to more recent publications may be found on my home page at <*http://home.acadia.net/userpages/arn/index.html*>.

3   A. Berleant (1991), *Art and Engagement*, Ch. 1 and *passim*, Philadelphia: Temple University Press.

4   This includes such 'remote' locations as Antarctica, the ocean depths and the highest mountains. Most wilderness areas are not primeval nature but regions that reflect the earlier and continuing effects of human action in the form of land clearing, erosion, strip mining, reforestation, acid rain and modifications of the surface of the land and in the distribution of water; in alterations of climate induced by the vast expanses of paved surfaces in urbanized areas, introduced species of flora and fauna, and now in

the desiccation of the ozone layer, to whose consequences in global warming and increased solar radiation no area of the planet is impervious.

5   See the discussion of the definition of environment in Berleant (1991), *Art and Engagement*, pp. 81, 224.

6   This may offer some explanation for exploitative practices toward natural resources, and for turning the edges of our streets and highways into linear refuse dumps. Yrjö Sepänmaa's *The Beauty of Environment*, the earliest comprehensive and systematic inquiry into environmental aesthetics, accepts the conventional usage. Although his sensitive discussion of the concept of environment retains its association with the external world of an observer, he expands its scope to include the cultural environment and the constructed environment, in addition to the natural one. See Y. Sepänmaa (1986, 1993), *The Beauty of Environment*, Denton: Environmental Ethics Books, p. 17.

7   A. Berleant (1964), 'The Sensuous and the Sensual in Aesthetics', *The Journal of Aesthetics and Art Criticism*, **XXIII** (2), 1964, 185–92. Gibson identifies five perceptual systems: the basic orienting system (movement), the auditory system, the haptic system, the taste–smell system and the visual system. 'Information about the world can be obtained with any perceptual system alone or with any combination of perceptual systems working together' (J.J. Gibson (1966), *The Senses Considered as Perceptual Systems*, Boston: Houghton Mifflin, pp. 55, 97). Also see J.J. Gibson (1976), *The Ecological Approach to Visual Perception*, Boston: Houghton Mifflin; and H.R. Schiffman (1976), *Sensation and Perception, An Integrated Approach*, New York: Wiley, pp. 119–21.

8   I use the term 'culture' here in its anthropological sense, exclusively. While this meaning is itself much discussed, it is perhaps safe to say that culture refers to the meanings, ideas, values, ideals, customs, skills and practical and fine arts that human beings learn as members of a given social group, past or present.

9   A rich body of material on perceptual experience continues to come from the phenomenological and existential traditions, following the seminal work of Husserl, Sartre, Heidegger, Merleau-Ponty, Schütz and others, in developing such concepts as body space, life space, lived space and lived time.

10 Geographers and anthropologists describe how different cultural groups develop distinctive ways of carrying on the many activities by which their lives proceed: food production, family organization, economic exchange, land use, ritual. They speak of the physical landscape that reflects these activities and that assumes distinctive patterns and shapes as a 'cultural landscape'. The concept of a *cultural aesthetic* is a correlative notion that emerges from the ideas about aesthetic perception I have been developing. A cultural aesthetic is the perceptual matrix that constitutes the distinctive environment of a society.

11 D.W. Meinig (ed.) (1979), *The Interpretation of Ordinary Landscapes*, New York: Oxford University Press, p. 3.

12 The distinction between 'environment' and 'landscape', then, must be drawn differently to mirror this new understanding. If environment is falsely regarded as objective, and if it joins landscape in being infused with the beliefs and attitudes of those who are part of it, what then is the difference between the two? Perhaps we can say that environment is the more general term, embracing the many factors, including the human ones, that combine to form the conditions of life. Landscape, reflecting the experience of an immediate location, is more particular. It is an individual environment, its peculiar features embodying in a distinctive way the factors that constitute any environment and emphasizing the human presence as the perceptual activator of that environment. We can express this somewhat differently by saying that landscape is a lived environment. 'Environment' is used here in this more general sense, but in discussing a region or in considering a specific location, it may be useful to particularize it by speaking of it as a landscape or as *the* environment or *this* environment.

13   W. Benjamin (1969), 'The work of art in the age of mechanical reproduction', *Illuminations*, New York: Schocken Books, pp. 238–40. What Walter Benjamin says about the changes in perception forced on us by film applies even more insistently in environment.

14   A. Berleant, A. (1991, ch. 4); A. Berleant (1992); A. Berleant (1997, 'Aesthetics and community', pp. 135–55); Y. Sepänmaa (1986, 1993); A. Carlson (1979), 'Appreciation and the natural environment', *The Journal of Aesthetics and Art Criticism*, **37**, 267–75.

15   On the relation between the appreciation of art and of beauty in nature, see Hepburn's classic discussion in R.W. Hepburn (1984), 'Contemporary aesthetics and the neglect of natural beauty', *'Wonder' and Other Essays. Eight Studies in Aesthetics and Neighboring Fields*, Trowbridge: Edinburgh University Press, pp. 9–35.

16   H.D. Thoreau (1966), *Walden*, New York: Norton, p. 61.

17   I. Kant (1790, 1951), *Critique of Judgment*, trans. J.H. Bernard, New York: Hafner, s.5. See also ss. 43 and 45.

18   The essays in the present volume by Brady and Rolston confront such issues. There is a growing literature on the interrelation of ethical and aesthetic values. Some other useful sources are M.M. Eaton (1997), 'Aesthetics: the mother of ethics?', *The Journal of Aesthetics and Art Criticism*, **55**, 355–64; a reply by A. Berleant (1999), 'Mothering and metaphor', *The Journal of Aesthetics and Art Criticism*, **57**, 363–4; and a response by M.M. Eaton (1999), 'The mother metaphor', *The Journal of Aesthetics and Art Criticism*, **57**, 365–6. See also H. Rolston (1988), 'Valuing aesthetic nature', *Environmental Ethics, Duties to and Values in the Natural World*, Philadelphia: Temple University Press, pp. 232–45; and E.C. Hargrove (1989), 'An ontological argument for environmental ethics', *Foundations of Environmental Ethics*, Englewood Cliffs, NJ: Prentice-Hall, pp. 191–201.

Chapter 2

Data and Theory in Aesthetics: Philosophical Understanding and Misunderstanding

Ronald W. Hepburn

This essay has two parts: both parts concern philosophy's understanding (or misunderstanding) of its subject-matter, its data – in the field of aesthetics. The first part considers aesthetics in its role as philosophy of art: the second part considers aesthetics as concerned also with the appreciation of nature.

Aesthetics as Philosophy of Art

Philosophers who write aesthetic theories have tended to see the key concepts of their account of aesthetic judgment and appreciation as grounded in their distinctive philosophical view of the human situation. The data on which their aesthetic theories are founded include their broad philosophical vision as well as their experience of works of art themselves and the writings of art critics. Moreover, aesthetic theory has often been seen, not as a detached, specialized, abstract, self-contained study that aims only at philosophical insight, but as having a potential impact upon art criticism and appreciation of the arts themselves at any time. The key concept or cluster of concepts that comprises the core of a theory, such as Imitation, Expression and Formal Unity, can be used to commend, celebrate, deplore or correct trends in art, and even sometimes to comment upon particular works of art.

Others today, however, see those views of aesthetics as thoroughly wrongheaded. Philosophers of art – they say – need to show a much greater modesty before artists and works of art. They must defer to those who have authority in the creation of art, an authority a philosopher does not have, *qua* philosopher: they must defer, not dominate or domineer or pontificate. Grand philosophical theories are sure to distort and misrepresent the arts, and so inhibit their development. Richard Kuhns makes a contrast between seeing painting in terms of 'the needs of a philosopher whose imperialism would overwhelm the arts and integrate them into a way of thinking about the ultimate nature of things' and seeing it in terms of 'the needs and actions of a painter whose tasks are immediate in both painterly and perceptual terms'.[1] The goals, idioms and styles of art are in continual change, sometimes gentle and slow, sometimes violent and revolutionary. Changes in the arts must be matched by changed aesthetics.

On this contrasted view, then, what is vital is that the arts develop through an inner dynamic which is theirs alone. Problems and challenges arise in any period and require highly specific insight and expertise on the part of artists to deal with them: once dealt with, new challenges will arise. Defenders of particularity in aesthetics can appeal to the side of Wittgenstein's aesthetic thought which opposed generalization. Let us focus our thoughts, he urged, on the bass that moves too much, the door or wall-picture, or indeed ceiling, that is now too high, now too low, and at last – Thank God! – just right.[2]

On this view, then, philosophers need to accept a circumscribed role. They must accept the actual ongoings in the arts (procession of movements, styles, fashions, revolts and counter-revolts) and refrain from trying to legislate what artists *ought* to be doing. We may be reminded of a (once popular) parallel view of moral philosophy, where the work of the philosopher is limited essentially to an overhearing and analysing of the current language of morals, rather than attempting to deepen or radically revise moral understanding.

No doubt it is good for the philosopher of art to be humble; but is this not carrying it too far? More wisely, I think, Flint Schier saw the value of art as 'emerging out of a particular structure consisting of other values, perfectionist and aesthetic values that exist independently of the art world'. 'If the value of art is ... radically incommensurate with, or unconnected to, our other values,' he wrote, it becomes a mystery how 'we ever come to be sensitive to the value of art.'[3]

A practicing artist may surely be moved *both* by pressures highly specific to the state of his particular art today *and* by his feeling for certain more pervasive, deep-running and long-lasting sources of aesthetic fulfillment; though he has maybe never articulated or analysed them. So may his reader or spectator or listener. If a philosopher reminds us of these sources, he is not necessarily bullying the arts; not all philosophers who propose theories seek to 'overwhelm' artists and arts. Neither (I venture to say) need they feel obliged to welcome whatever goes on under the title of 'art' and to trim their theorizing to accommodate it. Failures, mistakes and distortions in past philosophies of art do not entitle us to infer that the whole endeavor to ground aesthetic concepts in a general theory of values or metaphysic is misguided: it may just be highly complex and full of pitfalls.

Some Basic Aesthetic Values

Could we, then, sample and reaffirm some aesthetic values that (to one philosopher at least) do seem to be grounded in an understanding of the broadest human situation, and which are not replaceable by norms that emerge from the ever-changing practice of the arts themselves?

We can make most sense of them if we see some of these values as concerned to mitigate basic and necessary human needs that arise from our nature and situation in the world, as forms of our finitude: others express equally intelligible aspirations. None of these values by itself will generate a single-concept aesthetic theory but they may well furnish a cluster of explanatory key concepts, principles and ideals – some intriguingly interlinked. In particular, certain of them form pairs of contraries (or seeming-contraries) which, paradoxically, can be present together in experience of art. Indeed, it is a remarkable fact about the arts that they are able to satisfy several of these values simultaneously. Values proper to the arts, then, range from what we have no option but to cherish (consciousness, for instance) to what enlivens and enriches our experience through happy contingency – what we find can be done with particular pigments, strings, reeds, and the complex meanings and sounds of words …

Here are some reminders of these concepts and values, unsystematically and very briefly listed. They are of course as familiar as they are fundamental.[4]

Unity   Aesthetic experience celebrates what has been called ever the *same* triumph, the 'triumph of concentration over random dispersion'.[5] Unity is a necessary feature of all perception and reflection as such, but it is peculiarly intensified in aesthetic experience. One has to add: what is accepted as unity is constantly under review between artist and appreciator. It is only a small, but most significant, step from the 'necessary feature' to the historically relative.

Form   The holding together and grasping of a sensory complex as one object-of-experience already takes us close to concern with perceptual form, pattern and structure: a well-formed work of art offers more than usually effective deliverance from the inchoate, confused and chaotic, which oppress and defeat perception. Again, what counts as acceptable form in the various arts is continually open to persuasion and rethinking.

Plenitude   I shall use the word 'plenitude' for art's intensifying of conscious awareness through such means as the 'all-in' use of language resources in poetry, of sound resources in music, of spatial relationships in visual art. Through these, artworks can achieve a heightened, compressed, dense meaningfulness.[6] Behind these means to plenitude stand the values we attach to intensity and diversity of experience in general.

Communication and expression   In very many contexts, success in achieving plenitude (as density of meaning) is startling success also in communication. Indeed, another basic value of art is precisely its power to enhance and refine communication: to discriminate and express otherwise unattainably specific, elusively individual, emotional qualities, visions of humanity, visions of the world. Here again art speaks to a universal human need. Closely related is a concern with truth.

Truth   A serious work of art may be valued also as a distinctive way of seeing the world, as a reinterpretation or 'criticism' of human life, or of some limited but significant area of it – one that aims to illuminate, to express or reveal truth, by imaginative means. Conversely, it lowers the worth of a work if its vision is trite, clichéd or distorted.

Disengagement and vitality   'Disengagement', the contemplative or 'disinterested' attitude to aesthetic objects, was long unchallenged as a main feature, maybe the principal feature, of aesthetic appreciation. Today it has its critics. Developments in the arts – it is argued – make clear that the serious appreciator of the arts has to participate, to be involved, engaged, not a passive spectator. The appreciator's task can even sometimes involve actively completing the artistic process.[7] Here, it will be said, is a vivid example of a concept shaped by philosophy (chiefly eighteenth-century philosophy) that needs to be ousted in the light of current practice in the arts. Nevertheless, although I too want to deny that the appreciation of art is an inert and passive affair, I think that a broad, but not empty, conception of the disinterested and contemplative can still be defended.[8] It can be illuminating to explore it in conjunction with a companion-concept, one at first sight contrary to it, namely vitality or life-enhancement. Both concepts connect, once again, with values of a very wide and basic kind: love of calm and love of vitality. But how can such seeming-contraries work together?

Aesthetic experience (I want to say) involves disengagement from practical, acquisitive, utilitarian concerns of life; but that certainly does not make it a torpid or vapid kind of experience: in sharp contrast, it is experience closely akin to, and often directly involving, wonder – alert and vital. Such a coupling is hardly a novelty. Kant's aesthetics, for instance, wove together the strand of disinterestedness with repeated claims about the 'enlivening' or 'quickening' that come with the play of imagination and understanding. A contemplative attitude, stillness as well as vivid life, can be held essential components in human fulfillment. A fine work of art can maximize both values at once.

Schiller, in his *Letters on the Aesthetic Education of Man,* also bore witness to those deeply rooted values: indeed, more explicitly and eloquently than Kant. He describes mankind as progressively mastering both the outer and the inner turmoils that harass him, a movement towards equilibrium and inner freedom. 'What is man, before beauty cajoles from him a delight in things for their own sake, or the serenity of form tempers the savagery of life? ...he finds rest [*Ruhe*] nowhere but in exhaustion'.[9] Schiller conceives of a stage where aesthetic taste itself looks only to the exciting, the 'bizarre, the violent and the savage', and shuns 'tranquil simplicity' [*und vor nichts so sehr als vor der Einfalt und Ruhe fliehen*]. But more developed forms of aesthetic experience have disinterestedness and tranquillity, together with vitality. At its rapturous apex (described now in aesthetic–*religious* terms), it offers both tranquillity and vitality at their most intense.[10] It cannot be taken for granted that an art makes a genuine advance if it discards the stillness side of this duality and gives way unilaterally to the violent thrills of Schiller's 'earlier' stage of development.

'Paradoxical co-presence', the simultaneous realizing by art of goals that seem *prima facie* incompatible, can be identified in several other forms. It is true of some works of art that they are essentially extended in time, and yet our experience of them is also, in an important sense, time-transcending. Individual notes of music are transcended in a melody, melodies in a movement; syllables in words, words in phrases, lines, a whole short poem; yet all of these pass in continuous temporal flow, whenever performed. Freedom and inevitability make yet another pair. On aesthetic excellence in mathematics, for instance, Bertrand Russell once wrote that it displays 'in absolute perfection that combination, characteristic of great art, of godlike freedom, with the sense of inevitable destiny'.[11]

The Basis of Aesthetic Principles

Looking back to my title, what sort of 'philosophical understanding', then, do I claim lies behind the affirming of such principles and goals of art experience as I have been sampling? On what grounds can we urge the arts to respect and promote these principles?

I suggest that the values of art connect with the obverse of several basic limitations and deficiencies – forms of finitude – that are integral to the human condition. We delight in the vivacity and self-transparency of conscious awareness, as we are depressed when it flags and falls away towards torpor. Engagement with utilitarian tasks and demands disperses and dissipates the unity of being we strive for; so art experience is a highly prized heightening of consciousness, through the integration of the complexly connected components of artworks. Whether we are absorbed in the web of spatial relationships in a painting or of temporal materials in music, the outcome is a self-sustaining, intensified vitality.

Why should those paradoxically co-present 'opposites' be especially valued? Because in them the familiar *either-or*s of human finitude are replaced by something closer to the *both-and*s of metaphysical ideals. More generally, we are seeing how the basic values of art are not isolated or remote from the values relevant to other areas of life and thought. On this reading, and given that continuity, the philosopher of art is surely not excluded from pointing, on occasion, to values that some trends in the arts may be neglecting, or to permanently important tasks they are not fulfilling.

To say this is not to say, absurdly, that a philosopher is entitled, simply as a philosopher, to propose specific practical tasks for art. Nevertheless, the normative nature of the most deeply-grounded and pervasive principles does prevent the philosopher from being merely a recorder and analyst, or indeed a social scientist, even although some writers have seen the philosopher of art in that light. An aesthetics that is centered in sociology flattens out the philosopher's task and attempts to present him with already-processed, already-evaluated data concerning what is produced in the sphere of art by social forces, understood in historicist and determinist (that is, would-be scientific) style. Here as elsewhere, philosophers cannot rest simply in the role of neutral, quasi-scientific commentators, but they always rework their material, as they select, sift through and organize it. There is a relevant parallel in moral philosophy: for some moral philosophers' analogous commitment to 'scientific understanding' has been likewise uneasy and fitful: their avowed aim may initially be a 'science of man' but (like Hume) they may well end up alternating between something deserving that title, and the commending of particular acts and attitudes and the deprecating of others. (So in Hume the undogmatic, the humane and the critical are commended; and the 'monkish' is deplored.)

As I suggested earlier, we can acknowledge the deep values, rooted in a philosophical understanding of the human situation as such, without denying that there are also other, less abstract, values which do come and go, or are now emphasized and now soft-pedaled. The philosopher of art's understanding of his data has to be thought of as many-leveled, incorporating a hierarchy of values and aims. Some are derived from technical change, or are linked to developing traditions and movements: these can indeed be historically relative. Below them lie the deep, categoreal ones.

Critics of the arts implicitly or explicitly rely, in their interpretations and appraisals, on principles of different levels. It is not always easy to decide to what level a principle or value belongs: whether historically transient or deeply-rooted. I have been arguing, for instance, that 'disinterestedness' or 'disengagement' is more deeply entrenched in the hierarchy than its current detractors believe. That my 'deep' principles are neither archaic nor solely the subject of philosophers' theorizing, may, however, be readily shown. Here, for instance, is a critic of contemporary art drawing upon some of the deepest: Richard Cork commenting in *The Times* on paintings by Leon Kossoff. In particular, he wrote about

> a splendid picture called 'Here Comes the Diesel, Early Summer.' [The arrival of the train is enough to set] the whole picture into ecstatic agitation. Energy surges through the scene.... A quotidian stretch of industrial north London is transformed through Kossoff's avid vision into a place of wonder. The moment will soon pass, and the restless mobility of his mark-making implies a keen awareness of transience. But flux is arrested here, in all its turbulence, and endowed with the redemptive power of art.[12]

We note 'ecstatic agitation'...'energy'...'wonder.' There is 'keen awareness of transience', yet 'flux is arrested' – a splendid case of the paradoxical co-presence of contrary notions! Also art's 'redemptive power': 'redemptive' with its obvious religious resonance illustrates also a continuity between religious and aesthetic. We see too how recognition of even the most abstract-seeming metaphysical values can make an impact directly on the quality of an individual's aesthetic experience.

It is not only philosophers who are moved to philosophize in the presence of art: others tend to be far less inhibited than they! Many artists themselves have been powerfully influenced by a philosophical style or set of doctrines, although often in a popularized and simplified version. This being so, it would be strangely ironical if the aesthetic theorist alone had to occupy the place of a pure spectator of the arts and venture no philosophical comment or criticism that stems from his own understanding of his data.

Aesthetics and the Appreciation of Nature

A second set of questions about data and theory arises over the aesthetic appreciation of nature: there the objects of appreciation range from small-scale natural items, snowflakes, spiders' webs, shells, to landscapes, skyscapes, the immensities of space and time. We need to distinguish two areas of enquiry in this section. There is the question of 'understanding how' to manage, balance and orchestrate the various possible components of such experience of nature. And since understanding (here knowledge and belief) can feature also as one of the *components*, we have to ask: how far does it matter that we understand what is before us and constitutes the object of our aesthetic attention?

First, then, consider 'understanding' as it appears in the phrase, 'understanding how to approach and appreciate nature aesthetically'. In art appreciation we have various bodies of criticism to guide our responses; we have knowledge of developing genres and evolving forms. Not so with nature. What we engage in with nature is an aesthetic activity that is partly responsive, and partly creative, both receptive and formative. It is improvisatory and in important measure free. We deliberate where to let our attention settle: we decide whether to admit *this*, to soft-pedal or exclude *that*: perhaps how widely to let our attention range – for instance, a single shell, a beach, a whole visible stretch of coastline. Cognitive components can be of many kinds, historical, scientific or ecological. In aesthetic experience these will be fused with purely sensuous components, expressive qualities or formal qualities. And the cognitive factors themselves may generate new, distinctive emergent emotional qualities. In all this we are neither exclusively tracing nature as it is in itself, nor are we engaged in a wholly self-generated fantasy. To develop this account further, we need to spell out more explicitly some of those components and the factors we seek to synthesize, to unify into one aesthetic object.

Suppose I am contemplating the movement of deer across a hillside under snow. They emerge from the edge of a forest onto open country. In order to attend to the scene as an aesthetic object, how much more (and less) is required than sheer perception of events? For a start, once again there needs to be a wondering *disengagement* – disengagement from a utilitarian concern with forestry as commerce and animals as food, disengagement even from the network of cause–effect explanations. But not, I think, disengagement from concern with objectivity or with truth. We do want to be sure that it is *nature's* resources that we are experiencing and celebrating. In the aesthetic case, truth is incorporated not through the devising of illuminating theory, but in a memorable episode of experience. Or at least we hope it will be. Failure here can result from such factors as sentimental falsification or self-protective selectivity.

Whatever layers of thought, whatever understanding of nature contribute to the experience, we want also to retain a strong sense of the present actuality of this snowy hillside and these deer, as, on other occasions, the actuality of a particular river bank at dawn, or of a skein of migrating geese in flight, or of those towering cumulo-nimbus clouds around which one's aircraft is now manoeuvring its way.

Though we may draw upon scientific knowledge, we are not engaged in a scientific project: we are free also to encourage and foster emotional responses to the items or scenes of nature, responses in terms of human wants and fears, exultations and shrinkings of spirit.

In aesthetic appreciation of nature, we may even meet versions of those *paradoxically co-present* features for which I have been claiming importance in appreciation of the arts. Notable among these was tranquillity-with-vitality, unchanging form sustained by intense manifestation of energy: it has many parallels in the context of nature experience. I think of Romantics who saw in a waterfall precisely that combination of powerful energy and constant retention of form.

> What a sight it is to look down on such a cataract! [wrote Coleridge] – the wheels, that circumvolve in it – the leaping up and plunging forward of that infinity of pearls ... – the continual *change* of the *Matter*, the perpetual *sameness* of the *Form* – it is an awful Image and Shadow of God and the World.[13]

I think of Ruskin on the part played in natural beauty by what he described as 'the connection of vitality with repose'. 'Repose,' he claimed, 'demands for its expression the implied capability of its opposite, Energy.' 'Repose proper, the *rest* of things in which there is *vitality* or capability of motion...' for example, a 'great rock come down a mountain side, ... now bedded immovably among the fern.' Its 'stability' is 'great in proportion' to the 'power and fearfulness of its motion'.[14]

For another instance of this kind of complexity, our understanding of past states of nature may enter our perception of present states. As nature exists only in time and in constant change, we cannot exclude – as foreign to aesthetic experience of nature – imaginative realizations of earlier states of the object of experience, extensions of awareness back in time, whether recent or 'deep' time. These components can part-determine how we see nature now. Compare Simon Schama, commenting on his own book: '*Landscape and Memory* is built round ... moments of recognition ... when a place suddenly exposes its connections to an ancient and peculiar vision of the forest, mountain, river...'[15]

Once again, we can place such cases on a scale: at one end of it the appreciator's attention is very nearly absorbed in the perceived details of a scene in nature, although the 'contrary' principles are clearly enough acknowledged in the background of experience. (Ruskin describes a motionless yet intensely alive individual tree branch.[16]) At the other end are cases where one is focally aware of the full development in thought to which the schema of 'calm and vital', 'intensely still and intensely alive' lends itself. At the extreme point, those near-opposites appear in some memorable accounts of metaphysical perfection: the supreme being is conceived as unmoved, all-sufficient, in eternal repose and is yet at the same time life at its infinite intensity.[17] Our normal expectation is that increasing stillness means decreasing vitality, and that what enhances life will do so at the expense of tranquillity. But these are cases where both those highly valued modes of experience are in some measure simultaneously secured, and the thought of their complete, full conjunction can be taken at the least as marking an *ideal focus*.

It is worth adding that the theme of paradoxical co-presence should not be judged arcane or precious: it can be a feature of childhood experience. For example, in his book, *Passing Strange and Wonderful: Aesthetics, Nature and Culture*, Yi-Fu Tuan sensitively describes children's love of what he calls 'nooks'. A tree house, a hollow in bushes, or the like offer both a 'womblike hollow' and an 'open space', and can capture 'for the child ... the basic polarities of life: darkness and light, safety and adventure, indolence and excitation ... past and future cease to exist, displaced by a transcendent present'.[18]

What is it like to synthesize such diverse constituents as I have been listing into a unified aesthetic experience (for unity can be a key concept to us in nature, as well as in appreciation of art)? Consider some examples, in each of which a cluster of natural components makes an aesthetic unity-to-perception.

I perceive a landscape as *louring* or *threatening*; another has a *forbidding* or an *alien* look. I perceive a hushed landscape as *expectant*; a busy, variegated, brilliant landscape as *vibrant*. I see the cliffs and mountains of an island rising above a misty sea as *dreamlike* or *visionary*, or even '*unreal*'.

I look up at the full moon, and a sense comes to me of its *sphericity* and its *floating in space*. I look back to land or sea, and there comes to me now a sense of the earth as also a sphere floating in space. With that change, the emotional quality of my experience changes too. Now I feel the earth's isolation in space, chilling and thrilling at the same time. In terms of formal unity, there is a sense of the two spheres over against each other, in a silent opposition.

We are in the territory of Wittgenstein's *Philosophical Investigations*, the sections on the dawning of aspects and related experiences. What is it (Wittgenstein asks there) 'to *see* an object according to an *interpretation*?' 'Was it *seeing* or was it a thought?'[19] A little earlier, he asked: 'What does it mean to say that I *"see the sphere floating in the air"* in a picture?' '"The sphere seems to float." "You see it floating", or again, in a special tone of voice, "It floats!"'[20]

What is our *goal* in integrating such components into a single experience? We might ask ourselves whether the goal is to maximize emotional impact. But that might be attainable only by suppressing factors which we judge ought not to be suppressed – a strong element of illusion might do it! Watching a sunset, I could maximize my awe and amazement by elaborating a fantasy that the clouds are brilliantly lit golden palaces in the sky. Why not admit such illusion? Because it clashes with a conflicting criterion for desirable aesthetic experience: that it remain faithful to understanding how things really are. That checks my fantasy.

And yet emotional intensity and specificity are indisputably important features of aesthetic experience. Concern with them must check, for instance, a tendency to let theorizing or reverie weaken or obliterate them. The perceived sights and sounds of nature must count for far more than a trigger for reflection.

'Understanding how' to use such criteria in practice is a matter of making very rapid multiple practical judgments: to judge when one movement of the mind, if intensified further, will begin to encroach upon the deployment of another; when, for instance, particularity or poignancy is about to be lost, if the context, the scope of thought, or memory, or anticipation is further broadened. Often enough we will not even attempt to involve every factor or kind of component. But the most fully developed aesthetic approaches to nature may well be mindful of most of the factors I have mentioned, aiming to maximise the operating of each, consistently with the fullest acknowledgment of all the others.

How Far Should Understanding be Scientific?

So far we have been looking at the question of 'understanding how' to orchestrate the components of aesthetic experience of nature. Now we need to consider ways in which understanding can itself enter as *one of the components* of aesthetic experience of nature. In fact, the role and importance of understanding as a component is among the most debated current issues in this area. A recurrent question is, how far ought this component to be a strictly *scientific* understanding? As we look out upon a landscape, we can appropriate aesthetically the thought that this mountain range resulted from the collision of massive tectonic plates, which are still exerting their enormous pressures, unseen. Clearly, though, no single determinate scientific view of a landscape can constitute *the* one proper object of aesthetic appreciation. There is not only the perspective of geology, but also that of, say, crystallography, and a possible account in terms of fundamental physical theory. What we assimilate from the scientist's story has to be limited to what is imaginable – the surface geological, certainly, where we can imaginatively superimpose our understanding of some earlier state of the valley before us (while it was still under the ice, let us say). Or we may import in imagination, schematically, some of the evolutionary past of the living organisms now before us. Where we stop will depend essentially on the limitations of our imagination and knowledge to bring data of more than a certain complexity to bear on the scene at a given time, out of innumerable earlier states and stages, from the Big Bang onwards.

If we move from individual natural items to nature as a whole, our sense of its part-chaotic, part-lawful complexity, together with the mystery of its origin or of its always being there, may well prompt a respect or awe as a constant component in serious aesthetic experience. It will modify, and be modified by, features of the particular items we encounter, particular forests, sea coasts, moors and marshes.

Scientific understanding, as we incorporate it into an aesthetic experience, loses its evaluatively neutral character. It takes on emotional qualities that are dependent on our needs, anxieties, hopes and satisfactions. We delight also in other aspects of our aesthetic objects, such as formal organization, that are themselves dependent upon contingencies of observer's location, perspective and scale. Indeed, the realization of our humanly unique mode of enjoying the landscape – its relativity to our perceptual powers and limitations – can itself enter as a cognitive element in the experience. There can surely be no argument against the counterpointing of a scientific understanding of, say, a thunderstorm and a thoroughly 'life-world' mode of experiencing it, as *drama*: approach, climax and restoration of tranquillity.

It is true that on some occasions, before some landscapes, we may well say, 'Never mind understanding; let us just open ourselves to the beauty, the loveliness of it!' Why indeed not? Yet we may be unable to exclude from our experience a wistfulness on account of the fragility of the natural objects before us, and maybe a *frisson* of anxiety about their future. I am of course thinking of the moral imperative expressed powerfully in so much current writing – the imperative of ecological concern.

Some writers do indeed see our ecological responsibilities as demanding to be taken into account within an aesthetic approach to nature. We must respond to the predictions of scientists about nature's future states, seeing nature as threatened in a variety of what are to us grim and depressing ways. If we judge the near-extinction of some animal species to be sad or deplorable, because it is better to have maximal diversity of life-forms rather than their constant depletion, then (on this view) sadness must surely be an ingredient in our aesthetic appreciation of animals of that kind.

Are we then required, more generally, in *any* aesthetic experience of bird, beast, lake or meadow, to ensure that we 'build in' to our awareness some reference to threat of extinction or of coming harm? Perhaps the threat is from acid rain or from climatic change that will ultimately remove that item from the landscape. We also realize that, independently of ecological damage brought about by human beings, *all* of the planet's currently contemplated features will eventually, in the more distant future, be drastically altered and finally destroyed. Now this is a disturbing proposal: if taken literally, would it not amount to a self-sabotaging of aesthetic enjoyment as such? For a constant enveloping doom-laden expressive quality would obliterate discriminations of quality. A generalized, morally urgent environmental anxiety would be claiming a right to displace the luxury of 'fine tuning'. Worthy priority would here be given to environmental understanding and its moral implications, but with devastating effects on the aesthetic. Certainly, our cherishing of aesthetic experience must not be allowed to displace or override practical efforts to ameliorate environmental threats and dangers. But neither do those dangers have to dominate all our approaches to nature. There is room – and great need – for both concerns.

In a word: if we do see aesthetic awareness as essentially a heightening, an enhancing of discriminatory power, and therefore aiming precisely at the diversifying of experience, it would be supremely ironic if it became wholly obsessed with a generalized sense of environmental and planetary doom. This element of 'understanding' would surely have become wildly, usurpingly overemphatic. There can be no aesthetic requirement incessantly to go down the track that sets out from nature's rewarding, enjoyable forms and textures, dutifully adds the realization of how things stand with that same nature, in the longer term, and 'ultimately', until the global experience comes to be bleakly suffused with the thought of the transience of those loved objects. Items of nature, valued in considerable measure for the aesthetic experience they offer to us, would cease to provide that experience because of our very anxiety and foreboding over their continuance.

But how, and on what principle, can we resist that movement of mind? No doubt we could again simply say check the deployment of any one aesthetic component before the point at which it threatens to overwhelm others. But to invoke that stratagem on its own, in such a serious context and without further thought or preparation, might well seem *ad hoc* and facile.

We do, however, learn to handle an analogous situation in our perception of human beings through a kind of discipline of the attention: perhaps we can apply something of the same to our problem with aesthetic appreciation of nature. Think of a painting of an old man or woman, where the imminence of death and dissolution is signalled by an emphatic rendering of skull (just) beneath the skin. Though that can symbolize the *universal* human lot, we do not feel obliged to read in that same final state whenever we look at any human being – of no matter what age and condition – and so cancel any possibility of appreciating present human flourishing, animation and health. No, because that would amount to bringing forward gratuitously the loss of quality and discrimination. Can we deal in essentially the same way with the problem of nature's ephemerality as a component of aesthetic appreciation of nature? I think we can, to some degree at least. We can see that problem as setting a parallel challenge to the management of attention so as neither to evade, nor to be overwhelmed by, the depressive and destructive.

Yet another analogy can be invoked between aesthetic objects and persons, in this case with the relation between friends. In a close friendship, different levels of knowledge and concern are visited on different occasions. Some encounters will be light-hearted, skimming the surface only: others reach to the depths, in intimate awareness of the complexity of the other. Both levels are valued components of the friendship, though they are not of equal value. The relationship is not, and cannot be, conducted perpetually on the deepest level. There is an important element of freedom whereby the friends can blamelessly meet on the casual levels, provided that they are available to each other on the deeper levels as well. That freedom, I suggest, is a valuable feature of the aesthetic mode of experience also, too valuable a feature to be jettisoned.

Does Nature Possess Aesthetic Qualities?

We have yet to note a still more comprehensive challenge to the objective of responding to nature aesthetically and with understanding. That comes in any claim, whether from science or philosophy, that nature understood as it ultimately is, nature as it is in itself, does not possess qualities to which we *can* aesthetically respond: that the farther one goes towards understanding the world, the less scope remains for aesthetic experience. To think in the scientific background, consistently and in a thoroughgoing way, would dissolve away aesthetic perception, not enrich it. The qualities that we can appreciate aesthetically do not appear in the scientist's inventory of what fundamentally exists in nature. Moreover, the scientist's own understanding is itself expressed in terms known to be metaphorical, like wave and particle, (black) hole or string. These terms also are drawn from our life-world repertoire of perceptible events and the macroscopic entities involved in them, although scientists know well enough that these do not simply map onto the features of nature itself. And surely the same is true of much speculative metaphysics: metaphor abounds there also. It follows that nature-in-itself is still not being *directly* described. To realize this is to grasp how much greater is the gap between *aesthetic* perception and the nature we think we perceive.

In a lively article in *The Journal of Applied Philosophy*,[21] Stan Godlovitch asks how, within the context of an environmentalist concern for nature, we might develop an aesthetic of nature which is 'acentric', free of the anthropocentric and so enables us to 'appreciate nature on its own terms'. For Godlovitch, this does not mean merely that we build in our scientific understanding to the aesthetic appreciation of nature. 'Science,' he claims, 'is directed to forge a certain kind of intelligibility'; it 'de-mystifies nature by categorising, quantifying and patterning it'. If this is cognition, it is a 'human-centred cognition'. A more resolute intent to understand drives us – drives Godlovitch – to recognize nature as 'categorically other'. Only a 'sense of mystery', of 'aloofness' (more distant than the disinterested) and a 'sense of insignificance' are aesthetically appropriate and sustainable. Godlovitch allows us a sense neither of awe nor of wonder: only 'a sense of being outside, of not belonging'.

If we see the aesthetic as, above all, anchored to the ideal of maximally vivid, intensified and discriminating consciousness, then the thought that nature is ultimately unknowable will certainly not bring us nearer to that ideal: quite the contrary! Here, emptiness is all. We have a progressive canceling of sensory, perspectival and even scientific components, like the work of an over-zealous 'negative' theologian, who strikes out all our concepts in turn as inapplicable to deity in its infinite greatness. We start with 'plenitude': we risk ending with attenuation to nothingness. Must it be so too with our project of thinking our way towards a more adequate aesthetic of nature? Or (less pessimistically) should we conclude only that we cannot give the cognitive component total precedence over the other components of aesthetic experience, if we also want to go on understanding such experience in the way I have described it?

Of course, our grasp of nature is selective and partial; it leaves out both the vast and the minute that lie beyond the meagre zone of our receptivity. Surely, though, we can acknowledge that mystery lies beyond our awareness in every direction, but accept mystery as an enduring background to our benign exploitation of the bounded, the humanly scaled and the sensory – the factors that make possible aesthetic experience as we know it and value it. The sense of mystery can be integrated with these factors, rather than allowed to obliterate them.

I cannot agree that nature is 'categorically other than us, a nature of which we were never part', or that the aesthetic attitude should be 'a sense of being outside, of not belonging'. Surely it is wrong to characterize our situation in these terms. Why should we describe what we do not know of nature as 'belonging' to nature any more than we ourselves belong to it, and any more than what we do know of nature belongs to it? Why should we rule ourselves out from belonging, as if we had grounds for believing that we and our life-world had only a dubious claim to reality, compared with the unknowable nature beyond even the grasp of science? Whatever the *causal* relations between unobservable physical entities and the perceptible, phenomenal world, and between unknown and known, those dependencies do not entitle us to judge the life world, the phenomenal, *unreal*, or to place it low in a scale of degrees of reality. All we perceive from our own perceptual standpoint is actual, is nature, is *being*. Nature as it is in itself cannot exclude, has to include, the phenomenal. So understood, it remains a proper object of aesthetic concern.

Notes

1   Richard Kuhns (1995), *Mind*, **104**, 653–4.
2   L. Wittgenstein (1966), *Lectures and Conversations on Aesthetics, Psychology and Religious Belief*, ed. C. Barrett, Oxford: Blackwell, p. 13 and note 3.
3   Dudley Knowles and John Skorupski (eds) (1993), *Virtue and Taste: Essays on Politics, Ethics and Aesthetics in Memory of Flint Schier*, Philosophical Quarterly Series, Volume 2 , Oxford: Blackwell, p. 191.
4   From those fundamental key notions there lie short and obvious paths to familiar, 'monolithic' aesthetic theories – whether centering on such concepts as mimesis, 'significant form', expression or 'life-enhancement' – concepts none of which I believe to be individually adequate to serve as the foundation for such a theory. Aesthetic theory needs a plurality of interrelated and interdependent principles.
5   Quoted in my essay, 'Findlay's Aesthetic Thought', in Cohen, Martin and Westphal (eds) (1985), *Studies in the Philosophy of J.N. Findlay*, Albany, NY: State University of New York Press, p. 194; see J.N. Findlay (1967), *The Transcendence of the Cave*, London: Allen & Unwin, p. 217. I owe a substantial debt to Findlay's writing.
6   See also R.A. Sharpe (1983), *Contemporary Aesthetics*, Brighton: The Harvester Press.
7   Cf. Arnold Berleant (1991), *Art and Engagement*, Philadelphia: Temple University Press, p. 26.
8   Relevant here is Emily Brady (1998), 'Don't Eat the Daisies: Disinterestedness and the Situated Aesthetic', *Environmental Values*, 7 (1), 97–114.
9   Friedrich Schiller (1794–5, 1967), *On the Aesthetic Education of Man in a Series of Letters*, ed. and trans. by E.M.Wilkinson and L.A.Willoughby, Oxford: Clarendon Press, pp. 170–73, 210–11.
10   Ibid., pp. 210–11, 108–9.
11   Bertrand Russell (1967), *The Autobiography of Bertrand Russell, 1872–1914*, London: Allen & Unwin, p. 158, quoted from Yi-Fu Tuan (1995), *Passing Strange and Wonderful: Aesthetics, Nature and Culture*, New York: Kodansha International, p. 16.
12   R. Cork (1995), *The Times*, 27 May.
13   S.T. Coleridge, letter to Sara Hutchinson, 25 August 1802.
14   John Ruskin (1843–60, 1903–12), *Modern Painters*, London: Library Edition, vol. 4, pp. 115–16. Here is another example from a different field. In a book called *The Making of Landscape Photographs*, the author describes a scene with bright yellow autumn larch trees in a valley with hills on both sides and in the misty far distance. The brightness of the yellow trees suggests that they are directly and vividly sun-lit: but the light in fact is 'flat and diffused'. The effect is 'full of two contradictory things: calm and excitement ... drama and ease'. This 'must be the source of the pleasure' given by the scene (C. Waite (1992), *The Making of Landscape Photographs*, London: Collins and Brown, p. 91).
15   Simon Schama (1995), *Landscape and Memory*, London: Harper Collins, p. 16.
16   Ruskin, *Modern Painters*, vol. 4, p. 116.
17   Ruskin, *Modern Painters*, vol. 4, pp. 113 ff. Quoted also in R.W. Hepburn (1996), 'Landscape and the Metaphysical Imagination', *Environmental Values*, **5** (3).
18   Yi-Fu Tuan, *Passing Strange and Wonderful*, p. 22.
19   L. Wittgenstein (1958), *Philosophical Investigations*, trans. G.E.M. Anscombe, Oxford: Blackwell, pp. 200–204.

20   Ibid., p. 201.
21   S. Godlovitch (1994), 'Ice-Breakers: Environmentalism and natural aesthetics', *The Journal of Applied Philosophy*, **11** (1), 15–30; in particular, 18, 23, 26 and 27–8.

Chapter 3

The Two Aesthetic Cultures: The Great Analogy of Art and the Environment

Yrjö Sepänmaa

The traditional point of departure, when comparing art and the environment, has been to understand the environment through art.[1] This has led to an emphasis on representational art, because only imitation has been regarded as linking the imaginary world of art to the real environment. A similarity has thus been sought between reality and art. This requirement can be met easily, in a documentary sense, by photographs and painting, as well as by nature films or conventional literary depictions of nature. On a mythical and magical level, it is met by arts that do not directly attempt to achieve a direct likeness, but instead attempt to present symbolically a deeper correspondence, such as the kinship of all life or the suffering of nature.

An approach based on images is problematic, since the visual arts seem more and more to have no significance from the point of view of the environment. Art increasingly does not *depict* nature but operates in another relation to it, one that creates an alternative, an extension of reality, an imaginary world. The relation between art and the environment is in danger of remaining a matter of the relation between one kind of art and the environment. This comparison can be extended to other things, as well, particularly to art realized in the environment, such as environmental art proper and architecture. The question then is one of the overlapping of two separate things, not their comparison. If a fruitful basis for comparison cannot be found, the entire art connection must be rejected.

I do not wish to reject art as a fixed point, though I am not searching for a likeness. The essential relationship, the kinship of art and the environment, does not lie, after all, in a likeness that remains random. It lies, rather, on a more general level, in the analogy of their structures. It is just this kinship that is a good parallel, because it does not demand conventional similarity of appearance, a family resemblance, but a common ancestry. A connection then opens through this analogy, through the sharing of a common model that holds among aesthetic culture, experience, art and environmental education.

The Correspondence of Structures

The inspiration for the parallel that I have outlined comes from George Dickie.[2] Having spent an entire book searching for the contractual system of art, he ends with a guess that something similar might be found in the environment. 'I want to be cautious here. I am not saying that there are no conventional aspects involved in the appreciation of nature; there may well be some. If conventional aspects exist, however, they may be rather different from the conventions involved in the appreciation of art or they may be somewhat similar. If there are nature-appreciation conventions, they may have relations to art-appreciation conventions, and this possibility raises interesting questions: Which came first? Did the two grow up together? If one came first, does the later resemble the earlier in any way?'[3]

Dickie's questions were taken up by David B. Richardson, who outlined the possibilities of developing the idea from examples offered by Chinese art and by the amateur study of nature.[4] At the end of his examination, he presents his expanded Dickie-style institutional definition, in which the granting of status extends beyond works of art. The framework provided by a theory and operation according to conventions here too makes a work. For Richardson, however, this is not necessarily a work of art. 'I have extended the meaning of the idea of "conferring of status" on behalf of the art world beyond such performative acts as hanging an artifact in a museum to such performative acts as travelling to favourite mountain scenes and thus conferring aesthetic status on them.'[5]

In conclusion, the author nevertheless remarks, again committing himself to art, that the conventions of the examination of nature belong to the art world.[6] Thus he does not regard them as independent but only as variations of the conventions of art, and so restricts the perspective opened by Dickie. Despite their differences of emphasis, both Dickie and Richardson have seen the possibility of uniting these areas, and have opened a new and fruitful road to the treatment of the relation between art and the environment – the examination of the correspondence of structures.

Worlds and Sub-worlds

The pair being compared, therefore, is the *art world* (the system of art worlds) and the *environmental world* (the system of environmental worlds). The system of art worlds is formed by the art forms and the systems that maintain them,[7] the system of environmental worlds correspondingly by different types of environment and the systems that maintain them. They have their own groups of makers, intermediaries and devotees. Each side divides into similarly structured sub-worlds and these divide in turn as the common model is followed further.

There are, in fact, several environmental worlds (sub-cultures and sub-worlds), such as a natural state of things, an agrarian landscape or a built environment. There are several different kinds of makers and receivers, several different competencies. The acceptance of the analogy does not mean that it would extend to all levels and to every detail. In the case of environmental culture, there is an essential difference between a natural state and the work of humankind. Although the *ready made* is known in art, it is not a strong half of art in the same way.

Art and the environment are two contractual systems that branch out from a common family tree; aesthetic culture and general human aesthetic needs can be seen as their ultimate background. Thus aesthetic culture has two appearances, and internal structural analyses of both of them, art and the environment, are required. Both have a maker and a receiver, as well as persons and institutions at various levels; both acculturate their objects through their own processes. All of this is self-evident for art, as it is for the constructed environment and its components. It is true, for example, in the case of utensils, because in both art and the constructed environment human form-giving is significant. It is only nature in a natural state that is problematic. This is not so, however, when it is offered as an object for tourism, or when its components are separated as delimited objects for preservation. Here it resembles the art of the *ready made*. However, the cultural field does not stop here. Rather, as James Hillman puts it, 'Nature is always to some extent man-made, if not directly with our hands certainly always by our minds.'[8]

T.J. Diffey, referring to the universally admired heaths of his country, asserts that natural beauty exists, at least sometimes, quite as incontrovertibly as the hand pushed in front of the face of the philosopher G.E. Moore.[9] It is not possible to escape from beauty, nor is there any need to do so by talking about something else. If beauty is the real ground for preserving eskers, it should be possible to say this without appealing to less easily demonstrable aspects, such as the rarity of the flora or fauna. If we wish to preserve virgin forest because of its beauty, it should be possible to say so without having to appeal to the possible discovery of a cancer cure in one of the plants.

One explanation for the unity of conceptions of natural beauty mentioned by Diffey is the institutional structures regulating natural beauty and the use of power and control that takes place through them. There are officially delimited 'areas of outstanding natural beauty', nature trails and traditional landscapes, and there are information centers providing common basic information about these. Diffey continues by asking whether it is not true to say that these classified objects are kept on display to be looked at, teaching and giving us pleasure, in the same way as many works of art do.[10]

An institution, in the concrete significance of an outward structure, is therefore that which regulates and unifies modes of experience and also defines its objects. In the significance of an extensive deep structure it is the entire conceptual system.

There is no single environmental world, as there is also no single art world. Both worlds and their components branch out further and further from the same family tree, even having different appearances in particular cases. One's interest need not be directed at the entire diverse field. All the forms of the practice of art are not intended to be examined at once but only selectively and with a high degree of concentration. Nor does competence in one area of art imply competence in the others. Expertise has its limit. Naturalists have their own sphere, as do architects. Though ornithologists and building designers are both experts in their own aspects of the environment, the field of one may be strange and distant to the other.

When both art and the environment are regarded as conventional regulatory systems, it is possible and necessary to seek influences, not only from art sources but also from environmental sources and even from the ways environmental culture changes art culture through its own stimuli. One change lies precisely in the fact that environmental culture gives art the environmental performances that it has developed and made available. The two cultures meet without especially aiming at unity.

The Independent Common Life of Art and the Environment

The structural model of the art world offers an opportunity to see the environmental world, unnoticed but real. Its elements have always been visible, even when its conceptual form, which only theory can create, has not existed. This kind of derivation from art, however, is in danger of putting the environment in second place, as Richardson has done. The environment is easily forced into a foreign mode of observation by raising the similarities to art to a more exalted position than the environment's own system would grant them.[11] If the environmental institution had been more developed, it could have dictated terms to art. It is precisely this kind of prioritization that is assumed in the demand for representational art and realism in general!

Taking the environment as an original model would not, however, alter the traditional arrangement. What would be a real alternative to mutual dependence? I can only think of one: to avoid the creation of the boundary between art and non-art that has been so important and satisfying to traditional art philosophy. We could select the aesthetic object as the comprehensive term and leave aside questions of the status of individual objects. But then new questions would be encountered. Can an object be only and purely aesthetic, without specifically belonging to some form of art or type of environment? Can questions of authenticity and classification be passed over as inessential? Unclassified seeing is preliminary, and an object gains a more permanent form once it has been given its class, with its appropriate criteria for judgment.

We have come to a point at which the two models, that of art and that of the environment, have a similar appearance. First of all there is the maker of the object, second there is the object itself, and third there is the audience. Such a model still appears to be borrowed from art, but it reveals itself as a much more general structural model of culture institutions. Its first undeniable service is to show the fundamental unity of aesthetic culture. Art does not rise to a special position, but is dealt with in a broader group of cultural objects. Second, art is placed within a context of ideas and ideals, in which case aesthetics too gains features of cultural philosophy.

In this kind of framework, aesthetic works can be seen as meaningfully belonging together. Nonetheless, there is no guarantee that the greater totality will always be recognized. Concentrated, specific work takes place all the time in the art and environmental cultures. It is possible to examine both sides, their components, and components of components, each separately, as has indeed been done in the environmental sciences. The demanding task of aesthetics is to form an entirety out of these special areas.

The distance between the art and environmental worlds has supported different traditions within aesthetics itself. According to one's choice of approach, it has been possible to exclude significant whole sub-areas from the field. But because the question concerns two aesthetic cultures and therefore two parts of the culture of the humanities, these have never been problematically distanced from each other in the same way as the two cultures of the humanities and the natural sciences dealt with by C.P. Snow.[12] Recognizing the great analogy represents a new kind of affinity.

The search for the analogy leads to the discovery of openings and areas in both cultures that have never been analyzed. The differences that appear help to test their dissimilarities and to probe and search for their causes. On both sides there are trends that break up the testing of structures (such as anti-art and anti-environment): the disintegration of art also has its mirror image.[13] On the side of the environment there has been practically no attempt to create an avant-garde; traditional values of beauty have been sought, above all. The ugly environment has certainly not been the object of serious theoretical examination, though certainly the object of moralizing disapproval.

Like it or not, humankind has left increasingly visible marks on the environment. The symbiosis of humankind and the environment has conquered the most extensive areas of reality and is continually forming more. A treatment of the various degrees of artificial nature demands new 'humanists', a generation of depicters of the environment who trust human possibilities. The ambivalent photographs of such artist-nature photographers as John Pfahl are still relatively unknown, concentrating as they do on the fusions and collisions of nature and culture, such as an idyllic lake landscape with a nuclear power station in the background.[14] Skeet McAuley's photograph, 'Alaska Pipeline' (1990), shows a birch copse that *almost* covers the enormous oil pipeline running through it.[15] In contrast to the opposition of untouched and spoiled, which is already a cliché, the documentation, commentary on, and criticism of the effect of humankind on the natural world is one of the great challenges in nature depiction.[16]

Utopias

The second generation of anti-art after Duchamp wanted to question the very operating principles of the institution. Art tried to flee the normal systems of supply and distribution for the deserts of Nevada and, more conceptually, for unfulfilled and misleading promises, as well. Thus, for example, an exhibition catalogue might include a work that was not in the exhibition, while there might be a work in the exhibition that was not in the catalogue.

The direction of this experiment in playing with the rules is more radical than that of the first, in creating unconventional works. The issue is no longer the eternal standard of the norm and the anomaly, but an attempt to bring back the circle of challenge and counter-challenge, with anarchy lurking in the background as a consequence of deep breaches between them. When institutional theory arose from an attempt to avoid talking about the properties of a work, it was not able to protect itself against art that disputed the rules of the game and broke its framework. This theory, which refused to say anything about the object itself and concentrated on only talking about the framework, was unable to prepare itself for the fact that art would obviously turn next to breaking the framework.

Does the same threat exist on the side of environmental culture? The avant-garde introduced by landscape architecture has a parallel only with the first generation of anti-art, the presentation of unconventional works. This too has become a Pandora's box, which environmental art has already opened. It is difficult to see the second generation, because it would demand conscious institutional environmental thought, and that does not exist. How do you fix up that which is still unformed? But practice exists already and wild breaches are being directed against it. Dickie speaks of the minimum knowledge and skill required of members of the art institution. Analogously, environmental education could construct this kind of minimum knowledge by providing and determining it. Education would certainly then also provoke its counter-movement and protest. It might give an impulse to such expectations of novelty and surprise that harm a natural state but that accord with quite another rhythm, one that appears to be stationary from the perspective of a human life span, but which humankind has had time to produce changes in and which has even produced humankind.

A culture of discussion, which exists in the areas of art, is only just beginning in environmental culture, except for architecture and industrial design. Discussion provides the justification for bringing dispute into environmental culture. The initial result of successful environmental education, like art education, is disunity, confusion and dispute; that is, precisely the opposite of what has traditionally been expected of education. From this the elaboration of a positive solution can begin.

One factor that unifies the principles of environmental education is, however, always ecology and the diversity and durability it emphasizes.

Alongside the novelty and surprise of art stands a respect for the established presence and durability of the structures in nature in a natural state; that is, a respect for its basic character, which is naturally conservative (conservation). The artificial environment, too, has its own conscious and designed ecology. Nevertheless, space must still remain available for people to experiment and investigate. The ideal of the artificial environment is not the passive, humble reception of a 'perfect' work, but interaction: its value lies in our being able to participate in the making, in the inspiring attraction of incompleteness.

Dennis P. Doordan, who deals with narrow environmental simulation in natural history museums, such as a lava theater, sees a significant challenge in the integration of a human- designed ecological system and natural ecology.[17] He expands the problem to all meetings between things made by humankind and those in a natural state, of the built and the unbuilt, to situations in which two ecological systems, the natural and the artificial, must adapt to one another. The salvation of one demands the understanding of the other.[18]

The discussion leads to weighing up the utopias of art and the environment in groups and between groups. It forces an examination of the means of achieving utopias in art and environmental policy. The two cultures approach one another: art does not differ from the environment on the basis of its likeness. What is essential is the context and the difference of the way we talk about them. In art and environmental education, the two main branches of culture connect. Behind them lies the more enduring perception of the unity of aesthetic culture.[19]

Conclusion

Art and environment only occasionally meet on the surface level, but on a deeper level they have a close similarity: a common institutional structure. The basic similarity between them lies in the fact that in both cases an institution regulates production, transmission, and reception. In art, this institution is the art world; in environment it is the 'environmental world'. Together, these two form the aesthetic culture. In the same way as the institutional theory of art has met its challenge in anti-art, the institutional theory of environment will meet its challenge in anti-environment (artificial nature, avant-garde landscape architecture and so on). In handling these challenges, the two worlds differ. The art institution can freely and easily accept novelty and shocking innovation, even to its self-destruction; but the environment institution, because it deals with our common reality, must follow ecological guidelines. Thus ecology sets limits on the possibilities of ethically sound development of the environment. The environment institution might therefore outlive its parallel, the art institution.

Notes

1   Andrew Forge (1973), 'Art/Nature', in Godfrey Vesey (ed.), *Philosophy and the Arts. Royal Institute of Philosophy Lectures*, Volume Six, 1971–1972, London: Macmillan, pp. 228–41; R.W. Hepburn (1973), 'Nature in the Light of Art', ibid., pp. 242–58.

2   George Dickie (1974), *Art and the Aesthetic. An Institutional Analysis*, Ithaca and London: Cornell University Press; George Dickie (1984), *The Art Circle: A Theory of Art*, New York: Haven Publications. See also Arthur C. Danto (1964), 'The Artworld', *The Journal of Philosophy*, **61** (19), 571–84; T.J. Diffey (1969), 'The Republic of Art', *The British Journal of Aesthetics*, **9** (2), 145–56; T.J. Diffey (1991), *The Republic of Art and Other Essays*, New Studies in Aesthetics, general ed., Robert Ginsberg, Vol. 6, New York: Peter Lang; and Richard Wollheim (1980), *Art and Its Objects*, 2nd edn, with six supplementary essays, Cambridge, MA: Cambridge University Press.

3   Dickie (1974, p. 200).

4   David B. Richardson (1976), 'Nature-Appreciation Conventions and the Art World', *The British Journal of Aesthetics*, **16** (2), 186–91.

5   Ibid., pp. 190–91.

6   Ibid., p. 191.

7   Dickie (1984, pp. 71–86).

8   James Hillman (1984), 'Natural Beauty without Nature', in Pete A.Y. Gunter and Bobette Higgins (eds), *Present, Tense. Future, Perfect? A symposium on widening choices for the visual environmental resource*, Dallas, Texas: LandMark Program For the People, Incorporated, p. 67.

9   Diffey (1991, p. 279).

10 Ibid., pp. 275–6. On tourism, see Jonathan Culler (1981), 'Semiotics of Tourism', *American Journal of Semiotics*, **I** (I–2), 127–40.

11 On independence, see Arnold Berleant (1988), 'The Environment as an Aesthetic Paradigm', *Dialectics and Humanism*, **I**, 2, 95–6.

12 C.P. Snow (1956), 'The Two Cultures', *The New Statesman and Nation*, 6 October, 413–14; C.P. Snow (1959), *The Two Cultures and the Scientific Revolution*, Cambridge: Cambridge University Press.

13 This was brought out noticeably by the concentration on the avant-garde of the landscape in a congress on that topic. See Patrick M. Condon and Lance M. Neckar (eds) (1990), *The Avant-Garde and The Landscape: Can They Be Reconciled?*, proceedings, 'The Avant-Garde And The Landscape: Can They Be Reconciled?', Minneapolis: Landworks Press; note especially Diane Balmori, 'Change: A Landscape Manifesto', pp. 400–404.

14 *A Distanced Land. The Photographs of John Pfahl*, Cheryl Brutvan ed., New York: The University of New Mexico Press in association with Albright-Knox Art Gallery, 1990, plates 44–62.

15 Charles Hagen (1992), 'Tricky Attempts to Juggle Esthetics and Politics', *The New York Times*, Sunday, 14 June.

16 Andrew Ross (1992), 'The Ecology of Images', *The South Atlantic Quarterly*, **91** (1), 220.

17 Dennis P. Doordan (1992), 'Nature on Display', *Design Quarterly*, (155), 34–6.

18 Ibid., p. 36.

19 The idea of two aesthetic cultures has been developed also in Yrjö Sepänmaa (1986/1993), *The Beauty of Environment. A general model for environmental aesthetics*, Denton, Texas: Environmental Ethics Books, pp. 155–60, 'Postscript 1986–1993'.

Chapter 4

Art and Nature: The Interplay of Works of Art and Natural Phenomena

Arto Haapala

Does Art Represent Nature or *Vice Versa*?

Traditional introductions to aesthetics often begin with the representation theory of art: art represents nature. The roots of this conception are easy to trace. In both Plato's and Aristotle's theories the concept of mimesis played a significant role, and they have both had a considerable influence on modern philosophies of art. In *The Republic*, Plato puts forward a very critical view of painters: they are imitators who are further away from what Plato regarded as the truest reality, the world of ideas, than craftsmen who produce everyday objects. Aristotle, when discussing tragedy in his *Poetics*, regarded poetic activity as mimetic, although not necessarily mimetic in the sense of representing actual events of history but of representing possible or probable events. Poetry is more universal than history because it represents permanent possibilities of human nature rather than stories of individual human lives. Since Plato and Aristotle, the concept of mimesis has figured prominently in different accounts of art until the twentieth century.

When one considers all the different forms of art of today, it seems obvious that not all art is mimetic. Most music is not mimetic, neither is architecture: musical compositions and buildings do not represent anything. Literature and painting are the clearest examples of *mimesis*, but the ways in which representational paintings and literary works are mimetic seem to be very different. A picture of a horse resembles – in some sense of the word – a real horse, whereas a written description of a horse does not have any resemblance to an actual animal. There is one more consideration that makes things more complicated for the representation theory. One of the most obvious features of literary texts is that most of them are fictional: they are not about any actual people or events. They do not describe anything existing. So why is it that the representation theory is used as the dominant conception of art and for understanding the relationship of art and nature?

Perhaps at least a partial answer comes from the underlying ontological conception. There is a clear order of things: Nature – and reality more generally – comes first, art is dependent on and inferior to it. Without Salisbury Cathedral and the surrounding landscape, Constable could not have painted his *Salisbury Cathedral from the Meadow* (1831), and without the Lake District in northern England, Wordsworth could not have written all his poems about English nature. The very expression 'art and reality,' which is often used in philosophical aesthetics, suggests that there is a dichotomy stemming from the different ontological character of these things: one is real, the other is not. Nature exists independently of art and fiction, and its reality is taken for granted except in some philosophical contexts, whereas the reality of art and fiction is questionable even to the non-philosophical mind.

It is fair to say, I think, that the ordinary conception of art still relies heavily on this distinction, despite being questioned and criticized, for example, by postmodern theorists. When the concepts of reality and truth are questioned and relativized in the way that has been done in postmodernism, then the distinction between art and nature also becomes problematic. The concept of narration, in particular, has narrowed the gap between art and reality. If narration plays a role in the formation of our reality, and if there are no universal criteria for true or acceptable narrations, then the reality of reality, the stability and solidity of what we have taken for real, starts to shatter and may collapse altogether.

In this chapter I shall not, however, discuss the problems of art and nature in terms introduced by postmodern thinkers. The conception I put forward here is in many ways more conservative than, for example, the one identified with the generic term 'deconstruction', and it assumes there is something else in the world than narratives and texts. But I shall also problematize the common-sense conception of nature and reality and show the place that art has in the making of nature. I will defend a thesis that, against the background of the representation theory of art and the commonsense conception of the relation of art and nature, may sound radical.

A version of this conception was put forward by Oscar Wilde, in his typically provocative and paradoxical manner, as follows:

> Schopenhauer has analysed the pessimism that characterizes modern thought, but Hamlet invented it. The world has become sad because a puppet was once melancholy. The Nihilist, that strange martyr who has no faith, who goes to the stake without enthusiasm, and dies for what he does not believe in, is a purely literary product. He was invented by Tourgenieff, and completed by Dostoieffski.... The nineteenth century, as we know it, is largely an invention of Balzac.[1]

All this holds for the relation between nature and art too:

> At present, people see fogs, not because there are fogs, but because poets and painters have taught them the mysterious loveliness of such effects. There may have been fogs for centuries in London. I dare say there were. But no one saw them, and so we do not know anything about them. They did not exist till Art invented them.[2]

To use a Finnish example that I shall explore in more detail below, I could express the same idea as follows: the Finnish summer nights did not exist before the author F.E. Sillanpää invented them. My approach is, however, more moderate than the one Wilde formulated in the quotations above.[3] What is central is the notions of 'real' and 'reality'. What kind of reality are we referring to when saying that painters made London fog real or that we should be grateful to an author for the reality of Finnish summer nights? In answering this question, I draw from German phenomenology, Martin Heidegger in particular, and the idea of the 'life world'.[4]

Fiction and Reality

I shall concentrate on cases which *prima facie* seem to be especially challenging for the kind of conception I am advancing: fiction. If we relied on our common sense, we would have to talk about fiction in terms of non-existence: what is fictional does not exist. Non-existence has often been regarded even in the more sophisticated philosophical accounts as a necessary condition for something to be fictional, and it may even be argued to be a sufficient condition. Real is something that exists; fiction is imaginary and non-existent. At one level this difference obviously holds – fictional entities do not exist as physical objects – but it could be argued that fictions enjoy some other kind of existence than the concrete physical existence. This is what the outcome of the following discussion will be: fictions can sometimes enter our lives and our world but not as physical objects. There is no unbridgeable gap between art and reality, because art contributes in important ways to what there is in the world. Art and fiction can become important parts of our reality.

The fact that fictions are not physical objects prevents bodily interaction with them. When watching a movie or a theatre performance we cannot enter the world of fiction, nor can fictional entities enter our world. My entering the stage during a theatre performance does not save the heroine, although it will interrupt the performance. It is only in fiction that fictional characters can leave their world and, for example, start to look for an author, as in the play *Six Characters in Search of an Author* by Luigi Pirandello. But there are other kinds of contacts we have with fictions. The ontological gap does not prevent all interaction. One of the bridges crossing the gap is created by our emotional encounters: we respond to a moving story or to a horror film, even though we know it is 'only fiction'.[5]

We also acquire concepts and conceptual schemes from fictional works and apply them to our everyday surroundings. Fictional pieces can supply us with conceptual tools with which we structure the real world. This idea has been put forward by a number of philosophers, for example by Nelson Goodman, and it can even be regarded, at a certain level of sophistication, as a commonplace.[6] It is not an unusual experience, having read a novel with psychological insights, to see people with new eyes. There are Aljoshas, Dmitris and Ivans around us when we see the world in terms of Dostoyevsky's *The Brothers Karamazov*.

What this chapter is seeking, however, is not a theory of the cognitive role of art. The kind of epistemological significance described is a fact, but it is something that depends on and is restricted to individual readers or viewers. I may find Dostoyevsky's novel particularly illuminating because I can identify myself with it, but somebody else may well find it boring and epistemologically insignificant. This sort of epistemological importance does not have any wider applicability or cultural significance. In these cases fictions remain conceptual tools that are sometimes used for the structuring of an individual's world view. I am interested, however, in cases where fictions 'grow out' of their fictional context. Besides the fictional world, fictions sometimes acquire a cultural significance in another context that I shall call, following phenomenological philosophers, the life world. My argument is that different kinds of elements of a work of fiction can become props of the life world of a community. Some fictional characters can gain this kind of status; the most obvious examples are popular fictions, such as Donald Duck and Santa Claus. But characters in great classics, such as Anna Karenina and David Copperfield, can also enter our world as culturally significant entities. An atheist might well classify Biblical characters in this category: extremely influential fictions that have gained a firm place in the structures of our society. What is more relevant for this chapter is the role of what I call 'fictional ideas': they too can add to the reality of the life world. It is here that art and nature interact in such a way that the traditional representation theory is turned upside down.

We will come back to the notion of the life world in more detail below, but already at this stage it has become clear that the reality being discussed here is not the reality of physical objects. I am not saying that fictional characters and ideas could enter our world by becoming something tangible and perceptible. When I discuss the life world and its constituents, I am referring to another kind of reality than that of physical entities: cultural reality and cultural entities.

The Reality of Fictions

We continue by analysing some examples, taking two cases from Finnish literature and one from English. Aleksis Kivi's *Seven Brothers* is unanimously regarded as a classic in Finnish literature. It was completed in the 1860s at a time when there was very little literature actually written in Finnish. So Kivi's masterpiece can also be seen as a kind of starting point of Finnish literature. Before that the Swedish language dominated the Finnish literary scene. My other Finnish example is by F.E. Sillanpää. His novel, *People in the Summer Night*, was published in 1934. Sillanpää was awarded the

Nobel Prize for literature in 1939, and he is the only Finnish author to have won the award. My English examples come from William Wordsworth's poetry.

One of the central themes in Kivi's novel is the relationship of humans to nature. Nature is often seen as an opponent and a force to be fought against. The brothers have to suffer all kinds of obstacles nature sets them. But at the same time nature is their companion. Being rather wild and unsociable themselves, the brothers escape culture and civilization deep in the Finnish forests. Paradoxically, they are able to civilize and educate themselves in the wilderness. Their own wildness is calmed and each of them returns to live a more or less ordinary human life in the community. This is how one of the brothers, Lauri, introduces the idea of moving into the forest:

> Let's move into the bosom of the forest and sell wretched Jukola, or let's rent it to the tanner at Rajaportti. He has sent word to us of his willingness to close a bargain; only he wants possession for at least ten years. Let's do as I say and move with our horse, dogs and guns to the foot of Impivaara's steep heights. There we can build ourselves a jolly cabin on a southward looking clearing and live in peace far away from the bustle of the world and touchy people, hunting game in the forests.... There we'd be living like lords, hunting wildfowl, squirrels, hares, foxes, wolves, badgers and bushy bears.[7]

The conception of nature that Kivi puts forward is relevant for my argument. On one hand there is the traditional opposition between culture and nature, but on the other there is the idea that people are in some deeper sense a part of nature. This idea is also present in Lauri's persuasive and idyllic description. Despite all the obstacles that nature sets, wilderness is a companion to the brothers and they feel a deep sense of involvement with it. They were able to form their own little settlement in the forest. They had to make a tremendous effort and suffered a great deal to achieve the goal, but in the end they lived in harmony with nature.

It may well have been that Kivi originally intended to depict something that he saw was somehow typical of Finland – certain kinds of characters, a certain way of life. But as his novel gradually gained the monumental position it now has, the representational relation has changed. The views that Kivi put forward in his novel have become a part of the Finnish way of life. The kind of relationship between humans and nature Kivi portrays is deeply rooted in the Finnish national character. This can be seen in cultural practices, such as retreating to summer cottages during the summer months. The importance of nature for Finns, especially of forests and lakes, has become a cliché but it is no less true. When we consider the stature of Kivi's novel in the Finnish life world, we can understand its influence on the national character and on people's way of life.

Sillanpää also draws a lot from the connections between humans and nature. In his case, the concept of nature has a strong feel of pantheism: nature is a kind of divine force, and humans are essentially part of it. This connectedness of humans and nature and the divine character of Finnish nature are vividly described in Sillanpää's summer scenes. We return to the idea mentioned earlier in the chapter: the fictional origin of the Finnish summer, and its role in the Finnish life world. In many of Sillanpää's pieces, summer is portrayed in a very romantic manner. While there are other Finnish authors in this romantic tradition, Sillanpää is clearly one of the most influential. He opens *People in the Summer Night* with these lines:

> There is almost no summer night in the north; only a lingering evening, darkening slightly as it lingers, but even this darkening has its ineffable clarity. It is the approaching presentiment of the summer morning. When the music of late evening has sunk to a violet, dusky pianissimo, so delicate that it lengthens into a brief rest, then the first violin awakens with a soft, high cadence in which the cello soon joins, and this inwardly perceived tone picture is supported outwardly by a thousand-tongued accompaniment twittering from a myriad of branches and from the heights of the air. It is already morning, yet a moment ago it was still evening. The lark springs aloft, higher and higher, singing from above to the smaller, prettier warblers in the foliage and telling them what the morning looks like from a wider view.[8]

It could be argued of course that the Finnish summer, independent of novelists and other artists, is really nice, beautiful and perhaps even romantic. These qualities are not mere imaginative projections of those living in the summer months in Finland. I agree that people do experience the kind of qualities mentioned. There is a special light and clarity as the evening falls, and the twilight, as well as the brevity of the night, creates a distinct atmosphere, describable also in musical terms, as Sillanpää does above. But my claim is that it is at least partly because of art that the summer is experienced in such a way. Finnish literature has given Finns a romantic way of experiencing summer nights; or, to be more precise, literature has not only given ways of experiencing but has opened up the life world in such a way that people can experience it as having certain qualities.

Another obvious counter-argument is that not every Finn has read Kivi's and Sillanpää's novels. Even though they are both undisputed classics, the majority of Finns know them by their titles only, and there are those who are ignorant of these novels altogether. Is their experience different? Are they excluded from the wonders of nature and the loveliness of the summer nights? Of course they are not. Reading a particular novel is clearly not a prerequisite for perceiving and experiencing the qualities mentioned. My argument does not require this either; it does not depend on facts about individual readers and whether they have read something or not. My claim is that fictional ideas, that is, ideas introduced in fictional literature, can become embedded in the life world of a people.

This embeddedness is reflected in the popular images of different people. What is interesting is the lack of wintry scenes and especially snowstorms in early Finnish literature. It has been argued that it was only through the strong Russian influence that Finnish authors started to write about winter and especially to depict snowstorms, which are common also in the Finnish winter.[9] In the works of Pushkin, Gogol, Dostoyevsky and Tolstoy, winter and snowstorms play a role. It was especially through Tolstoy's influence that these were gradually taken up as themes in Finnish literature; however, snowstorms never gained any major significance. When we consider the popular images people have of Finland and Russia, it is clear that Russia is seen much more often in terms of winter than Finland. There seems to be a tendency to romanticize the Russian winter, a tendency that is lacking in the Finnish experience.

There is a correspondence, then, between certain literary themes and the ways in which cultures are portrayed and experienced. Again, I do not think it is too far-fetched to attribute some of the qualities of the life world to art, in this case to fictional literature. Let me introduce my final example and then explain in more detail the character of the world in which we humans live – the life world that exemplifies complex semantic properties and value.

William Wordsworth was a native-born Cumbrian who knew the Lake District and its mountains from an early age. One of the hobbies for boys at the time was collecting birds' eggs, and sometimes this involved climbing rocky mountain cliffs.[10] Together with fellow artists such as Coleridge, Constable and Turner, what Wordsworth brought into the English experience was a way to appreciate wilderness and landscapes previously regarded as hostile and dangerous. This was partly due to the interest that Wordsworth had in the theoretical discussion of the time; the concepts of the sublime and picturesque figure prominently in Wordsworth.[11] Besides his poetical works, Wordsworth wrote descriptive observations about his beloved Lake District, most notably a work entitled *Guide to the Lakes*.

Wordsworth's poetry is very much about the relation of humans to nature. It is one of the main themes in *The Prelude* (1805) and is present in many shorter poems, such as 'Lines Written a Few Miles above Tintern Abbey'. In Book VI of *The Prelude*, Wordsworth gives his famous account of the Alps, which has been influential in making the Alps a tourist resort, that is, an attractive place for everybody to visit.[12] But let me quote here the opening lines from *Tintern Abbey*:

> Five years have passed; five summers, with the length
> Of five long winters! and again I hear
> These waters, rolling from their mountain-springs
> With a sweet inland murmur. Once again
> Do I behold these steep and lofty cliffs,
> Which on a wild secluded scene impress
> Thoughts of more deep seclusion; and connect
> The landscape with the quiet of the sky.
> The day is come when I again repose
> Here, under this dark sycamore, and view
> These plots of cottage-ground, these orchard-tufts,

Which, at this season, with their unripe fruits,
Among the woods and copses lose themselves,
Nor, with their green and simple hue, disturb
The wild green landscape.[13]

David Craig argues that it was the Romantic tradition in poetry and painting – artists such as Wordsworth, Coleridge and Turner – that saw untamed nature, and especially mountains, as worth appreciating. Earlier, such places were regarded as 'frightening or plain useless'.[14] The way writers like Wordsworth described mountains also paved the way for mountaineering culture: mountains are there to be conquered and the views to be admired.[15] More generally, the tourist industry, which we now take self-evidently as linked to mountain areas, benefited considerably from the ways in which mountains were described by poets and painted by artists. For Wordsworth it was not only the mountains that counted, but the Lake District as a whole area, with different landscapes involving interaction of humans and nature. He was also very conscious in his efforts to educate people to see and appreciate the area that was a source of inspiration for himself.[16]

Art and fiction can change the world, and they can also increase the significance that nature has in the human world. In this respect, Heidegger's observations on art are on the right track: great works can open up, or 'set up', a world.[17] In my view, we do not have to assume that they would always or even typically open up a whole new world, as the temple did, in Heidegger's view, for the Greeks. Works of art often function on a minor scale of disclosure; they open parts of a world, such as the way in which people relate to nature, see and experience summer, winter and certain landscapes, such as mountains.

Life Worlds as Cultural Units

Let me now explain in more detail the nature of the reality I am concerned with here. I have already pointed out that I am not talking about the world in the sense of a collection of tangible entities. The reality I am referring to cannot be defined by reference to objects occupying a certain physical location. I am not denying the reality of the physical either: our society could simply not operate without different kinds of physical entities and without our acceptance of the physicality of these entities. To give a trivial example, we have to face traffic jams and crowds, and we experience them as physical hindrances making it difficult for us to move from one place to another. The world in which we exist is also a world in which physicality plays a crucial role. But tangible and perceivable objects are always something more than their mere physicality. We do not see physical objects but, for example, cars, and more particularly certain kinds of cars; we see other people, and not only nameless and faceless anonymous human beings but friends, acquaintances, shopkeepers, post office personnel; and we see the Alps and Mont Blanc, the Mountains in the Lakes and Sca Fell.

The human world is a meaningful totality, not a nameless collection of physical entities. I want to emphasize the 'human nature' of the life world. Distinctions such as culture and nature, and classifications such as wilderness and city, also have their origins in human interests. They are not in the objects themselves, in the sense that other distinctions and classifications could not be made. We make objects and events accessible to ourselves by naming and classifying them. This is already a form of 'humanizing' nature.[18] Besides naming and categorizing, we also evaluate. There are things that are condemnable, others that are praiseworthy. There are landscapes that are rugged and sublime, others that are uninteresting and dull. There are also cases in which we can say that a scene or an object possesses qualities such that it is serene and peaceful or lively and joyous, that is, qualities that in some sense of the word are 'expressive'. The human life world is thus complex, many-layered, and a qualitatively multifaceted whole.

Martin Heidegger has analysed the nature of the human world in many of his writings, such as *Being and Time* and the essay, 'The Origin of the Work of Art'. For Heidegger, the world is not something tangible and measurable: the world cannot be understood as a collection or set of physical entities.[19] To get a clearer picture of Heidegger's phenomenological conception of the world, let us consider more closely a particular example of a world, something that Heidegger calls the 'tool world'.[20] What is constitutive of the tool world is the different relations in which different pieces of equipment stand. A tool cannot function as a tool on its own: we could not build a house with just a hammer. In order for the hammer to function as a hammer, we need a number of other tools, such as a nail and a piece of board into which to hammer the nail.

These relations constitute a 'totality of equipment'[21] and this totality precedes each individual tool in the sense that the functionality of each singular piece presupposes the totality. This is why Heidegger can say that strictly speaking there is 'no such thing as *an* equipment'.[22] A hammer is a hammer only in the larger network; its nature as a hammer depends on this context.[23] The meaningfulness of a singular entity is defined by its relations to other entities, not to any particular object, but again to the totality of equipment. The fact that we produce different kinds of tools for different purposes demonstrates that we live in different tool worlds. It is self-evident to us that they are being produced to fulfill a multiplicity of functions. That these sorts of things are taken as 'matters of course', taken for granted without being reflected upon, indicates that we are also part of these structures. We have grown into them and they have become part of us as entities living in them.

This is how I understand life worlds more generally: they are structures that give us entities and events as *certain kinds* of entities and events. Life worlds are culturally determined totalities that define entities as meaningful and as valuable, or possibly as something to be avoided or despised. I am not referring only to functional contexts, tool worlds, but to all kinds of cultural units. Practices in the arts, the sciences, the humanities, in sports, economics, politics, and so on, all exemplify the kind of 'givenness' that is characteristic of life worlds. This is true of the role that nature plays in our life worlds, too. Depending on the meanings and evaluations that science, religion and economics, as well as literature and the arts, attribute to natural phenomena, nature appears differently in different cultural contexts. When we have lived in these structures long enough, or if we are born into them, the meanings and values of different things within them become part of our identities and so self-evident that we have to make an effort to realize and understand their presence and their nature. Most of the time we do not reflect the meaningfulness of politics, economics, the sciences or the arts. These cultural practices constitute ourselves as cultural entities living within these sorts of cultural worlds or life worlds.

Life World and Nature

Heidegger gives a detailed analysis of tools and their constitutive relations, as well as of the nature of the world and the notion of being-in-the-world.[24] But rather than going any deeper into Heidegger's existential ontology, I shall consider in more detail the role of nature in the cultural structures I have been exploring. He has useful things to say about this, too. In his analysis of tools, Heidegger touches upon the issue of how nature is revealed to us:

> Any work [tool] with which one concerns oneself is ready-to-hand not only in the domestic world of the workshop but also in the *public world*. Along with the public, the *environing Nature [die Umweltnatur]* is discovered and is accessible to everyone. In roads, streets, bridges, buildings, our concern [die Sorge] discovers Nature as having some definitive direction. A converted railway platform takes account of bad weather; an installation for public lighting takes account of the darkness, or rather of specific changes in the presence or absence of daylight – the 'position of the sun'. In a clock, account is taken of some definite constellation in the world-system. When we look at the clock, we tacitly make use of the 'sun's position', in accordance with which the measurement of time gets regulated in the official astronomical manner. When we make use of the clock-equipment, which is proximally and inconspicuously ready-to-hand, the environing Nature is ready-to-hand along with it. Our concernful absorption in whatever work-world [toolworld] lies closest to us has a function of discovering.[25]

Nature is disclosed to us by our activities within the life world. The way in which nature is revealed is not as something that nature truly is but as something serving our purposes. As Heidegger says, 'Nature is ready-to-hand', that is, in our life worlds we have humanized nature and her forces in the way that Heidegger describes. We build shelters for bad weather, bridges over rivers, tunnels through mountains. But not only do we take such concrete physical measures against nature. We also take advantage of natural forces: 'the wood is a forest of timber, the mountain a quarry of rock; the river is water-power, the wind is wind "in the sails"'.[26] We live together with nature, and make use of its materials and forces.

Even this picture is incomplete, however. We obviously also admire and respect nature as nature. Our attitude towards natural objects is more than just seeing them as tools for practical purposes. As I have pointed out, in cases in which we admire the aesthetic qualities of a natural setting – white mountain tops in the winter against the blue sky in the Lake District, or the colours of a late sunset in a Finnish lake during summer – we have taken nature into our life world and humanized it. It is clear that this kind of 'usage' is different from concrete physical utilization, but, from the point of view of the life world, the important difference is not in the concreteness of the usage. In the kind of aesthetic cases referred to, we can also talk about nature being disclosed to us in a certain way. We may then have a more respectful attitude towards nature, compared to cases in which we concretely use nature and her forces for our purposes.[27] Nevertheless, the qualities that nature offers for our consideration are determined by our interests and finally by values and meanings from which these interests arise. In an alternative world, natural phenomena might have only religious significance and no aesthetic qualities whatsoever. White mountains might not be beautiful but scary because they indicate, say, the anger of divinities. Although physically the same, the cultural significance of this natural phenomenon can be very different: indeed, to the extent that it is a different cultural object. Accordingly, the ways in which people in different cultural worlds relate to it differ considerably.

Life worlds are not limited to cultural structures in the narrow sense of cultural practices, such as arts, sciences, politics and so on, but cover the whole of human existence, including our relations to natural objects. The ways humans have seen and experienced nature have changed over time. In this sense, nature is of our making. Our relationships to nature have varied according to technical development, to changes in the scientific theories about nature, to changes in our religious beliefs, but also to the ways in which art and fiction have portrayed nature. Art is a significant factor in our life worlds, and its role in the formation of a life world should not be underestimated. It is often artists rather than historians who first give interpretations of historically significant events, such as military conflicts, and their interpretations are often more influential in the sense that they are more readily accessible to a wide audience than those of political analysts and historians. And, as I have tried to demonstrate, authors and artists are often the first to interpret nature, too, and through this they open up nature for the rest of us in a novel way.

Finally, it should be stressed once again that my thesis has not been a psychological one. I am not saying that fiction and art, more generally, simply offer new constituents for our perceptual and cognitive capacities, and that because of this each of us sees nature differently. My claim has been that art changes the world in which we live: our life world is different because art and fiction have changed it. Sillanpää did not actually change the temperature or light of Finnish nights in the summer, nor did Wordsworth alter the physical shapes of the Lake District. But what they both did was to give new a content to the life worlds in which they lived and which they shared with their contemporaries, and in which we still, to a certain extent, live. Wordsworth's and Sillanpää's life worlds as historical structures are parts of our life worlds too.

The human world goes through changes like these all the time. When our world changes, we change with it. We are in the 'webs of the life world',[28] not like spiders walking on a web but being distinct from it. We are in the web in the much more radical sense that the strands of the web go through us and determine what we finally are. This is the Heideggerian sense of 'being-in', which Heidegger characterized with the word 'care' (*Sorge*).[29] Our 'concernful being-in-the-world'[30] includes man-made as well as natural objects. This concernful existence has created, in the course of time, certain kinds of life worlds that give us, living in the present life worlds, objects as having properties and value. And so we can admire mountains and sunsets; we have certain kinds of relations to nature. All this is partly due to great artists such as Kivi and Sillanpää in the Finnish context, and Wordsworth, Turner and many others in the English life world. In the context of the life world, we can understand, and to a certain extent accept, Wilde's provocative claims and the logic of turning the representation theory upside-down:

> Where, if not from the Impressionists, do we get those wonderful brown fogs that come creeping down our streets, blurring the gas-lamps and changing the houses into monstrous shadows? To whom, if not them and their master, do we owe the lovely silver mists that brood over our river, and turn to faint forms of fading grace curved bridge and swaying barge?...For what is Nature? Nature is no great mother who has borne us. She is our creation.[31]

Notes

1 Oscar Wilde (1989), 'The Decay of Lying', in Isobel Murray (ed.), *The Oxford Authors: Oscar Wilde*, Oxford and New York: Oxford University Press, p. 230.
2 Ibid., p. 233.
3 When it comes to Wilde, however, one should always keep in mind that his reflections are often full of irony. In this case, it is not clear that he presents these views as his own.
4 I cannot go into the history of the term 'life world' (*Lebenswelt*). Edmund Husserl had already used it in his fairly early texts, but most notably in *Die Krisis der europäischen Wissenschaften und die transzendentale Phänomenologie: Eine Einleitung in die phäno-*

menologische Philosophie (1954), herausgegeben von Walter Biemel, The Hague: Martinus Nijhoff. A useful collection of Husserl's texts about the problems of the *Lebenswelt* is *Phänomenologie der Lebenswelt: Ausgewählte Texte II* (1986), Stuttgart: Philipp Reclam jun.

5   See Kendall Walton (1990), *Mimesis as Make-Believe – On the Foundations of Representational Arts*, Cambridge, MA: Harvard University Press, pp. 241–89.

6   Goodman uses the terms 'symbol' and 'symbolization' rather than 'concept' and conceptualization', but his line of thought is clear enough. For Goodman, art works are symbol systems, and the value of symbols lies in their capacity to serve our cognitive interests: that is, giving us tools to discover the world. See Nelson Goodman (1968), *Languages of Art*, Indianapolis: Bobbs-Merrill, pp. 258–60.

7   Aleksis Kivi (1952), *Seven Brothers*, trans. Alex Matson, Helsinki: Tammi Publishers, pp. 22–3.

8   F.E. Sillanpää (1966), *People in the Summer Night: An Epic Suite*, trans. Alan Blair, Madison, Milwaukee and London: University of Wisconsin Press, p. 3.

9   Annamari Sarajas (1980), 'Lumituisku: venäläinen aihelma' (Snow Storm: A Russian Theme), in *Orfeus nukkuu: tutkielmia kirjallisuudesta*, Porvoo, Helsinki and Juva: WSOY.

10 David Craig (1992), 'Coming Home: the Romantic Tradition of Mountaineering', in Keith Hanley and Alison Milbank (eds), *From Lancaster to the Lakes: The Region in Literature*, Lancaster: Centre for North-West Regional Studies, University of Lancaster, p. 29.

11 M. Brennan (1987), *Wordsworth, Turner, and the Romantic Landscape: A Study of the Traditions of the Picturesque and the Sublime*, Columbia, SC: Camden House, pp. 22–4, 69–77, 127–32; A.S. Byatt (1970), *Wordsworth and Coleridge in Their Time*, London: Thomas Nelson, pp. 259–60.

12 William Wordsworth, in Stephen Gill (ed.) (1984), *The Oxford Authors: William Wordsworth*, Oxford and New York: Oxford University Press, Book VI, lines 549–658; Craig (1992), pp. 33–4.

13 Wordsworth (1984, pp. 131–2).

14 Craig (1992, p. 27).

15 Ibid., pp. 34–5.

16 R. Noyes (1973), *Wordsworth and the Art of Landscape*, New York: Haskell House, pp. 83–8, 91–8; Byatt (1970, p. 261).

17 Martin Heidegger (1975), 'The Origin of the Work of Art', in Albert Hofstadter (ed. and trans.), *Poetry, Language, Thought*, New York: Harper & Row, pp. 44–5.

18 Arnold Berleant (1992), *The Aesthetics of Environment*, Philadelphia: Temple University Press, pp. 23, 194; Ronald Hepburn (1998), 'Nature Humanized: Nature Respected', *Environmental Values*, 7, 272, 274.

19 Martin Heidegger (1962), *Being and Time*, trans. John Macquarrie and Edward Robinson, Oxford, UK and Cambridge, MA: Blackwell, pp. 123–48.

20 Martin Heidegger (1979), *Prolegomena zur Geschichte des Zeitbegriffs: Marburger Vorlesung Sommersemester 1925*, herausgegeben von Petra Jaeger, Frankfurt am Main: Vittorio Klostermann, p. 260.

21 Heidegger (1962, p. 97).

22 Ibid.

23 Ibid., p. 98; Hubert L. Dreyfus (1992), 'Heidegger's History of the Being of Equipment', in Hubert Dreyfus and Harrison Hall (eds), *Heidegger: A Critical Reader*, Oxford: Blackwell.

24 Heidegger (1962, pp. 78–90, 149–224); Hubert L. Dreyfus (1991), *Being-in-the-World: A Commentary on Heidegger's Being and Time, Division I*, Cambridge, MA: MIT Press.

25 Heidegger (1962, pp. 100–101).

26 Ibid., p. 100.

27 Hepburn (1998, pp. 271–2).
28 Here I am using an expression from the title of Bernhard Waldenfels' book: Waldenfels (1985), *In den Netzen der Lebenswelt*, Frankfurt am Main: Suhrkamp.
29 Heidegger (1962, pp. 235–56).
30 This is not Heidegger's expression. In the English translation the term 'concern' is equivalent to the German 'Besorgen', by which Heidegger refers to our dealings with tools, objects ready-to-hand (Heidegger (1962, p. 237; Heidegger (1979), *Sein und Zeit*, fünfzehnte, an Hand der Gesamtausgabe durchgesehene Auflage mit den Randbemerkungen aus dem Handexemplar des Autors im Anhang, Tübingen: Max Niemeyer Verlag, p. 193). I am using the term 'concernful' in a broader sense here.
31 Wilde (1989, p. 232).

I am grateful to Emily Brady and Aarne Kinnunen for useful comments on this chapter.

Chapter 5

Nature Appreciation and the Question of Aesthetic Relevance

Allen Carlson

Mountain Gloom, Mountain Glory and Aesthetic Relevance

Marjorie Hope Nicolson opens her classic study on the history of nature appreciation, *Mountain Gloom and Mountain Glory*, with the following observations:

> 'To me,' said Byron's Childe Harold, 'high mountains are a feeling.' We comfortably agree, believing that the emotions we feel – or are supposed to feel – in the presence of grand Nature are universal and have been shared by men at all times. But high mountains were not 'a feeling' to Virgil or Horace, to Dante, to Shakespeare or Milton.... Today when tours ... have become synonymous ... with Mount Washington or Mount Hood, the Rockies, the High Sierras, Mont Blanc, the Jungfrau, the Alps or the Pyrenees, we assume that our feelings are the perennial ones of human beings. We do not ask whether they are sincere or to what extent they have been derived from poetry and novels we have read, landscape art we have seen, ways of thinking we have inherited. Like men of every age, we see in Nature what we have been taught to look for, we feel what we have been prepared to feel.[1]

After these provocative introductory remarks, Nicolson chronicles how, within a relatively short time span, our appreciation of 'grand nature', of mountains in particular, changed from 'Mountain Gloom' to 'Mountain Glory' – from seeing mountains as 'nature's shames and ills', as 'blisters' and 'tumours', the 'warts and pock-holes in the face Of th' earth' to viewing them as 'magnificent and glorious', 'the grandest, most majestic objects on the terrestrial globe'.[2]

Nicolson's account of this appreciative shift is compelling, explaining it in terms of changes in attitudes and information stemming from and embodied in not only poetry, novels and art, but also theology, philosophy, and science. The result is an impressive demonstration of how we, like 'men of every age', 'see in Nature what we have been taught to look for' and 'feel what we have been prepared to feel'. This demonstration forces to our attention an issue closely related to Nicolson's own main concern: the issue of the appropriateness to our aesthetic appreciation of nature of all these various forces and influences

61

that so effectively teach us what to look for and prepare us for how to feel. Nicolson's account is largely neutral concerning this issue, but it is yet one of the most central in the aesthetics of nature appreciation.

This chapter addresses this central issue of nature appreciation as a question of aesthetic relevance. The question is that of exactly how to appreciate nature appropriately and of exactly what is relevant to such appreciation. In other words, what attitudes, what points of view, what information, what knowledge should we acquire and cultivate in order to achieve a rich, appropriate appreciation of nature?[3] This question is approached by working through a number of different sources of attitudes and information, many of which Nicolson so convincingly demonstrates have shaped and continue to shape our aesthetic appreciation of nature. Eight different items are considered, each of which, following Nicolson, undoubtedly plays a significant role in influencing our aesthetic appreciation. However, the focus is primarily on the question of what role, if any, each *should* play in such appreciation: in other words, the question of which are, and which are not, relevant to the *appropriate* aesthetic appreciation of nature. The eight items are form, common knowledge, science, history, contemporary use, myth, symbol and art.[4] I also follow Nicolson in using mountains and mountain environments as my main examples throughout this chapter.

A Postmodern View of Nature Appreciation

Before considering these eight items, however, it is useful to note one point of view, which, were it correct, would seemingly make the whole question of what is relevant to appropriate nature appreciation pointless. It might be said that if, as Nicolson suggests, our appreciation of nature is so malleable that the seemingly momentous appreciative shift from 'Mountain Gloom' to 'Mountain Glory' could be accomplished within a relatively short time span – indeed, Nicolson claims 'within fifty years' – then it follows that anything and everything, and nothing in particular, should be considered essentially relevant to nature appreciation. This point of view holds that when it comes to the aesthetic appreciation of nature it is not a matter of appropriate or inappropriate appreciation, but simply a matter of 'the more, the merrier'. I call this point of view the postmodern view of nature appreciation because of, first, the obvious and much-made comparison between nature and a text and, second, one rather common postmodern position on the reading of a text. This is the position that in reading a text we appropriately find, not just that meaning its author intended, but any of various meanings that the text may in one way or another have acquired or that we may for one reason or another find in it. Moreover, and this is the key point, none of these possible meanings has priority; no reading of a text is privileged.

On such a postmodern view of nature appreciation, whatever attitudes and information we may bring to nature are seemingly as good as any other, for no reading of nature is privileged and thus nothing is essentially relevant. It makes no ultimate difference whether the attitudes and information are, on the one hand, those that gave rise to 'Mountain Gloom' or, on the other, those embodied in the poetry, art and science that made possible 'Mountain Glory'. Promoters of this view might find support for their position in Nicolson's insistence that in general our experiences of nature are a function of whatever conditioning we happen to undergo:

> What men see in Nature is a result of what they have been taught to see – lessons they have learned in school, doctrines they have heard in church, books they have read. They are conditioned most of all by what they mean by *Nature*, a word that has gathered around itself paradox and ambiguity ever since the fifth century BCE.[5]

However, Nicolson's observations also cast some doubt on the postmodern view. For example, after the above quoted remarks, she continues by noting that the particular change from 'Mountain Gloom' to 'Mountain Glory'

> was not merely a matter of literary language and conventions, though that played some part. It was a result of one of the most profound revolutions in thought that has ever occurred....it [was] motivated by man's conception of the world which he inhabits. Before the 'Mountain Glory' could shine, men were forced to change radically their ideas of the structure of the earth on which they lived and the structure of the universe of which that earth is only a part.[6]

Thus the overall message of Nicolson's observations seems to be that, although there are in fact differences in our appreciation of nature over time and place, this fact does not sanction the postmodern view that anything and everything, and nothing in particular, is relevant to nature appreciation. Rather, her observations suggest that how we experience and appreciate nature is ultimately a function of our deepest and most profound understanding of nature, and thus that the question of aesthetic relevance – that of what should and what should not play a role in shaping that appreciation – is not pointless but rather very much alive.

Consequently, I suggest, at least as a point of departure in our investigation, that in so far as we maintain a parallel between nature and a text, we assume a more modernist notion of reading a text. On such a view at least some readings are mistaken: misinterpretations that are simply read into a text. Likewise, some experiences of nature are mistaken: misinterpretations that are not the basis for appropriate appreciation. And thus there is the possibility of mistaken, inappropriate aesthetic appreciation of nature. I assume this modernist view of nature appreciation as we work through the above-mentioned eight items, asking of each what is its role, if any, in appropriate aesthetic appreciation of natural environments. My goal is to see if we can, concerning each of these items, escape being forced to accept something like a postmodern view.

Form and Content

With this background, we turn to the first of the eight items, form. By this is meant something like that which traditional formalized theoreticians, such as art critic Clive Bell, refer to as significant form, that is, aesthetically moving combinations of shapes, lines and colors. It is difficult to deny that the appreciation of form in this sense is a dimension of aesthetic appreciation of nature. Even Bell, whose focus is almost exclusively on art, allows for seeing nature as, in his words, 'a pure formal combination of lines and colours'.[7] Bell's idea is that of seeing a natural environment as it might look in a landscape painting by Cézanne, for example one of his many studies of Mont-Sainte-Victoire. And certainly Bell is correct in thinking that we seem to appreciate nature in this formal manner. In fact it is a dimension of the mode of appreciation that was, as noted by Nicolson, imposed on mountain environments by certain kinds of landscape art, and thus it is an important part of the story of the development of 'Mountain Glory'. It is also promoted in a less subtle way by popular presentations of natural environments, such as the calendar and postcard images of the mountains of our national parks, in which dominant shapes, strong lines and striking colors are emphasized. Such images facilitate a rather superficial, but yet quite common, formal appreciation of nature.

Consequently, I conclude that the skills, attitudes and information that facilitate formal appreciation are relevant to the appreciation of natural environments. However, having granted this, it important to resist the additional step that many formalist take. This is to insist that this dimension is not only a fundamental dimension of aesthetic appreciation but also the only dimension. Bell and other formalist are notorious for holding that consideration of form is all that is involved in aesthetic appreciation and that, by contrast, any consideration of content is irrelevant. However, there are many problems with this pure formalized position.[8] For example, concerning natural environments in particular, formal elements in themselves, that is, just shapes, lines, and colors, typically do not provide adequate resources for appreciation. This is in part because by reference to themselves alone the specific formal elements of a natural environment can hardly even be identified. The way in which they are identified is by reference to something other than themselves, typically by reference to the content of the environment.

As an illustration of this point, consider a formally impressive natural environment, for example a heavily forested mountain environment with one major and two minor peaks, and ask yourself: how many shapes does it have? Is the answer one? Or three? Or about three hundred? Likewise ask how many lines it has? The point is that, in order to identify the shapes and the lines in a natural environment, we typically make reference to content. If we say there is one basic shape, this is in part because one major thing, the major mountain peak, is present. If we say three, it is because three things, the major peak and two minor ones, are taken as constituting its content. If we say about three hundred, it is because we are taking each identifiable tree as identifying a particular shape. What these considerations demonstrate is that the formal appreciation of a natural environment in terms of shapes, lines and colors necessitates the essential consideration of the content of that environment. In short, in nature appreciation we cannot appreciate form without also considering content.

If formal appreciation requires us essentially to consider content, this takes us beyond pure formalism and beyond the first item of the eight topics previously indicated. It shows that content as well as form is aesthetically relevant. However, all of the remaining seven topics are in one sense or another content items. Thus the question is which and how many of these content items are relevant. Consider the first item after form: common knowledge. By this is meant the normal classifications and categorizations that we employ in our commonsense conceptualization of the world. It is in fact the knowledge that formalists such as Bell seek to exclude from aesthetic appreciation. Formalists ask us to see an environment as shapes, lines and colors and *not* as mountains and trees. Ironically, however, if the above argument is correct, this kind of knowledge is required for formal appreciation of nature, for it is by reference to these commonsense conceptualizations that we typically organize an environment. For example, we organize the above described mountain environment by reference to classifications such as mountain, peak and tree. Thus this basic kind of content is seemingly required for any aesthetic appreciation of nature whatsoever. It is an essential part of what is relevant for appropriate aesthetic appreciation.

Science and Nature Appreciation

The third item is science, by which I mean the natural history of environments as explicated by the natural sciences, especially geology, biology and ecology. I do not dwell on the role of scientific knowledge in aesthetic appreciation of nature here, as it has been discussed in detail elsewhere.[9] Nonetheless, it is useful to note briefly two arguments that demonstrate that scientific knowledge of nature is as vital to its aesthetic appreciation as is common knowledge.

The first argument notes that in an important sense scientific knowledge is simply an extension of common knowledge. A scientific conceptualization of a natural environment is finer-grained and theoretically richer than a commonsense conceptualization, but not essentially different in kind. Compare two descriptions of a typical mountain environment: first, a commonsense description of it as a series of peaks of rock jutting forth from surrounding rolling valleys; and, second, a scientific description of it as faulted igneous uplifts exposed by the erosion of surrounding sedimentary deposits. There is, of course, some conceptual movement from the commonsense description to the scientific one. However, this movement does not mark a change from aesthetic appreciation to something else. At most it only marks a change from superficial to deeper aesthetic appreciation. It constitutes a movement toward appreciation that is, in Nicolson's words, 'even more profoundly ... motivated by man's conception of the world which he inhabits'.[10] Thus, according to this line of argument, scientific knowledge enriches the appropriate aesthetic appreciation of nature that common knowledge initiates.

The second argument for the aesthetic relevance of scientific knowledge involves a comparison with the aesthetic appreciation of art. The argument takes for granted that in the appropriate aesthetic appreciation of works of art, knowledge that is provided by disciplines such as art history and art criticism is essentially aesthetically relevant. Moreover, the knowledge such disciplines provide about art is about the nature and the creation of works of art; in short, knowledge about their classification and categorization and about what might be called their 'histories of production'. And this is exactly the kind of knowledge that science provides about nature. For example, geology classifies and categorizes the elements of natural environments and tells us the story of how they came to be – their histories of production, as it were. Thus, for the same reasons that art critical and art historical knowledge are relevant for the aesthetic appreciation of art, scientific knowledge is similarly relevant for the aesthetic appreciation of nature. In light of this argument, and the previous one, I conclude that scientific knowledge is a part, together with form and common knowledge, of the basic relevant resources for appropriate aesthetic appreciation of natural environments.

Historical and Contemporary Uses of Environments

Does the above suggest that the remaining five items of the original list, history, contemporary use, myth, symbol, and art, are not aesthetically relevant? Are these five items only involved in what I call postmodern appreciation? In fact, the comparison with art appreciation seems to indicate this. Consider the next item, history. By this is meant the historical use of an environment rather than its natural history. The comparison with art appreciation seemingly suggests that the history of a particular natural environment in this sense is indeed irrelevant. This is because the history of a work of art, other than its history of production, is usually thought to be irrelevant to its aesthetic appreciation. For example, historical facts such as that a given work was first displayed in a certain place, then travelled here and there, and is now at a particular gallery would not normally be considered relevant to its aesthetic appreciation. For instance, is knowing that *Guernica* was displayed in New York City for many years and is now in Madrid relevant to its appropriate aesthetic appreciation? It seems not.

I suggest, however, that concerning the aesthetic relevance of history, rather than natural history, to natural environments the comparison with art appreciation is misleading. There is an important disanalogy between environments and works of art. It involves the fact that, typically, a work of art is completed at a specific point in time. What happens to it before that point is its history of production and, alternatively, what happens after this point of completion is its history. And typically while, as noted above, a work's history of production, like the natural history of an environment, is clearly relevant to its aesthetic appreciation, its later history is not. By contrast, however, there is no specific point in time at which natural environments are completed. For this reason their natural histories and their actual histories, their historical uses, are in a sense continuous; both constitute a single continuing history of production. The upshot is that for most environments knowledge of their continuing histories is vital to appropriate appreciation.

As illustrations of this point, consider two North American mountain environments that have experienced important changes in their recent histories: Devils Tower in Wyoming and Mount Rushmore in South Dakota. The former was set aside as the first United States National Monument in 1906. By this act it was removed from further development, and thus in a negative sense the act is extremely relevant to appreciating its present somewhat pristine state. Indeed, without this part of Devils Tower's recent history, the tower today might be crowned with golden arches or sculpted into a great stone Mickey Mouse. On the other hand, as is well known, Mount Rushmore was indeed sculpted, not into a stone mouse, but into likenesses of the heads of four United States presidents. Such a momentous moment in an environment's history is obviously relevant to its appropriate aesthetic appreciation. In a similar fashion, a less well-known mountain in South Dakota is currently in the process of being made into a sculpture of the Sioux leader, Crazy Horse. Without knowledge of this, it is impossible to appreciate appropriately the mountain's current, somewhat chaotic, state.

This last example, the current sculpting of a mountain into Crazy Horse's likeness, brings us to the fifth of the eight items, the contemporary use of an environment. However, once we see past the misleading nature of the comparison with art concerning historical use and thus understand the way in which the fourth item, the actual history of an environment, is relevant to its aesthetic appreciation, it becomes clear that this fifth item is equally relevant. The contemporary use of an environment, natural or otherwise, is continuous with its actual history just as that history is continuous with its natural history. All three are a part of its continuing history of production. Thus I conclude that all three are equally aesthetically relevant.

There is, however, a difference between the history of an environment and its contemporary use that is worth noting, if only because this difference tends to obscure the essential sameness of the two. This is that, seemingly in part because of our closeness to it, we as appreciators are more apt to regard the contemporary use of a natural environment in a negative fashion and thus look upon the results with aesthetic disgust. Consider, for example, the current uses of many mountain environments for strip mining and clear cutting. Few view the resultant environments positively. However, it must be recognized that, even if we regard such contemporary uses in a negative manner, this does not make knowledge of this part of an environment's history of production irrelevant to aesthetic appreciation. Here another comparison with art is helpful. Consider Michelangelo's *Pietà*. In 1972, it was damaged and reconstructed, with missing fragments replaced by a mixture of ground marble and resin. Most likely we regard this contemporary history negatively. However, given the way in which *Pietà*'s damage and reconstruction necessarily brought about changes in it, knowledge of this part of its contemporary history is essential to its appropriate aesthetic appreciation.[11] Likewise, knowledge of the contemporary uses of environments, regardless of the nature of our reaction to such uses, has an essential place in their appropriate aesthetic appreciation.

Myth, Symbol and Art

We have now considered the first five items and found all to be relevant to appropriate aesthetic appreciation of environments. This leaves the last three, myth, symbol and art. These labels indicate what are also *uses* of environments, just as historical and contemporary uses. In particular, they are the uses of environments within the mythical, symbolic and artistic creations of different peoples and cultures. However, these uses, unlike the previously considered more concrete physical uses of environments, do not seem to be directly involved in the making and changing of actual environments. Thus the issue is whether or not we have finally left what is essentially relevant to aesthetic appreciation and come, with these three uses, to items involved only in a postmodern account of appreciation. The question is: is knowledge of these three uses of environments thus irrelevant and therefore at best optional? Before addressing this question it is useful to illustrate briefly each of these kinds of uses.

The use of natural environments in mythical and folk traditions is common within most cultures. For example, in the traditions of some American aboriginal cultures, the previously described natural environment of Devils Tower is that of Mateo Tepee or 'Bear Lodge'. One such culture, that of the Kiowas, has the following myth about the formation of the tower:

> Eight children were there at play, seven sisters and their brother. Suddenly the boy was struck dumb: he trembled and began to run upon his hands and feet. His fingers became claws, and his body was covered with fur. Directly there was a bear where the boy had been. The sisters were terrified: they ran, and the bear after them. They came to the stump of a great tree, and the tree spoke to them. It bade them climb upon it, and as they did so it began to rise into the air. The bear came to kill them, but they were just beyond its reach. It reared against the tree and scored the bark all around with its claws. The seven sisters were borne into the sky, and they became the stars of the Big Dipper.[12]

Such mythical accounts are frequently closely related to what I term the symbolic uses of environments. For example, in part because of its role in this myth, the environment of Devils Tower is considered a sacred place by North American aboriginal cultures, symbolic of the very creation of the earth and the sky as we know it. They say that when Mateo Tepee rose from the earth, it was the 'birth of time' and 'the motion of the world was begun'.[13] Other natural environments have comparable symbolic roles within different cultures. As Nicolson clearly demonstrates, mountains and similar formations are seemingly particularly good bearers of such symbolic import. For example, Mount Fujiyama has a special symbolic role in the culture of Japan. And, of course, an environment such as that of Mount Rushmore, which was described earlier, has, for obvious reasons, symbolic importance for many Americans. Such examples can be multiplied almost endlessly. Consider not just Mount Rushmore, Mount Fujiyama and Devils Tower, but the mountains Nicolson mentions in the remarks quoted at the beginning of this chapter: Mount Washington, Mount Hood, the Rockies, the High Sierras, Mont Blanc, the Jungfrau, the Alps, the Pyrenees. And the list can go on and on, for example: Pikes Peak, Mount Kilimanjaro, Half Dome, Mont-Sainte-Victoire, Ayers Rock, Mount Edith Cavell, the Grand Tetons, Mount Ararat, Ship Rock, Mount Olympus. Each has a symbolic role for certain individuals, groups or cultures.

This brings us to the last of the eight items, that which Nicolson discusses definitively concerning mountains: the uses of natural environments in art. These uses include a number of different kinds of cases. On the one hand, many uses, such as that of Mount Fujiyama in Japanese art, involve mainly images of environments. Likewise, in Cézanne's many studies of Mont-Sainte-Victoire, the mountain is only a source of various images. On the other hand, there are uses such as those by environmental artists, such as Christo, where the actual natural environment is for a limited time a part of the work of art. Intermediate between these two extremes are the uses of actual environments in realistic photographic and cinematographic arts. For example, the photographic images of Ansel Adams, such as those of the Grand Tetons and of Half Dome in Yosemite National Park, are classic images of mountain environments of western North America. Equally classic, although perhaps in a somewhat different sense, are the uses of natural environments in many films. Consider, for example, the use of the environment of Mount Rushmore by Alfred Hitchcock in his 1959 thriller, *North by Northwest*, or the use of the Devils Tower environment by Steven Spielberg in the immensely popular 1977 science fiction film *Close Encounters of the Third Kind*, in which Devils Tower is the fictional landing site for visitors from outer space.

Having illustrated the mythical, symbolic and artistic uses of environments, we turn to the question of the relevance of these uses to the appropriate aesthetic appreciation of environments. Is knowledge of these uses essentially relevant to appropriate appreciation? Initially, a negative answer seems intuitive. After all, who would hold that, in order to aesthetically appreciate, for example, the environment of Devils Tower appropriately, we need to know about the Kiowas' creation myth of the formation of Mateo Tepee, let alone about Spielberg's story of humanity's first 'third kind' close encounter with aliens from outer space? Nor does Hitchcock's exciting chase scene across the faces of Lincoln, Grant and Jefferson seem relevant to the appropriate appreciation of Mount Rushmore. Intuitively, it seems plausible to abandon such images and information to postmodern appreciation.

Moreover, in addition to this intuition, there is a more substantial reason for skepticism about the aesthetic relevance of knowledge of mythical, symbolic and artistic uses of environments. Such uses are seemingly essentially different in kind from the other items previously considered. Knowledge of these items, especially of natural history, history and contemporary use, is relevant to aesthetic appreciation of environments at least in part because it tells us the stories of the histories of production of environments. It explains why environments are as they are and thus why they look as they do. By contrast, the mythical, symbolic and artistic uses of environments seemingly have nothing to do with their histories of production. Real environments are not changed by these uses. Unlike the natural history, history and contemporary use of environments, the mythical, symbolic and artistic uses seemingly leave environments just as they find them. The natural environment of Devils Tower was not remade by being called Mateo Tepee nor by fictionally hosting humanity's first big close encounter of the third kind. Likewise, Cézanne did not change Mont-Sainte-Victoire, nor did Adams alter the Grand Tetons. And even Christo religiously restores the environments he uses in his artistic creations to their original conditions.

In light of this seemingly significant difference between these last three items and the preceding ones, it is tempting to conclude that they indeed have no essential place in appropriate aesthetic appreciation of nature. Thus, concerning the mythical, symbolic and artistic uses of natural environments, it is tempting to accept the postmodern view of nature appreciation. Recall that this view allows that we may read in nature any of various meanings that it may in one way or another have acquired or that we may for one reason or another find in it. And, moreover, none of these possible meanings has priority; no reading is privileged. On the postmodern view, we may, if we like, read the environmental text of Devils Tower in light of the myth of Mateo Tepee and its great clawing bear; alternatively, we may contemplate it in light of tales of close encounters with childlike aliens, but there is absolutely nothing to chose between the two different readings: neither reading is privileged. Knowledge of neither is essentially relevant for appropriate aesthetic appreciation.

The 'Close Encounters Phenomenon' and Pluralism

However, there is something wrong with a postmodern view even for the mythical, symbolic and artistic uses of environments. The view does not do justice to the seeming importance and vitality of such uses. The problem is illuminated by what I call, after Spielberg's film, the 'Close Encounters Phenomenon'. It can be illustrated as follows. Even if we believe that knowledge of the use of Devils Tower in *Close Encounters of the Third Kind* is absolutely irrelevant to its appropriate aesthetic appreciation, we may find, if we have seen the film, that it is almost impossible to free ourselves from its images when we attempt to appreciate this environment. In a sense, we become caught in a state similar to that of the character in *Close Encounters* played by Richard Dreyfuss, who, because of an alien encounter that 'imprints' him with the image of the tower, cannot shake it from his mind. He finds himself possessed by it: he sculpts it in his mashed potatoes and in his shaving cream; he makes a large mud model of it in the middle of his living room. In a somewhat similar way, once we have had an 'imprinting' encounter with the film, it is difficult to shake its images from our minds. And they color our aesthetic appreciation of Devils Tower.

I think the 'Close Encounters Phenomenon' is both powerful and common. For example, whenever I look at a photo I took of my family standing in front of Devils Tower, I find it almost impossible not to imagine a large space ship emerging over the top of the tower. Likewise, having seen Hitchcock's *North by Northwest*, even only once and many years ago, I yet have difficulty seeing Mount Rushmore without imagining Cary Grant and Eva Marie Saint scampering in the moonlight next to Lincoln's face and crawling furtively under Jefferson's chin. Similarly, I expect there are native North Americans who imagine Mateo Tepee and the great clawing bear whenever they look at Devils Tower. And Half Dome and the Grand Tetons are seemingly seen by many mainly through the eyes of Adams. Moreover, this phenomenon has been explicitly noted by artists themselves. For example, even though Christo faithfully restores the environmental sites of his works to their initial states, when he was asked 'whether he thought that the canyon at Rifle Gap remained unaffected by having hosted *Valley Curtain*, he replied: "Perhaps not. Was Mont-Sainte-Victoire ever the same after Cézanne?"'[14]

The 'Close Encounters Phenomenon' reminds us that, to use Wittgenstein's image, our pictures hold us captive. The significance is that, because many of our mythical, symbolic and artistic images of environments do in this way hold us captive, these uses are after all more like the other uses than they initially appear to be. It is true that such uses are not a part of the history of production of actual environments and do not thereby explain how such environments look. Nonetheless, they yet have explanatory power concerning the ways that environments look to us, or at least with respect to the ways they look to those who are held captive by the relevant images. In this sense the mythical, symbolic and artistic uses of environments make, not the actual environments themselves, but rather the environmental images of an individual, a group or a whole culture – they shape imaginary environments in the individual or the collective mind. And thus knowledge of these uses does indeed explain the way environments look to certain individuals or to members of certain groups or cultures. Thus, although the explanatory power of the knowledge of these uses of environments is relative to specific contexts, it is yet in this contextually relativized way relevant to the aesthetic appreciation of nature.

The 'Close Encounters Phenomenon' suggests that, concerning even this dimension of nature appreciation, the postmodern view is not suitable after all. Rather, a related view which may be called 'pluralism' seems more correct. A pluralist view of nature appreciation accepts something like the comparison between nature and a text, in that it recognizes that we can read in an environment many of various meanings that it may have acquired or that we may find in it. However, for any particular reader, group of readers, or culture, or within any specific context, some of these possible meanings have, after all, priority and thus constitute privileged readings. Which readings are privileged and which not depends upon which imaginary environments of the mind hold sway for an individual, a group or a culture. In this way the pluralist view gives a contextually constrained role in our appropriate aesthetic appreciation of environments to mythical, symbolic and artistic uses. Nonetheless, the knowledge of such uses does not contribute to appropriate aesthetic appreciation in the same way in which knowledge of the actual histories of production of environments does. The latter is essential to the appropriate aesthetic appreciation of any appreciator whatsoever, while the former is significant only in certain contexts, only for certain individuals, groups or cultures.[15]

Conclusion

In conclusion, in light of a pluralist view of nature appreciation, we return to the question of aesthetic relevance. Just what is relevant to appropriate aesthetic appreciation of natural environments? Pluralism suggests an answer involving one central trunk of aesthetically relevant information comprising of the first five items of the original eight topics; that is, form, common knowledge, science, history and contemporary use, together with alternative branches of supplementary information comprising of the last three: myth, symbol and art. In appropriate aesthetic appreciation, the trunk is essential in any context, while different branches are relevant or not depending upon the context in question. Such a pluralist picture of appropriate aesthetic appreciation of environments accommodates our sometimes seemingly conflicting intuitions about what is relevant to the appreciation of nature. Similarly, it accommodates two of the main themes stressed by Nicolson:

that, on the one hand, our nature appreciation is in part 'derived from poetry and novels we have read, landscape art we have seen, ways of thinking we have inherited', while, on the other hand, it is yet rooted in our most profound 'ideas of the structure of the earth' on which we live 'and the structure of the universe of which that earth is only a part'.[16]

Notes

1 Nicolson, M.H. (1959), *Mountain Gloom and Mountain Glory: The Development of the Aesthetics of the Infinite*, Ithaca: Cornell University Press.

2 Ibid. The description of mountains as 'warts and pock-holes' is from John Donne's 1611 poem, 'An Anatomy of the World: The First Anniversary'. The phrases 'Mountain Gloom' and 'Mountain Glory' are from the headings of Chapters 19 and 20 of Book Five of John Ruskin's *Modern Painters*.

3 The classic formulation of the question of aesthetic relevance is in Jerome Stolnitz's 1960 textbook: 'Is it ever "relevant" to aesthetic experience to have thoughts or images or bits of knowledge which are not present within the object itself? If these are ever relevant, under what conditions are they so?' See J. Stolnitz (1960), *Aesthetics and the Philosophy of Art Criticism: A Critical Introduction*, Boston: Houghton Mifflin.

4 Elsewhere, I use the same line of thought as employed in this chapter in considering these items as possible topic areas for a correct curriculum for aesthetic education in landscape appreciation. See A. Carlson (2001), 'Education for appreciation: what is the correct curriculum for landscape?', *Journal of Aesthetic Education*, **35** (forthcoming in 2001).

5 Nicolson (1959), *Mountain Gloom and Mountain Glory*.

6 Ibid.

7 C. Bell [1913] (1958), *Art*, New York: Putnam's Sons.

8 See A. Carlson (1977), 'On the possibility of quantifying scenic beauty', *Landscape Planning*, **4**, 131–72; A. Carlson (1979), 'Formal qualities and the natural environment', *Journal of Aesthetic Education*, **13**, 99–114.

9 See A. Carlson (1979), 'Appreciation and the natural environment', *Journal of Aesthetics and Art Criticism*, **37**, 267–76; (1981), 'Nature, aesthetic judgment, and objectivity', *Journal of Aesthetics and Art Criticism*, **40**, 15–27; (1984), 'Nature and positive aesthetics', *Environmental Ethics*, **6**, 5–34; (1993), 'Appreciating Art and Appreciating Nature', in S. Kemal and I. Gaskell (eds), *Landscape, Natural Beauty and the Arts*, Cambridge: Cambridge University Press, pp. 199–227; (1995), 'Nature, aesthetic appreciation, and knowledge', *Journal of Aesthetics and Art Criticism*, **53**, 393–400; and (1998), 'Aesthetic Appreciation of Nature', in E. Craig (ed.), *Routledge Encyclopedia of Philosophy*, Vol. 6, London: Routledge, pp. 731–5.

10 Nicolson (1959), *Mountain Gloom and Mountain Glory*.

11 It might be thought that the damage to *Pietà* is similar to the earlier described travels of *Guernica* and thus not relevant to aesthetic appreciation. However, since the damage brought about permanent changes to the actual work, it is more similar to history of production than simply to history.

12 N.S. Momaday (1969), *The Way to Rainy Mountain*, Albuquerque: University of New Mexico Press.

13 Ibid.

14 See D. Crawford (1983), 'Nature and art: some dialectical relationships', *Journal of Aesthetics and Art Criticism*, **42**, 49–58.

15 Elsewhere, I consider a similar line of thought concerning mythological descriptions of landscapes. See A. Carlson (2000), 'Landscape and literature', in *Aesthetics and the*

Environment: The Appreciation of Nature, Art and Architecture, London: Routledge, pp. 216–40.

16   Nicolson (1959), *Mountain Gloom and Mountain Glory*.

Chapter 6

Embodied Metaphors

Kaia Lehari

Metaphor and Environment

Environmental experience never repeats itself but changes constantly and possesses multiple meanings. It is both conscious and unconscious, for joined and intertwined in environmental experience are memory, imagination as a bodily state and the immediate experience of perception. Furthermore, the core experience of place and of the path, which are the basic elements of a living environment, lies in its meaning. In both the urban and rural landscapes, a person's physical involvement in nature is the deepest layer of the environmental condition and the source of its meanings. Moreover, the natural world is the basis of all mental and spiritual worlds. According to Edmund Husserl, lived experience, *Erlebnis,* is flowing and altering, depending on changes both in subject and object, as well as on intersubjectivity. The basic layer of experience is the primary feeling of reality, *protodoxa.*[1]

For Maurice Merleau-Ponty the body is the zero level of environment. Environment is neither external surrounding nor subjective imagination but the immediate, mutual and reciprocal relation of a person as an embodied spirit in the world. The invisible can thus fill me and occupy me only because I who see it do not see it from the depths of nothingness but from the midst of itself. I, the seer, am also visible. What makes the weight, the thickness, the flesh of each color, of each sound, of each tactile texture, of the present, and of the world is the fact that he who grasps them feels himself emerge from them by a sort of coiling up or redoubling, and is fundamentally homogeneous with them. He feels that he is the sensible coming to itself, and that, in return, the sensible is in his eyes as if it were his double or an extension of his own flesh. Things, whether here or there, now or then, no longer exist in themselves, in their own place and in their own time. They exist only at the end of those rays of spatiality and of temporality that are emitted in the secrecy of my flesh.[2]

The immediate present world of things surrounding us has meaning only because it includes both the latent past and future as their extending spatiality. A person is dependent on both his or her history and geography. At the same time one's lived experience and its phenomenological order are the primary, underlying foundation to the objective order, which is secondary. By placing

75

the phenomenological order first, Merleau-Ponty surpasses the dualism of the subject–object. A logical consequence of this is giving up any confrontation between the rational and the linguistic, the cultural and the natural, the visible and the invisible. In human culture, time and space are not anything external to a person; rather, we are involved in creating them. The style of a person's being-in-the-world is embodied by her culture.[3] The communication of one culture with another is carried out through this 'wild' area from which we all originate.[4]

Various signs make the body conscious of itself. We use signs to bring our chaotic world of feelings and cognition into order. Semiosis, or the way in which something acts as a sign, combines body, environment, spirit and culture. All types of signs: indexes, icons and symbols (to use Peirce's basic triad), as well as their hybrids, are used on different levels of environmental experience.

Metaphors hold a special place in this process. Metaphor is the cognitive phenomenon that converts actual feelings into artefactual conceptual structures.[5] It is a fundamental form of thinking, one by which a person makes his environmental state conscious. According to Peirce, metaphors constitute a type of *hypo-icons*, potential signs with only a limited signatory status. *Hypo-icons* participate in primary experience in a special way. Metaphors stand parallel to something else, according to the nature and state of the representator.[6]

A metaphorical relation to the environment involves both natural and conventional markings. As a result, the cognition of meanings is always also partially intuitive, unconscious and thus pre-semiotic. The metaphorical process, in a broad sense,[7] involves metonymy, synecdoche and also the symbol, and is a fundamental form of thinking. Metaphor concentrates, combines and helps to make different kinds and levels of environmental experience conscious.

A great number of metaphors have appeared and remained in use in almost all spheres of life that concern a person's relations to the natural environment. Paul Ricoeur[8] calls such metaphors 'key metaphors', metaphors that have a special metaphysical power, a primordial metaphorical character. They can also be called 'archetypal metaphors'. Using the sun, light, heat, the earth, water and fire as metaphors is a global practice. Their symbolic meaning goes back to ancient times and is celebrated in mythology and religion.[9] Earl R. MacCormac finds that myths develop from metaphors. When the metaphorical character of root-metaphors is forgotten and they are taken as absolutes, myths come into being. This is essentially the same both in the ancient faith that a notion may embody and in science.[10] The archetypal metaphor *metaphor* is 'home'. A fireplace is a focal point and symbol of home, home itself: *caput mundi*. From the Sumerians to preliterate cultures today, the sun and the sky, earth and water gods function as the mother or father of mankind. The basic archetypes in both nature and townscape are 'path' ('way') and 'place'.

Metaphorical Place

The three main sources in forming the metaphorical meaning of place are (1) experience of the body; (2) experience in the natural environment; and (3) life-experience in an artificial and designed urban and rural environment. These three realms of experience provide the context for each new, immediate experience of place. One universally valued place is the navel of the earth (*omphalos, umbilicus*). It is one of the archetypal metaphors which, as a symbol for the center of the earth, has supported other symbols denoting the center, such as the *axis* of the earth and the tree of the cosmos. This metaphor created myths and rituals in Delphos and in India, and was utilized as well by American Indians, Yakuts, Fenno-Ugrian peoples and Aborigines in Australia. The Greeks believed that the ocean also has a navel and that the Temple of Demeter, located in the center of Sicily, lies on the navel of the world and is the place through which Persephone entered the bosom of the earth to reach the underworld of Hades. The navel of the world is also the location, when on earth, of Agni, the god of fire in the Vedas and in Hindu mythology. The poetical power of the navel as the symbol of the center has not died away but survives to the present day in the languages of different nations throughout the world.

The metaphor of the head appears in the names of mountains as a latent metaphor in toponymics. It is grounded on an analogy that crosses the borders of language and culture to characterize a round form on the top, as *caput montis*, Golgotha and Capitolium. Functionally, the most important town in a state is the capital, *capitale, Hauptstadt* and so on. In the name of the upper town in Tallin, Estonia, *Toompea*, the formal analogy (hill as the head) and the political relevance of the place (seat of the superior power) have been combined. Similar latent metaphors are also hidden in the names of the town's main street, its main building and its main square in the German, Finnish and Estonian languages.

In Estonian and in Finnish we come across other anthropomorphic metaphors referring to different forms in nature, particularly in the topography of coastal areas: a mountain or a hill has a back, a head, a foot, a nose and a leg. 'Head' can stand for headland, a spring can be thought of as an eye, a throat as a narrow strait and so on. All these are dead metaphors that have survived in language in the form of a concept, a language form or a name. Among the old street names in Tallinn we find Long Leg (*Pikk Jalg*), Short Leg (*Lühike Jalg*), and a Neck of the Old Market (*Vanaturu kael*).

A whole range of metaphors appears in townscapes. Their meanings are based on symbolical forms of nature, as when the town is described as a bog, a forest, a desert, an island, a river or a hill. In the town, jungle laws hold sway. A street becomes a river whose flow carries us along, and we are drowned in a flood of people. Home becomes an island confronting the sloughs of the underworld. Several archetypal metaphors have retained their value, but their meaning has shifted, sometimes assuming the sheer opposite meaning. Myths about the mountain, the forest, the island, the sea or ocean, the bog and other places deemed sacred stem from archetypal metaphors. These places may become celebrated mythically and religiously. In town, an alluring bright light can be misleading, like a will-o'-the-wisp in a marsh or a swamp, and lead us to a ruinous amusement establishment.

The two opposite elements in the bog – an island and a marsh grave – can have an identical meaning. The slough can be a shelter for someone, just as a protected island can be a safe place. In a bog the two substances of water and earth merge to become an almost indistinguishable mixture. An island, on the other hand, with its dry earth, is a protected place, a place of order in the midst of a wet and bottomless chaos. Original place identity can shift to a total loss of identity. An archetypal metaphor taken from nature is covered with a new layer of meaning derived from the social and cultural context of the town, and a tension between new and old metaphors arises. The multiplicity of meanings increases, as the original metaphors never disappear completely but glimmer through the new layers, waiting like a phoenix to be born again from its ashes. To make archetypal metaphors conscious requires vertical cognition, penetration through the opaque layers of meaning.[11]

The metaphorical character of landscape has been widely applied to the experience of human-made environments. Generations of architects and mayors have dreamt of a town that could operate like clockwork. The most widespread synecdoches characterize the town as a museum, a prison and a fortress. Depending on which basic function is chosen, the town is represented in a given context by its most characteristic part. A number of such metaphorical relations are mutually convertible. We can think of a castle as a town or a town as a castle; we can look at a town as a prison or at a prison as a town; and so on. Such a revolving movement changes the field of meanings each time, making it more compact, if not wider. The etymology of names can experience a revival; nest-words can come to life. For instance, the Estonian word for 'town' (*linn*) is derived from the word '*linnus*', which is synonymous with 'fortress' (castle). In the Finnish language a word derived from the same root is used in the meaning of 'prison'. Historically, the fortress was a prison, a castle and a town. An analogous language game can be played with the English word 'borough', the German word '*burg*' and the French words '*bourg*' and '*bourgade*'. The historical context and protective function of the early towns has been fixed in many place names. Their dead metaphors await recognition.

The convertibility, ambivalence and intertwining of metaphors, and their different states (alive, half-alive, dead) affect our immediate perception of place differently each time, since lived metaphors are changeable. Metaphors of place are connected with culture myths. When we perceive a town as an island, its normative coloring can come from the myth that man is a Creator, a Master or an Engineer. The town is then an island of order in the midst of chaos, a place of civilization and culture in the midst of wild and chaotic nature. We admire ourselves through the town, a human creation. Such a town can turn into a fetish – the created itself becomes Ruler and Master. We really do adore such a town.

A second variant of a cultural myth is the imagination that civilization protects people against dangerous and wild nature. The town then becomes a shelter, a home that offers protection. Since nature is alien, the closure of the town is in contrast to the openness of nature, in the same way that the island in the sea is enclosed while surrounded by openness. Perceived this way, the town is also a nest, a den, a stronghold. The stronghold on an island is the safest shelter.

A third variant that can be identified is the culture myth according to which the town is a meeting place, an island of intensive communication, of the exchange of information and a place of culture amidst sparse mental emptiness. A whole range of metaphors can be associated with this myth: the town as a museum, as a book, as a historical text and as a theater. At the same time the town can be contrasted with the natural environment the other way round. When we perceive the town as a slough, a bog, a desert or a wild place, it then contains the criticism of the vices of civilization. The natural landscape then becomes like the Garden of Eden, where the relations between people and between people and nature are clean, immediate and based on honesty and love. Such a culture myth has been influenced by the ideas of Rousseau and Tolstoy and by events like those in Robinson Crusoe, together with agrarian mystification.

These three variants are old, indeed, but they are not aged myths. They stem from different root-metaphors which, being made conscious, stand for the town as a place, and continue as the context of new metaphors of place. Mythopoetical stratification is like a mental bed or setting that surrounds our concrete aesthetic evaluation of the environment. A whole range of archetypal metaphors embodying common human experience stem from the depths of history. They die repeatedly, to be born again in order to serve cognition as symbols. And then they may fall again into a latent state, to be drowned in the depths of time.

Metaphorical Path

Home and town are archetypical places. Path, walk and journey are also archetypes. The town and the path embody the two opposite ways of life: one located and the other nomadic, for presence and movement are two equally important and substantial ways of being.[12] Place comes into being at the spot where the paths of people, services, goods, experiences, thoughts and feelings cross. The meaningfulness of place derives from that meeting. One of the symbols of place is a crossroads, the mythical and magical crossroad, for paths create and determine the place.

Perception is connected with movement, beginning from retinal movement, quavering and ending in the movement of the body.

My mobile body makes a difference in the visible world, being part of it; that is why I can steer it through the visible.... In principle all my changes of place figure in a corner of my landscape; they are recorded on the map of the visible. ...The visible world and the world of my motor projects are each total parts of the same Being. This extraordinary overlapping, which we never think about sufficiently .... Immersed in the visible by his body, itself visible, the see-er does not appropriate what he sees; he merely approaches it by looking, he opens himself to the world....It is a self through confusion, narcissism, through inherence of the one who sees in that which he sees, and through inherence of sensing in the sensed – a self, therefore, that is caught up in things, that has a front and a back, a past and a future.... Visible and mobile, my body is a thing among things; it is caught in the fabric of the world .... But because it moves itself and sees, it holds things in a circle around itself. Things are an annex or prolongation of itself; they are incrusted into its flesh, they are part of its full definition.[13]

For Merleau-Ponty the idea from moving from place to place lies in the seeing, in meeting the being at the crossroads, thus encountering one's belonging to the world. The result is an extension of the private world, assembling and absorbing a number of things in one's personality. This means an increase in self-realization and the styling of one's way of existence in the world. We move around, wander around, drive around and look around. The road from home has two directions: we leave; we return. The final point of each journey is home – the place of all places, if not directly in the physical sense, then at least metaphorically. The mythical heroes Gilgamesh, Inanna, Orpheus, Odysseus, Aeneas, Kalevipoeg (and the shamans) return to the universe with a message after visiting Heaven or Hades. The motif of the prodigal son is repeated in the archaic myths, religions and arts of both East and West. The way home is the last stage of a journey. Departure and arrival occur in the same place. The journey to home is a circle.

The metaphorical road is used in mythopoetical texts in connection with meeting one's fate, as a trial that consists in overcoming difficulties or attaining wisdom. It is mostly characterized by its linear quality. The direction and course of a road are connected with a discourse of time, for movement along the road is temporal. Our traditional concept of time is linear and is of Judaeo-Christian origin, with which the idea of a linear road is associated. However, we cannot treat it too simply, for the path as an intentional object is an intricate complex whose linear essence is embodied in a line full of knots, returnings, circles and crossings.[14] This is the path of stories about memory and experience.

The spatialization of time has enjoyed support from Aristotle to Heidegger. Both a circle and a straight line are images of space–time. Death, the end of the path through life, is the beginning of a new life beyond. The idea of redemption accords with the idea of a linear earthly path through life, a delimited segment of eternal time. The dualisms of finite–infinite and of mortal–immortal do not exclude; rather, they include a belief in a return to prehistoric purity, to the time before the original sin, which means both the beginning and an eternal life in the Garden of Eden. The ideas of a man being formed from the dust of the ground, the resurrection of the mortal body, human burial in the ground and other such rituals are connected with the circle. Mythopoetical images, the line and the circle, are not part of Euclidean geometry. They are archetypal metaphors, existential constants, embodying universally recurring experience. They are in use as both visual and word images, as imagination and notions. Their historical (vertical) coherence is guaranteed by their metaphorical ground and core. Movement along the path also has nothing to do with geometry. It is rather an irregular movement that depends on the complex relations of the body and topography, memory and imagination, perception, knowledge and environment. A moving man can change his direction and levels, but he always ends where he started out, returning to himself. Prehistoric time in its spatialized form involves cyclical development, which is circular, an eternal return.[15] Home is not the only holy place that makes us move in circles: holy places within sacred and profane space have the same effect. A symbolic return to the beginning guarantees regeneration.

Circular movement has been a subject throughout history, from prehistoric myths to the philosophy of the twentieth century. The Absolute Idea revolves in a spiral pattern to reach self-cognition and return to its former position. In Heidegger's early theory of cognition, the central motif is a train of thought. Husserl, Heidegger and Merleau-Ponty all speak of the necessity of returning to the beginning of thinking, of starting a new circle of cognition. Heidegger's *Holzwege*, written in 1949, indeed all of his post-war work is, in a way, a philosophy of return. The road itself, as a place, is closed; it is a world of its own, a circle of departure and return.[16] A road embodies the style of human movements, whether it be the movement of body, feeling or thought.

Embodied metaphors are the expression of a style. Re-embodiment means a change in style, the style of being. Walking can have metaphorical meaning as a ritual journey or simply as a general symbol. The journey as embodiment of a life style can be made conscious as a metaphor, but it can also be subconscious. When it is latent, it belongs to the style of a person. Movements, gestures, facial expressions, all the devices of body language play an expressive role without being done consciously and without intention. We perceive the style of being of another person through our ability to transfer our own experience, which becomes involved through catharsis and empathy. This ability is possible because of our common human experience of the body. Motion is the more metaphoric the farther away we move from the immediate somatic experience in our perceptual process. The mental meaning in a symbolic gesture has almost completely overshadowed that of somatic ones.

The circle is not only a metaphor embodying the style of a kind of motion; it is also a symbolic image standing for a situated presence, a home or a town. In the literature of the history of settlement, the oldest known ideogram denoting town is often mentioned. Its Egyptian hieroglyph consists of a cross and a circle around it.[17] This symbol indicates the origin and function of towns, a location at a crossroads and protected by a circular wall, rampart and moat. The cross symbolizes the meeting-point; the circle stands for compact homogeneity of a community, as well as its border with a strange area and the physical, moral and mental barriers that are created. Both the cross and the circle denote places in cartography. Graphically, the cross in a circle develops into a grid, resembling a spider's web on the maps and referring to exact places and roads in the landscape.

The network of streets is connected with the network of roads, and these connect towns with other places. The network is not only a cartographic symbol; it is a topographical scheme and an iconic sign, as well, denoting (representing) movement on real landscape. The network is a symbol that represents different natural and artificial roads. Its hydrological terms are the hydrographic network, the observation network of subsoil and ground water, the network of water reservations, and so on. The natural network of waters in the moors consists of low watering patches, bog pools, springs, lakes and brooks, and thus of places and paths of circling waters. These all have physical equivalents in nature. In mathematics the net method, net analysis, net graph and grid are used. 'The classical cognitive method in the humanities reminds us of a net, where one moves from a knot to another and, as a result of this, forms a "screen of knowledge" with a texture that resembles a fabric. This becomes more dense through study'.[18]

The density of the net corresponds to the amount of knowledge. The nets of information and communication, virtual and Internet, mark invisible connections. The net has become a notion denoting conceptual schemes. The experience of using a net is very old and derives from more than the movement of a traveler. Ancient hunters, warriors and fishermen netted booty or haul. The spider has been often mentioned as an example for humans in using the net. According to Democritus and Empedocles, man as a weaver is a disciple of the spider. According to the Veda scriptures and ancient Hindu mythology, the cosmic threads (or winds) bolster the universe as breathing animates a human body. The thread of threads is Brahman or Atman or God. The earth is bound to the sun by threads. In Rig-Veda two sisters, the Night and the Dawn, are ceaselessly weaving the sun. The sun itself is a cosmic spinner and weaver. In the Upanishads it is compared with a spider thousands of times. In Bhagavad-Gita Krishna weaves the world. The cosmic spider is identified either with the sun, the extrapersonal principle (Atman-Brahman), or with the god. Weaving symbolizes a cosmogonic act.

The idea that all living things, existing and real, in as well as outside of time, have been created forms the basis of archaic Hindu thinking. Connection and integration are necessary for real being. What has been created remains connected with the Creator. The world and beings there are not free. Living means being connected and dependent either on God, the Principle, the world or other beings. In Song VII of Homer's *Iliad*, Zeus has a golden rope. In the *Laws*, Plato compares man with a marionette made by the gods and pulled by threads. The sacred, golden thread should be preferred to other threads, for it holds the world together. The image of the net as thread, rope, chain or string is ambivalent. The net connects and ties as well. This can mean either a privileged status as one of the elected (immediately connected with the Creator) or the lack of freedom. Thus the spider's web can simultaneously be a road and a net for communicating information.

The net as arch-metaphor embodies experience in different spheres, both in motion and in action or making. At the same time, these two spheres of experience are similar in their formal result, the emergence of the net. In all the meanings and forms of existence mentioned above (metaphor as visual, figure of speech, notion and real structure or object), the net guarantees free movement either along earthly paths, in water nets, in the Internet, or in a cosmic web. At the same time, the direction and limits of movement are conditioned by the net's configuration. Our relations with nature, society and other people are subjected to the dialectics of freedom and inevitability, hence the ambivalence of nets. Such an ambivalent meaning lies at the core of the net as arch-metaphor, and it does not disappear even if the metaphor should die. The embodiment of different kinds of experiences may have only a structural similarity, yet these experiences are linked by the deeper meaning of the net, simultaneously linking and limiting their motion on any level. As live or dead metaphors, the cross, the circle and the net are so universal in their multiple meanings that they seem to confirm the argument of Gaston Bachelard that 'the inversion of an image proves its significance, confirms its perfectness and naturalness'.[19]

We are never completely conscious about the movement of our bodies. Moving up or down, along rectilinear, circular, sinuous or zig-zag paths has archetypal symbolical meaning. The archetype, changed into a stereotype, is an unconscious part of motion experience. It is a potential image and a linguistic form that, even if half-consciously and unclearly expressed in words, involves aesthetic experience as part of lived experience. Dynamics has its own metaphors, in which the power of motion, direction and tempo are embodied; statics has its own ones: balance, harmony, unity and accordance. The path embodies the first and the place the second experience. The style of Being is embodied in both of them.

The Metaphorical Character of Acting and Making

Humans are beings who make things, thus shaping their environment. The style of being in the world, that is, the way of life, cultural properties, technological possibilities and the like, is embodied in things. The embodiment of mental values in art has always been an age-old problem (now actual, again) in the philosophy of art and aesthetic theory. This has been interpreted in contemporary theory of architecture and design, emphasizing new aspects. Metaphorization is not only the investigation of the problems of objective entities. The activity of making things and shaping environment also deserves attention.

The human field of activity is so extensive, practically unlimited, that here I can dwell only on some examples of arch-metaphorical activities and makings associated with one another. *Weaving* as an archetypal activity has been mentioned above. In everyday life we do not perceive the metaphorical core of this activity. It is rather an activity requiring technical skill based on the repetition of the same movements, which fosters psychological automatism. As a mythopoetical process, however, weaving is an activity of creating the world, a profound and symbolic substantiation.

Covering is an activity of ancient origin whose primary biological meaning has been buried under deep cultural layers. Covering is, in essence, ambiguous. The following are some of its multiple meanings:

1   Covering as a protection against cold, rain, snow and other natural occurrences. The skin is the oldest covering of the body, both for birds and animals, as well as people. Furs, carpets, blankets and clothes cover the body, the floor and the wall. The roof covers the home. Plants are protected by special transparencies, such as glass. Covering keeps things warm.
2   Covering to hide from a strange eye. Windows are covered, which is a two-way hiding. The external world is hidden, the inner space closed, and the possibility of looking in from outside disappears. The naked body, which is *taboo*, needs to be covered. Smoke screens, fog, hedges and trees, also create visual seclusion.
3   Covering for physical isolation as restriction. Clothes mark the outline of the body, walls close the town and garden of the castle. The door or gate covers the entrance and interrupts the way for the stranger. In the world of animals, the marking of territory by odor serves to cover it.
4   Covering of one material with another. This can be either to isolate, hide or protect, and for pragmatic or aesthetic reasons. As ice covers a body of water, humans cover water with a bridge, build a timber path into a bog, pave roads with asphalt or harder materials.

In architecture, finishing materials protect and hide structures. In the nineteenth century historicist and eclectic influences led to hiding buildings behind a decorative façade. This kind of covering is also used in postmodern architecture. In ceramics and metalwork, glazes and enamel cover weak and ugly material. Coloring, varnishing and painting are all coverings for wood, canvas, cardboard and other such materials. Covering for the purpose of hiding is ambivalent. It is both a protective and a concealing activity. By covering, people become involved in the activities of things, displaying both motherly and fatherly care in protecting plants, animals and human life, and in their power to imprison, restrict, isolate, hide and conceal.

Covering as arch-metaphor thus has an ambivalent meaning with a double core. Covered ground and uncovered earth are both values, but different styles of being are embodied in them. The state of being covered is a value: when the table is laid, it is a symbol of wealth. Naked is poor, as with the *sans-culotte* in the French Revolution. Empty hands, empty life. In fact, empty and naked are often synonyms. In war or in sport, as well as elsewhere, fields of action are covered by people: they are full of people. When a cheque has cash cover, it is good. A synonym for 'covered' is 'full'.

Cover, as a metaphor, often coincides with the common metaphor of 'container'.[20] Restriction, as an action, also has an independent, symbolic meaning, in addition to its pragmatic one. Setting limits creates identity, whether by creating the boundary of a body, a family or a state. A *border* both connects and separates an object in relation to its surroundings, as in vineyards, in gardens for growing apple trees and berries, and in pleasure gardens. Cutting, trimming or shearing are ways of regulating the growth of hair and beards in men, the manes of horses, the hair and tail of dogs, but they are also ways of containing them. Such activities are both pramatically and symbolically meaningful and aesthetically motivated.

Throughout the history of military technology and politics, the protective function of the *border* and the means of transgressing it have been a main concern. Besieging and crossing the border is a drama of breaking and destroying identity, on physical, moral and symbolical levels (own–alien, in–out, and so on). The image of the border is mostly linear, whether as a circle, curve, or straight line. Cover is associated with the ground, the surface of the body and natural forms, the geometrical abstraction of the latter being a plane, concave or convex surface. Surfaces encircle volume. The deeper meaning of linear, plane, volume and spatial images takes us back to the arch-metaphors and to the archaic imagination, which gave rise to them.

Archaic experience with natural forms and materials has been realized in different construction techniques: (1) from an eggshell, skull, shell and gourd to the invention of ceramics and the Gothic vaulted ceiling, and from there to shell construction in contemporary architecture and plastics in furniture; (2) from megalithic architecture to the system of buttresses; and (3) from wickerwork and genuine elastic materials to contemporary hanging constructions.

All those developing lines of technological devices are solutions to one and the same problem, that of creating a *container*. The search for a technological equivalent of the shell, the cover and the enclosing plane has been directed toward creating relations between inner and outer. The metaphor of the container thus embodies the dialectics of inner and outer. It is used as a universal device of perception, both as an image and as an idea, and this both as a lived and a latent metaphor. An egg, a pyramidal pile of granite and a woven nest are arch-metaphors, embodying the perfection of a created form. The everyday routine that people follow is full of stereotypical perception, images, feelings, thoughts and actions. Rediscovering the archetypal metaphors embodied in that routine is one way of overcoming stereotypes. Stereotypes and archetypes are not opposites. A stereotype rests on a dead metaphor. Each stereotyped activity is a simple re-use of a human value or experience; it is repetition without any creation. This is the survival of the archetypal metaphor, where the original idea has been forgotten and lies buried under the layers of culture.

Conclusion

Both latent (dead) and active metaphors operate in environmental experience. In a paradoxical way, metaphors that are linguistically dead or are not perceived are nonetheless lived metaphors, establishing a basis for the sense of place and experience. If we can find suitable wording for it, a dead metaphor can revive verbally. Lived experience is also metaphorical, however, just as much as the experience expressed in words. The metaphorization of environment occurs not only in conscious, figurative, verbal thinking. Any gesture, movement or activity, and the most various relations between the body and environment, are non-verbal forms that can have metaphorical meaning. Because they change an environment into multiple meanings, these numerous lived metaphors, in their intertwining, inverted, multilayered dispositions and in their shifting meanings, are prerequisites for aesthetic environmental experience. The final phase of metaphorical cognition lies in making it conscious.

Metaphorization can be characterized as the basic web of aesthetic perception, constructing the double fabric that binds us to the world, where conscious and unconscious, sensuous and mental, objective and subjective, stereotypical and archetypal are intertwined. Archetypal metaphors change in the course of history into cultural stereotypes that remain unconscious but nevertheless affect our environmental experience. Active metaphors that are clearly expressed provide a layer of meanings or a cultural context. Their aesthetic function is to guarantee the living and dynamic relation between humans and their environment, where reciprocal re-embodiment continuously takes place. This relation can be reverential, uplifting, wistful, heroic or some other emotional experience. Environment can also evoke *catharsis* through a process of empathy. The role of imagination is of the utmost importance in metaphorization. If the environment becomes our *alter ego*, it will help us overcome alienation and attain harmony through reciprocity in our relations with ourselves, with nature and with other people.

Notes

1   C. Macann (1993), *Four Phenomenological Philosophers. Hussel, Heidegger, Sartre, Merleau-Ponty*, London and New York: Routledge, pp. 36–43.
2   M. Merleau-Ponty (1968), *The Visible and Invisible*, Evanston: Northwestern University Press, pp. 113–14.
3   M. Merleau-Ponty (1963), *The Structure of Behavior*, Pittsburgh: Duquesne University Press, p. 120; M. Merleau-Ponty (1968), *The Visible and Invisible*, p. 139.
4   M. Merleau-Ponty (1968), *The Visible and Invisible*, p. 115.
5   M. Danesi (1994), *Messages and Meanings: An Introduction to Semiotics*, Toronto: Canadian Scholars' Press, p. 107.
6   C.S. Peirce (1932), 'Elements of Logic', in *Charles Sanders Peirce, Collected Papers II*, Cambridge, MA: Harvard University Press, p. 277.
7   G. Lakoff and M. Johnson (1980), *Metaphors We Live By*, Chicago: University of Chicago Press; M. Danesi (1994), *Messages and Meanings*.
8   P. Ricoeur (1977), *The Rule of Metaphor. Multidisciplinarity studies of the creation of Meaning in Language*, Toronto, Buffalo and London: University of Toronto Press, p. 289.
9   M. Eliade (1989), *The Myth of the Eternal Return. Cosmos and History*, London: Arkana.
10 E.R. MacCormac (1976), *Metaphor and Myth in Science and Religion*, Durham: Duke University Press.
11 M. Merleau-Ponty, M. (1968), *The Visible and Invisible*, pp. 177–9; 221–7.
12 Yi-Fu Tuan (1990), *Topophilia. A Study on Environmental Perception. Attitudes and Values*, New York: Columbia University Press.
13 C. Norberg-Schulz (1971), *Existence, Space and Architecture*, London. Studio Vista.
14 M. Merleau-Ponty (1964), 'Eye and Mind', in J.M. Edie (ed.), *The Primacy of Perception*, Evanston: Northwestern University Press, pp. 162–3.
15 J. Hillis Miller (1992), *Ariadne's thread: story lines*, New Haven and London: Yale University Press, pp. 4–6.
16 M. Eliade (1989), *The Myth of the Eternal Return. Cosmos and History*, London: Arkana.
17 M. Heidegger (1980), *Holzwege*, Frankfurt am Main: Vittorio Klostermann.
18 E. Jones (1966), *Towns and Cities*, Oxford: Oxford University Press.
19 C. Norberg-Schulz (1985), *The Concept of Dwelling*, New York: Rizzoli International.
20 A.A. Moles (1967), *Sociodynamique de la culture*, Paris and The Hague: Mouton.
21 G. Bachelard (1942), *L'eau et les rêves*, Paris: Librairie Jose Corti, p. 124.
22 G. Lakoff and M. Johnson (1980), *Metaphors We Live By*, Chicago: University of Chicago Press.

Chapter 7

Urban Richness and the Art of Building

Pauline von Bonsdorff

A temple, related to its site, or the interior of this temple, is for us a kind of complete grandeur in which we live…. We are, we move, we live then in this work of man![1]

In this chapter I want to reflect upon the built environment as the creation, responsibility and joy of humans, but also in relation to nature, for the construction of the world is a continuing, many-sided process. The chapter begins by placing architecture within the wider context of human habitation, where buildings not only frame activities but are also themselves conceptually framed by them, for activities are perceptible in urban space, both directly and through the traces they leave. After this, I shall point to various kinds of urban diversity and processes of environmental diversification, arguing that diversity is an intrinsic as well as systemic value of any environment, cultural or natural. Then, through a discussion of some overall aesthetic qualities of the urban habitat, I shall indicate how diversity is often positively related to the perceived beauty of urban areas. This habitational perspective on the aesthetics of built environments emphasizes qualities related to what the environment both suggests and offers for physical activities, as well as for thinking, dreaming and meeting other people. The chapter concludes with some reflections on the interrelations of the art of building and environment, focusing on the complementary tasks of respecting the environment as it is, on the one hand, and, on the other, of adding something to it by following a vision.

Placing Architecture

Architecture is often called the mother art, for various reasons which I shall not enumerate here. Suffice it to say that buildings, usually in very concrete ways, comprise the other arts and human cultural activities generally, which take place mostly in built spaces. We read, listen to music, see performances and look at paintings in rooms that frame the objects of attention and influence how we perceive them. We also work, eat, sleep and enjoy the company of other people in rooms, and are ourselves framed, supported and delimited by built spaces. Furthermore, buildings themselves are typically framed by other buildings or built structures, such as streets, roads or bridges. This is particularly the case in urban and semi-urban environments, the kinds of environments where the greater part of humankind live today.

If buildings are irreducibly part of human habitats,[2] our understanding, perception and experience of buildings are always mediated by our idea of the human activities that take place in them and by our own personal relation to an environment. As a cultural phenomenon, architecture is socially and politically constituted: it is part of the contexts, structures and institutions that, at the same time, it makes visible. A building is not just a building; it is a building of a particular sort: a residential house, a barn, an office building, a church or a school. Both in ordinary environments and in the praised and admired masterworks of built space, the relevance of function is undeniable. When we are touched by the humane dignity of a residential neighborhood or by the play of light in a sacred space, our knowledge of the purpose of the building is inseparable from our feeling of gratitude or reverence.

If it is a truism to say that we inhabit the built environment, the point of this truism is that our basic relation to it is one of habitation or dwelling. While I shall discuss some specific aspects of this later, I want to emphasize here the general aesthetic relevance of such a perspective. In the aesthetic response to and judgment of built environments, habitability is a central criterion. It is also a generous one, for built environments are habitable in different ways, which depend in part on the local landscape, climate and culture. In addition, we inhabit the environment in many ways, not just in acting according to goals, performing tasks or going from one place to another, but also in meeting people by chance, spending time, reflecting, talking and dreaming. These and other aspects of life should be kept in mind when we consider how benign an environment is. 'Habitation' therefore is preferable to 'use' as a key concept in our relation to the built environment, for 'use' suggests an instrumental relation with little room for the reflective, receptive and genuinely interactive aspects of environmental experience.

A habitat is the kind of environment where a particular species typically lives. The human habitat is thus an inherently normative notion, in that it implies suitability for the needs and habits of our species. This does not mean, of course, that the habitat is fixed or unchanging. Animals adapt to changes in the environment, with humans as no exception, and needs can be fulfilled in different ways in different environments. Furthermore, cultural or spiritual needs often arise in a particular environment. We might invest ourselves in the wide open views, gently rolling fields, thick forest or abrupt seashore of the region where we live, and miss these features deeply if we move to a different place. Likewise, cities are good in different ways and are valued for different reasons by people of different tastes, habits and temper.

If the idea of a habitat is normative, so is architecture, a term often reserved for the best or most outstanding buildings which represent the art of building. To think of architecture as normative is legitimate as long as architecture is understood as a challenge and possibility that pertains to any building. However, if combined with an institutional definition of architecture, which considers only renowned buildings or buildings designed by renowned architects, this term may become counter-productive.[3] The risk in a narrow understanding of architecture is that the rest of the built environment falls outside the scope of aesthetic consideration and criticism. Yet quality or interest are by no means limited to spaces designed by architects. The challenge of art and aesthetic value – of richness, pleasure and beauty – is important all the time and in all kinds of buildings. Furthermore, in the everyday experience of environments, the masterpieces do not typically stand out as separate objects but appear in a more fragmentary manner, now from this side, now from that, quite in the same way as their more mundane companion buildings. Often the theory of architecture considers its object from the designer's point of view, forgetting the inhabitants and the transformations that are bound to take place in the cultural context. But the contexts of architecture that make buildings meaningful are multiple and in many ways unforeseeable, always changing and evolving.

I want to focus on the potential aesthetic value of urban environments, where I shall rely on a generalized and, to some extent, an ideal idea of a city.[4] It is essential to this idea that the city is not homogeneous. Thus it harbors a certain resistance to planning and design, which are among the fundamentals of architecture, when considered as an art of building and construction. The discussion of urban diversity is intended to substantiate the suggestion that the aesthetics of the built environment is not just about volumes, spaces, forms and materials, but also about the way life appears to be lived here and now, and about how it has been and could be lived. The aesthetics of building has a narrative dimension, which includes both history and imagination.

Urban Diversity and Processes of Diversification

We do not normally pay conscious attention to the elements of an environment, but perceive it in a way that appears synthetic, even to ourselves. We also get to know an environment gradually, acting and feeling ourselves into it, in a process that is informed in important ways by previous experiences. Thus we can recognize qualities in environments we have not visited before as immediately meaningful to us, although misinterpretations may occur. This is especially true of the social and cultural dimension of a built environment, which is inseparable from our perception of it, particularly as habitat or place. Inhabitants mark and transform their habitat according to their way of life, needs and habits, and places are often seen as places because they have a character, because they are places of or for someone.

It might feel natural to think of the city as primarily a human habitat, but cities are also the habitat of a number of other species.[5] Although we humans have a tendency to conceive of ourselves as different from the rest of nature, it is worth remembering that our relation to other species includes cohabitation in cities, as well, and while we may not like some of our co-inhabitants, they all add to the diversity and richness of a city. In what follows, I shall discuss mostly human and cultural urban diversity and from different perspectives – the relation of the city to its surroundings, the role of management and planning, the impact of traffic and transport, building construction and history – but without forgetting the importance of non-human nature in human habitats. First I want to look at the way a city is situated in a larger, non-urban environment, and how this influences its urban character.

While cities earlier were normally surrounded by countryside and sometimes bounded by a wall, urban areas today tend to blur into semi-urban, suburban or industrial land, interspersed with highways and possibly occupied by fairly large and similar-looking buildings that serve as hotels, supermarkets, warehouses or industrial buildings. Present-day surroundings are often as strange, uncivilized and easy to get lost in as a forest with beasts and bandits would be. In spite of this, the central urban area can be as clearly separable from its surroundings as in earlier times. Compared to the semi-urban surroundings, which many people only move through, the central urban area is where one goes in order to spend time or to see new things and new people. Cities are regional centers of commerce, culture and other activities that benefit from the presence of different people. They also attract new people. Those who arrive from abroad as immigrants or refugees often prefer to settle in a city rather than in a rural environment, where a newcomer stands out more clearly.

In addition to being the center of a region, a city is also centered in its political organization, which consists of a variety of parallel structures and sub-structures. A city is a human creation not just because its tangible forms are made by humans: it is also an immaterial structure made of communication and other networks and various communities, as well as of ideas and images. Because of their multiplicity and because activities tend to take place in unpredicted ways, diversity characterizes most cities, whether considered as built environments or as places for living, work and leisure. But the way urban management deals with and responds to diversity, with control or tolerance, is of crucial importance. One may note that, especially from the point of view of individual inhabitants, centralized control has many disadvantages. As Paul Chemetov has argued, it can hinder the processes of appropriation and can nurture the idea that others are responsible for the area that basically belongs to its inhabitants, thus increasing the probability of neglect and even discomfort.[6]

Human diversity in public space can also be supported by planning. Street life is richer if activities of a different character can share urban space, so that people who otherwise would not seek each other's company are to some extent present to one another. In particular, one might emphasize the mix of private businesses and public services. For example, to locate an old people's home and a school in the vicinity of a big business corporation and a public building may support the view that a human community is not and need not be a homogeneous group. This is worth emphasizing, since there is a trend towards increased monofunctionality of urban areas and spaces. If business, night life, administration, culture and residential areas are separate, the chances of straying into people different from oneself are certainly reduced.[7] While diversity may then exist on the map, the simultaneity of different life forms and activities in a particular situation will be absent.

The principle of mixing residential and other functions is by no means obsolete. It creates a situation in which people do not just visit or work in an area but are at home and dwell there, thus contributing to the character and atmosphere of a place. In a sense, residents occupy a place permanently even when they are not on the street or in the houses. Signs of habitation, such as benches outside or curtains and flowers in the windows, signal that human life is going on in the area. It may be noted that people also tend to inhabit their places of work by personalizing them, if allowed to, but on the whole the professional relationship to a place is less engaged than the relationships to one's home.

In today's cities, traffic often decreases the chances of experiencing human diversity. In the car, people are typically either alone or in the company of others whom they already know. They are by and among themselves. The vehicle constitutes an enclave of private space, while shared urban space is outside. In contrast, using public transport or walking puts us in company we have not chosen, and although surprises in the bus or train are not always pleasant, they are about ways of being human rather than about driving styles or traffic jams. Further, besides constituting an environment where many people spend several hours daily, roads transform the areas they cut through. Main traffic arteries have a largely destructive impact on adjacent areas. They typically produce noise and pollution and hinder the mobility of pedestrians, cyclists, animals and other non-motorized road-users. The freedom of movement, often used as an argument for building new roads, is a freedom for those who use cars, and literally stands in the way of the freedom of others.

Modern construction, whether of roads or houses, differs from that of earlier eras in both scale and technique. It changes the urban environment more radically and fundamentally, both visually and by its impact, for example, on ground water and air temperature. When building takes up more space and goes deeper into the ground, less of the environment as it existed before is left to itself. Compared with the continuous transformations which have characterized practically all human habitats, recent change is often radical replacement. The ensuing eradication of temporal depth is especially true within specific areas, so that to become aware of the temporal depth and layers of a city, one often has to go from one area to another.

In renovation and reconstruction there is also the real risk that areas could be transformed into historical images, where the complexity of the processes that took place and the imperfection and heterogeneity of time are hidden.[8] Yet there are also cities alive with history, such as Rome, where history is present as part of modern life. Large parts of its history may be unknown to its citizens, yet age is perceptible in the urban fabric, and this indicates change and continuity. In the muteness of traces that do not declare their cause, this material history of human activities influences the built environment in a way that is similar to the impact of natural processes or the weather. The traces are indubitable but are suggestive more than informative. Precisely for this reason, they contribute a sense of otherness that cannot be provided for in other ways. The past that is thus present rather than represented provides a thick context for our present and future. We may relate to history in various ways, by subjecting ourselves to it, neglecting it or seeing it as a generous ground on which we are dependent, but on which we live and which we utilize with discernment and judgment.[9]

The relation of a city to nature is similar to its relation to history, in that both are necessary conditions for fully human life. Yet there has been a tendency to treat as true nature only those areas where the human impact is minimal or imperceptible, while the presence of nature in all human habitats has been overlooked.[10] As with history, the possibility to perceive and live with nature has irreplaceable existential value to a thinking human being, although this is potential rather than necessary. Nature can stimulate reflections on how things are born, grow and die, how life forms are interdependent and vulnerable, and how strong the vitality of nature is as a whole. These are our personal conditions as well. Nature can appear as a world parallel to that of human society and culture, a world in which we can reflect more freely by going out into it, by drawing it in, and by letting our minds wander among its riches. Undoubtedly, it is a realm of unsurpassed sensuous richness.

To sum up, human, natural, social, cultural, historical and political diversity is an intrinsic value that cities have, and unpredictability is an essential part of it. To realize that we are not and cannot be in full control is an important insight which, once realized, helps to improve our life with others, socially and politically, as well as in nature.[11] Moreover, if allowing and making room for different life forms improves the life of individuals, groups and society as a whole, diversity can also be a seen as a systemic value.[12] One could argue at length for the importance of allowing different forms of life: existentially, to realize one's own place as one individual among others; socially, to enrich life; politically, to increase the understanding and tolerance of different viewpoints.[13] I shall only add one reflection to this: to understand and appreciate diversity might not be necessary if it were not for the fact that the world we live in is diverse. This does not seem to be a contingent feature. In fact, diversity tends to increase over time as things take their course. Furthermore, the diversity of the world is an important part of what makes the world interesting aesthetically, culturally and scientifically. In addition, environmental diversity can help to increase our self-understanding and ethical growth.

Aesthetics of the Habitat

In aesthetic reflections on the habitat, it is most fruitful to understand aesthetic value in a broad or deep sense. The aesthetic dimension then includes not only the sensuous pleasures of the environment: its vistas, light and color, its sound and smellscapes and how these relate to the moving and sensing human body. It also includes what the particular environment suggests about human and natural life in general and in relation to the individual person each of us is. Let me suggest, roughly, that the kind of aesthetic value we would call beauty is actualized when we reflectively perceive an object or a situation and feel a pleasure, and where elements of surprise and recognition, joy and gratitude are often included. The pleasure is about how things appear to us, where the appearance is a synthesis of all the object's perceptible elements, features and qualities, which in turn are influenced by the perceptual skills, knowledge and basic values of the perceiver.[14]

This description is not meant to exclude the possibility of aesthetic experience. It focuses in particular on the beautiful and neglects the sublime, and privileges harmony over dissonance.[15] On the other hand, if it is accepted that our habitat suggests who we are, personally and collectively, although it does not define or determine this,[16] there is reason to strengthen and support benign and generous rather than difficult aesthetic environmental qualities. The built environment can stimulate our thinking, our dreams and our imagination in various ways, and make suggestions about what is not immediately present, but at the same time it always constitutes the real world in which we live. Life is probably richer if we are tempted to turn toward and not away from our immediate environment.

Beauty and harmony are worthwhile goals, especially for the design of public, common, shared areas and buildings. This implies neither a pacification of human life nor false illusions, for a building is not a picture. Representation in architecture is not straightforward imitation; a building, rather, represents the activities it houses by standing for them and framing them in a particular way.[17] Further, while buildings constitute a shared and relatively permanent aspect of human life, they are still just one part of it, for the human condition is extremely complex and many-sided. However harmonious the physical surroundings are, problems and conflicts arising from social and cultural reality may continue to exist, but it is unwarranted to think that they should be introduced through building. This is not to say that sublimity, boldness, even less variety or dynamics, are banned from the design of the built environment. On the other hand, variety often already exists on the building site, in which case an aesthetic goal of building might be to respect variety and to create or support the overall character and individuality of the place. The ideal of environmental harmony proposed here is inclusive rather than exclusive, and in a social sense, as well: an attunement of elements so that they do not conflict aggressively.

What is common to the key notions of 'affordance', enticement, generosity and recognizability that I shall shortly discuss is that they relate to the way the environment is or can be inhabited. These aesthetic environmental qualities also apply to environments that do not belong to the canon of architecture but are the result of various, sometimes conflicting, intentions and of social and natural events and processes that, strictly speaking, were not intended at all. The aesthetics of the habitat, understood as an investigation into its potential aesthetic values and resources, will treat it as both 'art' – intentional and expressive, and as 'environment' – natural and given. Clearly, these two sides are not separate in concrete and particular situations.

The term 'affordance' was introduced by the psychologist J.J. Gibson in order to refer to what an environment offers in terms of the possibilities to perform activities and fulfill needs.[18] A boulder, for example, can afford the possibility of sitting, as does a bench, and both offer the possibility of resting. Berries and other edibles, whether found in a market or in the forest, afford us the possibility of nourishing ourselves and enjoying their taste. Especially in the human context, there is also reason to apply the idea of affordance beyond basic, physical needs to aesthetic, social and cultural aspects of life, such as the possibility of enjoying sensuous richness, meeting other people, talking, thinking, reflecting and imagining. These needs can be met by ensuring that there are spaces where one can and wants to linger and that the appearance of the built environment is rich and varied. However, an environment can be poor in social and contemplative affordances, while at the same time it fulfills the needs of transport, food and shelter.

Enticement, a second environmental quality, can be understood as a special kind of affordance, or as environmental promise. Grant Hildebrand describes the paradigmatic case 'as a view and opportunity for movement from one space to another whose features are only partly revealed', emphasizing that enticement conceals 'significant elements of what lies ahead'.[19] The perceiver is tempted to move forward to see how it looks, but even if he does not, the mere suggestion of a view adds pleasure. While Hildebrand limits his discussion to visual and spatial features, the term could also be applied fruitfully to aural, olfactory, even gustatory environmental promises. For instance, when walking on a lively street, the smells of restaurants or the faint chatter from cafes in inner courtyards tempt us by promising gastric and social experiences or simply a moment of rest and reflection. Enticement could even illuminate the charm of a ruin, which allures us into reflecting upon its temporal depth. Part of the charm, in all these cases, is that one does not know exactly what awaits us at the other end.

A third key term, generosity, has been used by Edward Relph to indicate a perceived quality of the way an environment is inhabited. In particular, it mirrors the care of inhabitants for their environment. 'Generosity is manifest in flowerbeds in front yards, in idiosyncratically decorated houses, in storekeepers sweeping their sidewalks, and perhaps even in landscaping and urban design that improve the appearance of a place but probably do little to increase profits or win votes. This spirit is an expression of spontaneity and creativity. ... Generosity is doing something for its own sake.'[20] It tells, on the one hand, about belonging and dedication on the part of inhabitants, who give of their time and work to the environment. On the other hand, it offers pleasures to visitors. The inhabitants' rich relationship to their environment thus makes it more habitable to others, as well.

A fourth quality, recognizability, likewise facilitates both the possibility of feeling at home and the use of urban space. It comprises orientation and legibility and thus the ability to find one's way in an environment.[21] But if this were all, the quality would be important mainly for visitors, since inhabitants know an area anyway. Recognizability is not just about the spatial and visual clarity of a city, but also about multisensuous qualities, atmosphere and historical continuity.[22] The particular memorable and dependable character of an area may be based on various features: a particular blend of smells or of languages. These various elements should be kept in mind, especially in times of rapid construction, not because all of them should be preserved but in order to ensure continuity. Recognizability is not the opposite of change but it presupposes continuity, which alone makes change meaningful.

Affordances and enticement, generosity and recognizability make an environment more habitable and, as a rule, both support and are supported by processes of diversification. This does not mean that diversity should be maximized by every means possible. Diversity has more to do with respect, sometimes subtle and sometimes easily perceived, for the plurality and heterogeneity of places and life forms that evolve over time, than with the number of different things or the magnitude of their difference. Planning and design can make room for and support diversity, but they cannot by themselves create it. Further, a diverse environment provides room for human individuality. Diversity and the receptivity of built environments towards human and other individuals may engender a quality of space, a feeling that there is room for full and many-sided existence, and that we are allowed and welcomed but not defined or delimited by our habitat.

An Art of Balance and Vision

Let me finally reflect upon the idea of architecture as an art in relation to the challenges and opportunities of urban environments. If diversity and habitability are important qualities of urban environments, the art of building should be an art of caring for and enhancing the existing environment, except in cases where it is ugly beyond repair. The art of building would then primarily be an art of balancing which, in addition to considering buildings, takes the natural and the social environment seriously.[23] To build would be a way of inhabiting or dwelling, as Martin Heidegger suggested, playing upon the German word *bauen* (to build) and its affinity to dwelling (*buan*).[24] To build by dwelling is to inhabit thoughtfully.[25] But inhabitants do not just use buildings and spaces; they also make them, adjust them to their needs, adorn them, fill them with light, sounds and voices, and bring in things and animals and other people. We all leave traces on the earth, take part in cultural practices and make choices with real consequences.

If building can thus be conceived ideally as thoughtful dwelling, how we inhabit our environment can also be seen as part of the continuing process of constructing our world physically and mentally, as co-responsible for it. Neither perspective is value-neutral. In addition, the idea that to dwell is inevitably also to build emphasizes that how we live is a concern shared with other people and species, affecting ecosystems and biotic communities.[26] This constitutes the ultimate frame within which to evaluate how good our habitats and our collective and personal ways of life are. And while I have focused on urban living as the dominant and growing human condition, it should not be taken for granted that this represents the most benign form of human life. In particular, much speaks for the respectful cohabitation with nature and in the urban human setting, too.

Nevertheless, to balance the natural and social environments with urban reality is not simply to adapt. As construction, architecture is never just *bricolage*, a combination of items; it is making according to general principles or to the principles of a particular building. Some buildings are buildings of grace, where order and clarity appear non-repressively but with hope and dignity as the expression of dreams and ideas. A building can suggest another world untouched by the physical and moral imperfections of concrete reality and which is perpetually out of reach, yet it is meaningful because it appears in this world.[27] Here one might recall that architecture has often been given the task of embodying the basic values of a culture or a society.[28] If fulfilling such a task were possible, a building would then make visible what society strives towards. However, in addition to foundational values, one should think about how a building necessarily and even unintentionally mediates the institution and functions it serves. Any building, but especially public buildings, contributes to making society, which is always in the making. At its best the beauty and balance of a building can inspire hope and joy, belief in life and human society, and a will to continue to add richness to it. Thus the utopia of architecture, this most tangible of human practices, exists as a direction rather than a place.

Human habitats are combinations of environment and art, landscape and technology, non-human nature and human culture. But the fact that architecture is a human creation does not mean that good architecture imposes human values on the environment or that imposing human values is always good. Reflecting on examples of excellent, graceful and dignified building around the world, it seems rather that the success of architecture as a symbolic and functional marker of human culture is proportional to the extent to which it respects and enhances the larger environment, creating conditions for human life without destroying other life forms. It is scarcely far-fetched to say that all species strive to build well, and this is one basic aspect of the normativity of architecture. But the human condition differs from that of other animals through our capacity to transcend our immediate conditions through thinking and dreaming, to which one must add our unsurpassed technical capacities. Fortunate in many respects as these capacities may be, it seems more than possible that, when human dreams and hopes are channeled into technological vision, this contributes to a blindness to the environment as it is, which then becomes uninteresting or unimportant. However that may be, it is apparent that physical construction today is often destruction, with built structures that reduce rather than add to the diversity and beauty of their environment.

To abandon vision, hope and the possibility of utopia is not a feasible answer. As an art, architecture was always visionary. The world being built does not yet exist, and so even the most convinced pragmatist cannot escape envisioning how it might be. Here lies, perhaps, the greatest risk and the greatest possibility and the greatest challenge for modern building (and, one might add, for environmental politics at large). The responsibilities involved in building, which is a tangible transformation of the world, are huge: responsibilities toward the present in its multiplicity, toward the future, and toward the past. A worthwhile task today is to cultivate a vision of architecture that does not look away from the human and natural environment but looks seriously at it with respect and generosity.

Notes

1   Valéry, Paul (1924), 'Eupalinos ou l'architecte', in *Eupalinos ou l'architecte, précédé de l'âme et la danse*, Paris: Librairie Gallimard, pp. 75–221.
2   Susanne K. Langer suggests that impermanent structures such as ships or camps can also be relevant for the understanding of architecture as an 'image of life' of a particular culture (Susanne K. Langer (1953), *Feeling and Form. A Theory of Art Developed from Philosophy in a New Key*, London: Routledge & Kegan Paul, pp. 94–5, 99).
3   For discussions of architecture as art, see Roger Scruton (1980), *The Aesthetics of Architecture*, Princeton: Princeton University Press, pp. 6–16; Anthony Savile (1993), 'Architecture and Sculpture', in *Kantian Aesthetics Pursued*, Edinburgh: Edinburgh University Press, pp. 157–80; Karsten Harries (1997), *The Ethical Function of Architecture*, Cambridge and London: MIT Press, pp. 270–91; and Adolf Loos (1985), 'Architecture', in Y. Safran and W. Wang (eds), *The Architecture of Adolf Loos*, London: Arts Council of Great Britain, pp. 104–9. For a useful discussion of an evaluative vs. an institutional understanding of art, see Richard Shusterman (1992), *Pragmatist Aesthetics. Living Beauty, Rethinking Art*, Oxford and Cambridge: Blackwell, pp. 169–235.

4   My approach to the city is indebted to authors such as Walter Benjamin (1997), 'One-way street' and 'A Berlin Chronicle', in *One-Way Street,* London: Verso, pp. 45–104, 293–346; Richard Sennett (1990), *The Conscience of the Eye. The Design and Social Life of Cities,* New York: Aldred A. Knopf; Paul Chemetov (1996), *20 000 mots pour la ville,* Paris: Flammarion; and Witold Rybczynski (1995), *City Life. Urban Expectations in a New World,* New York: Scribner. For a fuller discussion of some of the ideas dealt with in the following, see Pauline von Bonsdorff (1998), *The Human Habitat. Aesthetic and Axiological Perspectives,* Lahti: International Institute for Applied Aesthetics.

5   For example, in Helsinki around thirty species of mammals live permanently, and if those are added who visit now and then, the number grows to 50.

6   Chemetov, Paul (1996), *20 000 mots pour la ville,* pp. 61–75.

7   The 'walled-in, private enclaves called common-interest housing developments' are among the most extreme examples of attempts to create homogeneous communities; see M. Christine Boyer (1996), *CyberCities. Visual Perception in the Age of Electronic Communication,* New York: Princeton Architectural Press, pp. 151–75.

8   Cf. Ada Louise Huxtable (1997), *The Unreal America. Architecture and Illusion,* New York: The New Press, pp. 15–36.

9   The last alternative is suggestively described by David Abram (1997), *The Spell of the Sensuous. Perception and Language in a More-Than Human World,* New York: Vintage Books, p. 214. A useful warning about the cult of memory is provided by Tzvetan Todorov (1995), *Les abus de la mémoire,* Évreux: Arléa.

10 It might be noted that these tendencies are counter-balanced by the rise of urban ecology. By 'nature' I mean organic nature of different kinds but also elements such as weather and temperature and even the given topography of areas. To 'nature in experience' belong the elements that we experience as existing independently of human intentions. Cf. Pauline von Bonsdorff, (2000), '"Nature" in experience: body and environment', *Nordisk estetisk tidskrift,* **19,** 111–28.

11 Ladelle McWhorter (1992), 'Guilt as management technology: A call to Heideggerian reflection', in Ladelle McWhorter (ed.), *Heidegger and the Earth. Essays in Environmental Philosophy,* Kirksville: The Thomas Jefferson University Press, pp. 1–10.

12 Holmes Rolston (1994), *Conserving Natural Value,* New York: Columbia University Press, p. 177.

13 For the political argument, see Hannah Arendt (1958), *The Human Condition,* Chicago and London: University of Chicago Press; and Julia Kristeva (1989), *Étrangers à nous-mêmes,* Paris: Fayard.

14 No dualism between appearance and reality is supposed here. For a defense of the importance of knowledge in aesthetic appreciation; see Allen Carlson (1979), 'Appreciation and the natural environment', *Journal of Aesthetics and Art Criticism,* **37,** 267–75; and Allen Carlson (1995), 'Nature, aesthetic appreciation, and knowledge', *Journal of Aesthetics and Art Criticism,* **53,** 393–400. For a discussion of basic values as an 'attitudinal framework', see Robert Elliot (1997), *Faking Nature. The Ethics of Environmental Restoration,* London and New York: Routledge, pp. 16–23.

15 If beauty connotes an experience of harmony between experiencer and object of perception, the sublime connotes dissonance, for the object of perception exceeds, in one way or another, the mental capacities of the experiencer. This understanding of the beautiful and the sublime has its roots in Immanuel Kant (1990), *Kritik der Urteilskraft,* Hamburg: Felix Meiner Verlag, pp. 39–113.

16 For a warning against environmental determinism, see Stanford Anderson (1991), 'People in the physical environment: The urban ecology of streets', in Stanford Anderson (ed.), *On Streets,* Cambridge and London: MIT Press, pp. 1–11.

17 For more detailed discussions, see Karsten Harries (1997), *The Ethical Function of Architecture,* pp. 84–133; or Pauline von Bonsdorff (1998), *The Human Habitat. Aesthetic and Axiological Perspectives,* pp. 160–71.

18 See J.J. Gibson (1966), *The Senses Considered as Perceptual Systems*, Boston: Houghton Mifflin Company, p. 285; and for an extended use of the term, see Pauline von Bonsdorff (1998), *The Human Habitat. Aesthetic and Axiological Perspectives*, p. 31.

19 Grant Hildebrand (1999), *Origins of Architectural Pleasure*, Berkeley, Los Angeles and London: University of California Press, p. 55.

20 Edward Relph (1993), 'Modernity and the reclamation of place', in David Seamon (ed.), *Dwelling, Seeing and Designing. Toward a Phenomenological Ecology*, Albany: State University of New York Press, p. 37.

21 Kevin Lynch (1960), *The Image of the City*, Cambridge and London: MIT Press. Cf. Christian Norberg-Schulz (1980), *Genius Loci. Towards a Phenomenology of Architecture*, London: Academy Editions.

22 On atmosphere, see Gernot Böhme (1995), *Atmosphäre. Essays zur neuen Ästhetik*, Frankfurt am Main: Suhrkamp; and Gernot Böhme (1998), *Anmutungen. Über das atmosphärische*, Frankfurt am Main: Suhrkamp.

23 The adverse idea is 'building for the map', where buildings are considered important according to the publicity and reputation they earn. Cf. Kenneth Robert Olwig (1991), 'The Nordic environment – identity and symbolism: the insider's and outsider's view of the landscape', in Nina Vakkilainen (ed.), *Built Environment – Identity – European Integration*, Helsinki: Helsinki University Press.

24 To continue the etymological suggestions, in Swedish, the verb *bo* means 'to live (somewhere)', also 'to nest'; *var bor du?* is 'Where do you live?' The noun *bo* means nest. The verb *dväljas* emphasizes staying in a place, indicating permanence and feeling at home; a *däld* is a dell.

25 Martin Heidegger (1954), 'Bauen wohnen denken', in *Vorträge und Aufsätze*, Pfullingen: Günther Neske, pp. 145–62.

26 On the 'land ethic', see Aldo Leopold (1970) *A Sand County Almanac. With Essays on Conservation from Round River*, New York: Ballantine Books; or J. Baird Callicott (1989), *In defense of the land ethic. Essays in environmental philosophy*, Albany: State University of New York Press.

27 Valéry, Paul (1924), pp. 132, 184–5. Firmness and durability can answer to a similar metaphysical longing.

28 See, for example, Ludwig Wittgenstein (1987), *Vermischte Bemerkungen*, ed. Georg Henrik von Wright and Heikki Nyman, Frankfurt am Main: Suhrkamp Verlag, p. 134; or Martin Heidegger (1972), 'Der Ursprung des Kunstwerkes', in *Holzwege*, Frankfurt am Main: Vittorio Klosterman, pp. 32–3.

Chapter 8

Front Yards

Kevin Melchionne

Stranded

I left New York City in the fall of 1988 to attend graduate school at the State University of New York at Stony Brook on eastern Long Island. The campus was set in a suburb of single-family homes on curving cul-de-sacs. With few apartment buildings in the vicinity of the school, students banded together to rent houses in the many sub-divisions surrounding the school. We hopped from one lease to the next, seeking winter leases with luxurious beachfront views or cheaper rents inland near the Expressway. Some yard duties were usually expected of tenants, so in addition to plowing through Gramsci and Habermas, I periodically found myself pushing a lawnmower around weed-choked pachysandra.

I had not envisioned yard work as part of my studies at graduate school, although, in my case, it turned out to be an important complement to contemporary cultural theory. Despite the premium placed on context and identity in cultural theory in most graduate programs in the early 1990s, there seemed to be no way to acknowledge my own situation as an inhabitant of a vast suburban sprawl, far from the bookstores, cafes and bars of a city or college town. Sensing a close link between cosmopolitan intellectualism and urbanism, a sizable minority of faculty members and graduate students chose to trade four hours of commuting for a Manhattan address. Abetted by the academic workweek, others transformed modest suburban hobbies such as boating, house restoration and gardening into considerable accomplishments. But, for the most part, these endeavors remained safely (and, probably, happily) beyond the scrutiny of their own scholarship. For the official record, the Stony Brook campus was a cultural and scientific outpost in the desert of suburbia.

A few years into my residency, as I grew more comfortable occupying a suburban home, I began to undertake modest renovation projects in exchange for breaks on the rent from the landlord. I planted a vegetable garden, put a picnic table in its center and edited my dissertation while eyeing beanstalks for aphids. Despite my own pleasure in working on the house and garden, my thinking was guided by assumptions about the cultural poverty of the North American suburb, which I attributed to its aesthetic and sociological homogeneity. In this respect, I was the inheritor of a long-standing tradition. Critics had long fought a losing battle against the overwhelming centrifugal momentum out of urban centers with reminders of their cultural superiority. Responding to the wave of suburbanization between the end of the First World War and the stock market crash, urbanist Lewis Mumford described the outer reaches of Brooklyn as a 'dissolute landscape' and 'no-man's land'.[1] This was not to say that Mumford was enamored with the American city. Indeed, he understood that its shortcomings, namely, cramped living quarters and a lack of open space, stood as the very explanation for the growing flight to the suburbs. The suburbs, however, compounded architectural poverty with a lack of cultural amenities.[2] Its 'interminable blank streets' were, in Mumford's words, 'as dull and depressing as those from which the frantic suburbanite had escaped'.[3]

The attack on suburbia was renewed in the wake of the second expansion, following the Second World War. With tract housing spilling out beyond America's industrial centers, others joined Mumford's critical voice in cautioning against the dulling conformity of suburban life. Popular sociology books like William Whyte's *The Organization Man* (1956), John Keats' *The Crack in the Picture Window* (1957) and Peter Blake's *God's Own Junkyard* (1964), as well as novels like John Marquand's *Point of No Return* (1949), helped to establish a picture of a culturally barren suburban landscape.[4]

The balloon-framed cracker box with its prim front yard figured prominently in the critique of suburbia. It was as if the front yard, in tandem with the gray flannel suit, was the leitmotif of corporate conformity. But whereas the gray flannel suit has faded into fashion history, replaced by chinos from The Gap, the front yard remains part of the suburban ideal and, so also, a standard prop in anti-suburban barbs. On this view, the social conformity of the suburbs finds expression in the aesthetic homogeneity of the front yard. Indeed, the front yard is usually characterized as a monolithic horticultural form, stretching across North America with unwavering predictability and with utter disregard for climate. Fred Schroeder provides this tidy characterization of the typical front yard: (1) a neat lawn without visible division from neighbors; (2) foundation plantings, usually evergreens like junipers, yews, spruces and broad leaf evergreens; (3) a specimen ornamental tree; and (4) shade tree by road.[5]

While variations on this ideal–typical model can be detected, the lawn, that is, the grass itself, is the one element rarely missing from the yard. In fact, the basic front yard might be still sparer than Schroeder's, reduced to the lawn itself and the foundation plantings, without which the North American front yard seems especially barren. For this reason, the lawn has come virtually to stand for the front yard. In fact, most recent attention to suburban vernacular horticulture has focused upon the lawn.[6] Beyond the lawn, the yard is thought to be remarkable only in examples of eccentric deviation: as a verdant stage for pink flamingos, cast concrete lawn jockeys, or fiberglass gnomes.

But the front yard is more than a bland transcontinental carpet marked occasionally by the goofy lawn ornament. While property values and peer pressure favor conformity, the design and maintenance of a front yard may be seen as a cultural practice marked by creativity. Like that other important suburban pursuit, do-it-yourself home improvement, gardening is a mix of investment, consumerism and art.[7] A well-tended front yard is an investment in so far as it can enhance the value of a property. However, gardening is also a potentially creative practice in which gardeners buy mass-produced supplies available in chain nurseries and national seed suppliers for gardens of their own design. Creativity begins when homeowners move beyond the developer's filler to put together a composition of their own. Thus consumerism supports and channels, but does not replace, creativity.

The standard front yard provides a basic template or default version, a minimally acceptable format which may be enhanced by more ambitious gardeners. At its default level of lawn and bush, the front yard is not so much a work of art as a point of departure for motivated gardeners who, while still keeping within its framework, introduce greater plant variety and design variations. The default model also allows suburbanites – whose large tracts may contrast with their lack of substantial gardening knowledge – to cope with the responsibilities of ownership. Many people do not choose a suburban address in order to garden. They come for quality public schools, safety and, increasingly, because that's all there is. The default model provides the indifferent homeowner with a clear benchmark of minimal effort.

Backtracking

As the first horse car suburbs began to spring up in the middle of the nineteenth century around the centers of major cities like New York, Philadelphia and Chicago, aesthetes began to articulate a vision for the homes and gardens to be built in these new developments.[8] To live in the country for non-agrarian reasons requires a motivational ideal, a concept of the pastoral, a composition of domesticated nature. These developments were modeled closely on the English garden. The English garden aesthetic arose in the eighteenth century, in opposition to the formal garden of sharply pruned bushes, set within a formal axial structure, most famously embodied in André Le Nôtre's design for the garden at Versailles. The English garden, in contrast, offered meandering circuits of paths amidst gently rolling hills and irregularly formed ponds and brooks. Although often as contrived in design as its formal counterpart, the English garden reflected a conception of beauty as natural, pastoral, seemingly discovered and not made.

The slow process of popularizing the English garden took on momentum with the laying out of public parks in major cities. The widely circulated writings of Andrew Jackson Downing helped to establish the desirability of the picturesque setting for the suburban cottage.[9] Early suburban developments followed closely upon the construction of these parks. Indeed, the influential project of Riverside (1868) outside Chicago was laid out by the designer of Manhattan's Central Park (1858) and Brooklyn's Prospect Park (1866), Frederic Law Olmsted. The 1868 design for Riverside established standard set-backs for all houses and eliminated partitioning walls between lots. In 1870, Frank J. Scott published what is taken to be the first book codifying the suburban landscape, applying the values extolled by Downing to the problem of profitable real estate development.[10] He built his own development, Scottwood, in Toledo, Ohio in 1874. By the end of the nineteenth century, the house and lawn model of development could be detected in the suburbs of every major city in the country. Mass suburbanization may be seen as the next step in the Americanization of the pastoral ideal, extending the privilege of living in a park to the middle classes.

The post-war suburban development is the culmination of this eighteenth and nineteenth-century tradition of landscape aesthetics. The English garden's meandering paths are found again in the curving lanes of the North American sub-division development. The 'park' becomes the ensemble of front yards facing these lanes. Suburbanites enjoy the entire 'yardscape', to use Cynthia Girling and Kenneth Helphand's term, not just their own property.[11] The effect of a park is formed out of the aesthetic uniformity of contiguous properties. Private developments and public spaces (such as schools and parks) as well as natural features like lakes and streams merge into a shared aesthetic whole. The homeowner is a caretaker of a parcel of a collective aesthetic project.

However, the front yard did not spring fully formed from the minds of urban designers, landscape architects and real estate developers out of a desire to democratize the English garden. The emergence of the front yard as an ornamental garden dominated by the lawn required shifting functions inside and outside the house, as well as changing relations between urban centers and fringes. Trolley and rail lines enabled access to sparsely populated suburbs, where developers with ambitious aesthetic visions had access to sufficient land and political control to realize their visions.[12] Technological changes in the late nineteenth and early twentieth centuries made possible changes in the distribution of functions within the house and yards. The introduction of indoor plumbing and the decline of petty animal husbandry, along with orchards, woodsheds and garbage heaps, allowed for the sanitizing of the backyard and the removal of functional fencing in the front. The sanitizing of the backyard permitted its use for more leisure activity. The popularity of the lawn itself required the development of practical mowing machinery, along with hybridization of grass species that make up the modern lawn.[13] Over the course of the twentieth century, as the backyard became more amenable to leisure, the front yard became more ornamental and the front porch receded to a vestigial organ with only symbolic significance. The ornamentalizing of the front yard was extended further by the automobile. Passing traffic created more street noise and less pedestrian activity, hence there was less occasion to use the front yard for the satisfying, haphazard encounters with neighbors that are now the mark of nostalgia for small-town America. Today, the lure of television and air conditioning makes the yardscape an almost entirely vacant scene, save for the periodic mower. The pristine, park-like effect of the suburban development rests now on this reliable vacancy.

These shifting functions made it possible for the English garden aesthetic to take hold on a vast scale. But they would not have been enough to create the North American suburban landscape, as we know it today. By itself, each front yard lacks the flowing qualities of the English garden. It is small and the overall yardscape is parceled out among many private owners. The challenge for early designers like Olmsted and Scott was in translating the gently flowing hills of the English garden into the more profitable framework of the quarter acre lots of the suburban tract. The desire for a unified landscape motivated them to insist on conformity within a development. The park effect required blurring the divisions between properties by removing or lowering fences so that properties could blend into a single landscape. Modern regulations prohibiting or, at least, limiting the height of fences stem from the desire to maintain the park-like flow between yards. Regulations defining set-backs, allowable lot coverage and street layout, as well as zoning regulations segregating commercial, industrial and residential functions, also reinforce the ideal of pastoral uniformity.[14]

Finally, the success of the front yard lies partly in its relatively easy maintenance. Notwithstanding familiar complaints about the tediousness of mowing, the typical front yard is in fact not a labor-intensive ordeal. Nor does it depend on extensive horticultural knowledge. With its emphasis on a large lawn and hardy, evergreen planting, regular mowing and annual pruning are usually sufficient to maintain a serviceable front yard. Although one can certainly design a garden with even slighter demands (such as alternative ground covers like meadow lawns and pachysandra that do not need mowing, or a heavily wooded site), most serious gardening involves an intensive year-round engagement, a knowledge of pests and of the suitability of species for one's grounds that is unnecessary for the standard front yard.

Practice

Since the value of one's property is often connected to the attractiveness of neighboring ones, the suburban homeowner is under implicit pressure to conform to neighborhood standards. Regulations limiting grass and fence height in the front yard are common. Yet the ubiquity of the default version of the front yard cannot be accounted for solely by regulations. For instance, there are no regulations prohibiting a highly wooded lot, where shade might eliminate the conditions for a lawn and, hence, the burden of cutting it.

Foundation plantings, although ubiquitous, are not required. There is an unspoken consensus as to what constitutes an appropriate lawn. What are we to make of this uniformity? How much uniformity is there in fact? Or rather, in what respects is the uniformity of the front yard most evident? What are we to make of the variation that nevertheless remains? Is uniformity an undesirable goal for such a socially visible form?

Preminda Jacob argues that, whereas the overwhelming emphasis of scholarly and popular commentary on the front yard has been on its homogeneity, a closer look at individual plots often reveals idiosyncrasies that distinguish the homeowner from the group.[15] The lawn is but one piece of the larger composition, involving trees, shrubbery, flowers and their relation to the house itself. We can attribute differences in the front yard to, among other things, historical evolution, regional style and, at times, sheer personal motivation. Availability of leisure time and the presence of children are also factors, with the former usually facilitating the enhancement of the yard and the latter curbing it. Beyond the degree of rigor in its maintenance and the extent of coverage, the lawn figures little in this practice. It is part of the 'default setting'. As the involvement of the homeowner increases, a greater variety of plantings is introduced and the lawn shrinks. The lawn is a stage for the display of the house and plantings. Upon that stage, we can detect several respects in which practice retains some diversity.

Homogeneity is greatest where the default version is least tampered with. Homogeneity is most apparent at the level of the enclave or development, especially when it is new. A group of houses will be erected by a developer as a single construction project. By virtue of shared materials, techniques and layouts, as well as current fashion, the houses will share aesthetic affinities even as they may sport superficial decorative variations. Likewise, the yards will also share a style. Not only will the lots be similar in size; they will usually have the same layout and selection of ornamental foundation plantings.

However, as suburbanization continues over several generations, architectural styles and land use patterns change. In a given area, one is likely to find a patchwork of developments built over the course of several decades. Each new development will bring stylistic variations to the house, as well as to the front yard. Immediately adjacent enclaves will possess somewhat different architectural and horticultural forms, while remaining within the same basic format of detached houses, lawns and foundation plantings. The result is homogeneous residential developments within a suburban landscape itself fragmented into stylistically distinct residential clusters.

Time, too, plays a role in diversification. Individual owners leave their mark upon a property, adding to the house and introducing new plantings. Indeed, the very maturity of the plantings in a yard will do much to influence perceptions of uniformity or variety. New homes will not be shrouded by stately oak and maple trees and, in older yards, a mature tree may wither and be replaced by a rock garden covering its roots. So it is easy to understand

Mumford's response to outer Brooklyn at the onset of its development. Driving or taking a train through any recently constructed sub-division, one is likely to be struck by the uniformity of the buildings and yards. However, cutting across sub-divisions, and hence across time, differences in architectural and gardening style emerge.

Despite the impression of timeless stability, front yards, like everything else, are subject to changing fashions. Plantings fall out of favor and new ones are introduced.[16] Yard designs follow similar patterns. For instance, stylistic change can be detected in the decline of the common privet and boxwood hedges, rarely seen now in plantings around newer constructions. Hedges were used not only to divide properties but also to offer a degree of privacy when grown tall along the front or side of a property. Still more commonly, they lined walks and driveways, emphatically underlining the major components of the yard design. The decline of the hedge is due, not to the decline in popularity of lawn division, but to a decline in the popularity of the hedge's rectilinear formality, which evokes a dourness out of keeping in newer suburbs where ornamental kale and fountain grass are having their day. Like the hedge, the picket fence is another powerful image of the suburban yard. However, the source of its status in the American dream is difficult to come by, for, in fact, the picket fence is much rarer than its reputation might predict. The picket fence is a precursor to the suburban park; it was used to enclose the kitchen garden, protecting it from wandering livestock. Picket fences were opposed by early visionaries such as Andrew Jackson Downing.

Though often overlooked as a factor, effort, simply put, is often enough to distinguish a front yard from the default version. Some homeowners simply try harder than others, spending more time in the yard on conventional tasks. Even in fairly typical front yards, differences in effort will manifest themselves in well-clipped hedges, weeded beds, freshly planted annuals and manicured sod. This maintenance work is integral to the craft of gardening, and its absence can undo the most brilliant and ambitious planting. When a garden is distinguished by effort, it is not so much what is planted or how it is laid out but the degree to which it is tended. Through this aesthetics of effort or 'excess of norm', to use Jacob's term, a front yard may stand out from the common lot by embodying conventional values perfectly.

The shortcomings of the standard view of the front yard are particularly evident when it comes to lawn division. The suppression of divisions between lawns seems to be axiomatic for the effect of the suburban park desired by Olmsted and Scott. However, unified lawns are in fact quite rare, especially in older suburbs, where the accumulation of individual decisions overlays the default version. In the vast majority of suburban developments, property divisions come to be marked over time by low fences, overgrown hedges or clustered ornamental plantings. Only in communities self-consciously adhering to the park ideal is yard division uniformly suppressed. In fact, the home in the park effect is most effectively realized not through the shared aesthetic of a neighborhood of single family houses, but rather the shared property of the condominium, cooperative or luxury rental development. With its permanent maintenance staff, the complex succeeds in attaining a level of control over the landscape far beyond what is possible by neighborhood consensus.

Although the front yard is a transcontinental form, regional conditions often lead to extreme departures. The difficulty and cost of maintaining grass in the Southwest has led a growing number of homeowners to resort to a concrete or gravel front yard. These yards are often planted with native plants such as cacti that can withstand the region's arid climate.[17] The gravel and cactus style is a measured departure from the dominant continental style. On the one hand, it relies on local plants and eschews the green lawn. On the other, it remains firmly within the framework of Scott's low-maintenance/high-control suburban plot within a low-density suburban development. Cacti replace rhododendra, and gravel, grass.

Conclusion

There are good reasons for the default version of the front yard. Its ease of maintenance allows the tenders of front yards some degree of control. Its clear terms guide the uninspired. However, the homogeneity of the basic front yard offers an aesthetic value as well. As John Brinckerhoff Jackson has observed, 'There are landscapes in America separated by hundreds of miles that resemble one another to a bewildering degree.'[18] Yet Jackson does not experience a consequent lack of beauty. He finds beauty not so much in the distinctiveness of American domestic landscapes as in their gentle variation of a 'distinctive American form'. Jackson uses the phrase 'classical sameness', the rhythmic repetition leading to subtly varying order, to describe the vernacular landscape. Whereas this landscape often sinks to monotony, even the relative homogeneity of a scene does not, for Jackson, preclude our engagement with it: 'over-familiarity with the scene has compensations; it teaches sensitivity to change'.[19]

The front yard is one piece of this bewilderingly familiar landscape. Nevertheless, it is marked by modest variations on its conventions that are the mark of artistic intention. Alongside the monolithic green carpet growing to the curbs of Mumford's 'interminable blank streets' lie subtler departures: attentions to color, adventurous plantings, well-calculated designs, grand trees planted as saplings by long-departed newlyweds. Jackson points to an attitude that may work best with vernacular culture: rather than discerning authorship and its genesis, the lover of the front yard derives pleasure from the countless permutations of the general form. Rather than the masterpieces that transcend it, the lover of the vernacular appreciates the form itself for its capacity to sustain these variations.

Notes

1   L. Mumford (1921), 'The Wilderness of Suburbia', *New Republic*, **28** (September), 44–5, cited by G. Teyssot (1999), 'The American Lawn: Surface of Everyday Life', *The American Lawn*, Princeton: Princeton Architectural Press; and R. Baxandall and E. Ewen (2000), *Picture Windows: How the Suburbs Happened*, New York: Basic Books.

2   Over twenty years later, Mumford's very definition of suburbia in *City Development* was still in terms of what suburbia lacked rather than what it offered: 'distant dormitories where, by and large, life is carried on without the discipline of rural occupations and without the cultural resources that the Central District of the city still retains in its art exhibitions, theaters, concerts and the like' (L. Mumford (1945), *City Development*, New York: Harcourt, Brace and Company), p. 20.

3   L. Mumford (1921), 'The Wilderness of Suburbia', 44–5.

4   See reviews of this literature in S. Donaldson (1969), *The Suburban Myth*, New York: Columbia University Press; D.P. Sobin (1971), *The Future of the American Suburbs: Survival or Extinction*, Port Washington, NY: National University Publications; P. Rowe (1991), *The Making of the Middle Landscape*, Cambridge, MA: MIT Press; and R. Baxandall and E. Ewen (2000), *Picture Windows*.

5   F.E.H. Schroeder (1993), *Front Yard America: The Evolution and Meanings of a Vernacular Domestic Landscape*, Bowling Green, OH: Bowling Green State University Press.

6   See F.H. Bormann, D. Balmori. and G.T. Geballe (1993), *Redesigning the American Lawn: A Search for Environmental Harmony*, New Haven, Yale University Press; V.S. Jenkins (1994), *The Lawn: A History of an American Obsession*, Washington: Smithsonian Institution Press; and G. Teyssot (1999), 'The American Lawn: Surface of Everyday Life'.

7   K. Melchionne (1999), 'Of Bookworms and Busybees: Cultural Theory in the Age of Do-It-Yourselfing', *Journal of Aesthetics and Art Criticism*, **57**, 247–55.

8   H.C. Binford (1985), *The First Suburbs: Residential Communities on the Boston Periphery, 1815–1860*, Chicago: University of Chicago Press; and J.R. Stilgoe (1988), *Borderland: Origins of the American Suburb, 1820–1839*, New Haven: Yale University Press.

9   For the impact of Downing, see J.K. Major (1997*), To Live in the New World: A.J. Downing and American Landscape Gardening*, Cambridge, MA: MIT Press.

10 F. Scott (1870), *The Art of Beautifying Suburban Grounds*, New York: D. Appleton.

11 C.L. Girling and K.I. Helphand (1994), *Yard, Street, Park: The Design of Suburban Open Space*, New York: John Wiley and Sons.

12 K.T. Jackson (1985), *Crabgrass Frontier: the Suburbanization of the United States*, New York: Oxford University Press; and R. Baxandall and E. Ewen (2000), *Picture Windows: How the Suburbs Happened*.

13 V.S. Jenkins (1994), *The Lawn: A History of an American Obsession*.

14 M. Southworth and E. Ben-Joseph (1995), 'Street Standards and the Shaping of Suburbia', *Journal of the American Planning Association*, **61** (1), 65–81.

15 P. Jacob (1992), 'A Dialectic of Personal and Communal Aesthetics: Paradigms of Yard Ornamentation in Northeastern America', *Journal of Popular Culture*, **26** (Winter), 91–105.

16 A.M. Coats (1992), *Garden Shrubs and their Histories*, New York: Simon & Schuster.

17 C. Grampp (1987), 'The Well-Tempered Garden: Gravel and Topiary in California', *Landscape*, **30** (1), 41–7.

18 J.B. Jackson (1984), *Discovering the Vernacular Landscape*, New Haven: Yale University Press, p. 67.

19 Ibid.

Chapter 9

Aesthetics, Ethics and the Natural Environment

Emily Brady

Conflict

Have you ever had the uncomfortable feeling of enjoying something that you know is harmful? Such experiences are not uncommon, and they occur frequently in aesthetic experience. Leni Riefenstahl's film of the Nazi spectacle, *Triumph of the Will*, has stirring music, great choreography, coordinated uniforms and accomplished cinematography. It is hard to take your eyes off the brilliant images but your disgust in the celebration of Fascism and genocide compels you to turn away and leave the cinema. The problem is, as Mary Devereaux puts it, 'Riefenstahl's film portrays National Socialism (something morally evil) as beautiful.'[1] In this example, you enjoy a fine film, an artwork that clearly has aesthetic merit, but what it portrays is morally repugnant. The serious moral defect of the film overrides whatever aesthetic value it has.

There are a variety of other cases where the conflict between moral and aesthetic value is brought out and resolved in different ways: cases where something is morally dubious but aesthetically brilliant, such as the film, *Pulp Fiction*, or the play, *The Merchant of Venice*, but where the moral defects are tolerated for the sake of aesthetic value; cases where there is disagreement about which values should take precedence – moral or aesthetic; and cases where the very conflict between moral and aesthetic considerations is the main issue, as in Oliver Stone's film, *Natural Born Killers*, which could be seen as both a commentary on and an example of the aestheticization of violence.[2] The cases are distinguished according to the way we prioritize values in each one.

In these cases and others, we may understand the differences between them in terms of where the moral offence is located. First, artworks and other aesthetic objects may cause offence to their audience, as did several works in the recent controversial British art exhibition, 'Sensations'. Second, someone or something is actually harmed in an aesthetic context. A model is sexually abused in the course of sitting for an artwork or an actor is killed because of lax security or safety on the set.[3] Some audiences will find it difficult to appreciate artworks when they know some harm was caused in their making.

Turning to the natural environment, this type of case is very common.[4] We cause varying degrees of harm to the natural environment in many of the things we do in relation to it. (Whether such harm is justified is another question, of course.) Specifically, I am concerned with situations where harm is caused in order to achieve some aesthetic goal. A familiar one is the destruction of a natural area to create a neat and tidy park. Given that one has knowledge of the place before and after the change, two responses are most likely. There will be people who enjoy the new park as a place to wander, walk the dog or read a book. They are pleased with the change and place more value on the new aesthetic and recreational value of the place than the ecological harm caused by the change. Other people will probably avoid the park on principle, for they may feel that the sense of place has been destroyed – the mood of the place has changed, particular smells and other aesthetic qualities are gone, and ecological damage has been caused – and they would rather not have anything to do with it. Coming to the park for the first time, without knowledge of its history, it is likely that one simply takes it for what it is, and there may be no conflict in values.

Third, there are cases where humans *indirectly* harm something to serve an aesthetic goal. The problem of non-native plant and animal species has created serious debate in environmental conservation. In Britain, a particular variety of rhododendron has been introduced that causes real harm to native ecology. *Rhododendron ponticum* was brought to Britain from Portugal and Spain in 1763.[5] The bright, colorful flowers of this common bush have strong aesthetic appeal and it is valued highly for this reason, even attracting special bus tours in late spring, when the bush blooms. *Rhododendron ponticum* is toxic to mammals and, in addition to the dense shade it creates, its roots release poison into the soil which kills most plant and insect life. In Wales's Snowdonia National Park, eradicating this species is a conservation aim in order to protect native ecology, and also, undoubtedly, in an attempt to keep the park wild rather than to support its less genuinely natural species. The tourists want to keep the plants and are horrified to learn that they are destroyed. The debate over non-native species is complicated and it raises a host of issues I cannot address here. I cite it because it is a common case of conflict between aesthetic, cultural and other values, on the one hand, and ecological and moral values, on the other.

In all of the cases discussed above, some aesthetic consideration or aim conflicts with our moral obligations to nature. The offense is against nature, and it is the environment that has been harmed or has suffered damage at the expense of aesthetic value. There are also, of course, situations where there is little or no conflict between moral and aesthetic value, where the two exist in harmony. In Britain, this might be exemplified by the traditional and appealing English countryside of fields, stone walls and hedgerows, as opposed to the wide open fields of industrial farming that destroy important habitats.[6] Or, in terms of negative value, the feeling of loss experienced on witnessing a scarred landscape – a huge quarry or new highway – has both a moral and an aesthetic basis.

The aim of this essay is not to attempt to resolve conflicts between the moral and the aesthetic. Rather, it is hoped to untangle the many strands of this difficult area in order to reveal the sources and logic of this conflict. To achieve this, two opposing philosophical positions are considered concerning the relationship between aesthetic and moral values: 'moralism' and 'autonomism'. I shall defend a moderate version of autonomism; that is, I argue that aesthetic and moral value are distinct values, but I also set out where aesthetics and ethics interact.

Moderate Moralism

The conflict discussed above would be clear to most people. That the conflict exists in the first place would seem to show that aesthetics and morality are distinct domains, different values that often conflict *because* they have different bases. But this is really the crux of the matter, for some philosophers would argue that the two types of value are not as separable as they might first appear.

Generally, the position called 'moralism' presupposes that moral value and aesthetic value are not distinct. There is a radical version of this approach and a more moderate version. 'Radical moralism' holds that aesthetic objects – artworks, architecture, design objects, landscapes, natural objects, environments – are only appropriately appreciated and evaluated through moral judgment. A basic tenet of this view holds that art has instrumental value. Art is for moral or political ends rather than 'art for art's sake'. Plato and Tolstoy are usually cited as proponents of this position. For example, Plato argued that the only poetry acceptable in his ideal state of the Republic is that which represents virtuous characters, characters who can inculcate the young guardians of the state to act justly themselves. If the aesthetic object has no moral value then it also has no aesthetic value. (Because I am more concerned with the subtle arguments of the more moderate versions of these positions, I will not elaborate further.)

'Moderate moralism' is a view held more recently by some Anglo-American aestheticians. Noël Carroll, for example, holds that 'some works of art may be evaluated morally…and that sometimes the moral defects and/ or merits of a work may figure in the aesthetic evaluation of the work'.[7] This version does not argue that works should always be evaluated morally, or that *every* moral defect should figure in aesthetic evaluation, but it does take the view that, with many aesthetic objects, moral considerations are unavoidable. To support this claim, the reason usually given is that a moral stance, that is, a concern for humans and what they do, is part of the appreciative stance we take to many aesthetic encounters. In the arts this is most common in narrative artworks such as novels. It is argued that very often our aesthetic and moral interests are so intertwined that they become inseparable. Sometimes some moral concerns, such as their role in the portrayal of a character and its actions, are central to the aesthetic effect of the work. Carroll asserts that 'moral presuppositions play a structural role in the design of many artworks'.[8] Also, while it is sometimes thought that moral considerations detract from aesthetic attention and take us outside the realm of aesthetic appreciation, moderate moralists insist that moral interest increases our engagement and focus by drawing us further into the narrative or content of the work.

This view sounds reasonable and, relative to radical moralism, it is. Its strongest claim is that we cannot disentangle moral and aesthetic interests. In our approach to art, we are emotionally affected by characters and we care about how their lives turn out, even if they are only part of a fictional world. We are dismayed when injustice prevails because we disapprove of injustice in the real world. These emotional responses are just what the author bargains for; they are an integral part of the imaginative response expected of fictional narratives and in that respect they may be seen as inseparable from the aesthetic impact. After all, this is how tragic drama works.[9]

According to the moralist, this means that some of our aesthetic judgments are necessarily bound up with moral judgments. An important consequence of this for aesthetic evaluation is that in most cases a moral defect will count as an aesthetic defect. This needs clarification. Narrative art often has moral content; it shows itself in the way characters are developed and ways they act in relation to others in the fictional world they inhabit. Bad things happen in these fictional worlds, and these may be a crucial part of the plots and something we find interesting and enlightening. A moral defect occurs when the moral content is suspect. For example, a novel which clearly takes a sympathetic attitude toward violence against women will be rejected regardless of any aesthetic merit because this sort of moral defect creates an aesthetic defect. Similarly, given that one objects to the glorification of Fascism, Leni Riefenstahl's aesthetic representation of it will also be rejected. The film is immoral and so it is just a bad film. It is in this sense that aesthetic and moral values become inseparable for the moralist.

Cheryl Foster has put forward what appears to be a moralist position in relation to the aesthetic appreciation of nature:

> [A]n attitude that expresses continued enjoyment in an explicitly acknowledged destructive situation indicates a lack of harmony between the perception of beauty and the greater value of life itself. This disjunction between pleasure and the context of pleasure is at bottom irrational: to appreciate genuinely destructive situations is to approve them, and continued (or universalized) approval of this sort would lead, given what we now know through environmental science, to the destruction of life itself. Life provides the context and conditions for aesthetic pleasure.[10]

Should one find a deeply colored, striking sunset less beautiful upon discovering that much of the color is due to the proliferation of sulphur dioxide in the air?[11] On Foster's account, we cannot find the polluted sunset beautiful: to do so would be to condone life-denying qualities. She wants to show why we have a moral responsibility to change our aesthetic judgment of the sunset if we know its existence is somehow harmful:

> To continue to admire it would be to lend aesthetic approval to an unnecessary process which has life-denying consequences.... Individual aesthetic judgments are rooted in the perceptual features and patterns of the object's surface, but the practice of aesthetics, both productive and appreciative, takes place within a wider context of life-enhancing ethical considerations. That is, the manner and material of human presence in the natural environment, whether aesthetic, practical or whimsical, is subject to ethical appraisal.[12]

Foster appears to support a moralist position in so far as aesthetic and moral values are inseparable. A moral defect must count as an aesthetic defect in the sunset case. It is not hard to see Foster's point. How could we continue to feel delight in the presence of something that is harming the environment? Yet something seems to be wrong in her reasoning, and in the reasoning of moralists more generally. Why is it that aesthetic value has to take the fall too in these situations? Morally, we do feel compelled to suppress our enjoyment – we feel disappointed, betrayed and concerned about environmental damage – but these reasons are moral, not aesthetic. After all, nothing has changed in the aesthetic qualities of the sunset: the colors remain beautiful. What *has* changed is that we have come to know that the cause of the beauty is harmful, but that is a moral issue and not an aesthetic one. It makes no sense to say that we feel aesthetically compelled to suppress our pleasure. What is actually happening in the sunset case is that aesthetic value remains high, but on *moral* grounds we may decide to turn away from the scene before us. By turning away we end the aesthetic experience altogether without changing our aesthetic judgment. Some spectators may continue to enjoy the scene, but with an added feeling of poignancy. Their aesthetic delight is accompanied by the conflicting moral feeling of sympathy in the face of pollution's harm. Still others will feel no conflict at all. From Foster's perspective, we experience a shift in perception such that we no longer find the sunset beautiful, and in so doing our aesthetic judgment changes.

Moderate Autonomism

Let me try to explain these points further. Moralists cannot argue that aesthetic disvalue follows from moral disvalue until they have shown how a moral flaw constitutes an aesthetic flaw. Once again, the two values have different bases. Aesthetic value is primarily concerned with perceptual qualities and the emotional and imaginative responses connected to them, as well as the meanings that come through appreciating these qualities. In this respect aesthetic evaluation is generally restricted to perceptual, emotional and imaginative experiential states rather than significantly cognitive ones. Moral value is primarily concerned with making choices about how one ought to act, and how one ought to treat humans and the rest of nature. This is not to say that moral considerations are not part of our aesthetic experiences, or that aesthetic considerations are not part of moral deliberation. But aesthetic and moral value are nevertheless distinct and require judgment on their own terms. I may wish to support the eradication of a non-native species on moral grounds, but it would not be inconsistent for me to continue to find that species aesthetically appealing.

The view that I am sketching out is 'moderate autonomism'. It is called autonomism because it argues that aesthetic value lies within the autonomous domain of the aesthetic. It is described as 'moderate' to distinguish it from its extreme form, 'radical autonomism'. Radical autonomism holds that moral considerations and moral evaluation have no role in aesthetic appreciation. Unlike moderate autonomism, it rests on a formalist view of art and argues that the aesthetic response rests purely on formal properties of aesthetic objects. The works of Clive Bell and Oscar Wilde are often cited as representating this position.[13] Moderate autonomism offers a much more acceptable version of this kind of view because it does not deny that moral value can play a role in aesthetic appreciation and argues only for the clear separation of aesthetic value and moral value. A recent version which I support is put forward in the context of art by James C. Anderson and Jeffrey T. Dean:

> [M]oral criticism of a work can *surround* [my emphasis] aspects of the moral subject matter of a work, i.e. the moral content of a work can contribute to or detract from aesthetic aspects of a work. What distinguishes our view...is our claim that it is never the moral component of the criticism *as such* that diminishes or strengthens the value of an artwork *qua* artwork. In short, both sorts of criticism are appropriate to works of art but the categories of moral and aesthetic criticism always remain conceptually distinct.[14]

Even moderate autonomism may be hard to accept because it might still seem that in our aesthetic experiences it is unclear how the aesthetic and the moral can be teased apart. This may be because, phenomenologically, the two concerns do feel as one in many cases. However, conceptually speaking it is not so difficult to maintain the separation.

In his discussion of 'aesthetic offences' against nature, Stan Godlovitch sets out one useful difference between aesthetic and moral offenses that helps to support the moderate autonomist's case.[15] Aesthetic offenses may be characterized as acts of 'tastelessness': they arise 'in the form of an objectionable intervention; when nature has been uninvitedly sullied or soiled by gratuitous human intrusions which bespeak interference, carelessness or indifference'.[16] His examples include 'littering a beach, defacement of cliffs by climbers, tearing up paths by mountain bikes, stripping hills for ski runs, river-damming, raw sewage disposal, decimation of species, etc.'[17] The perpetrators of these offenses are human beings rather than nature. Godlovitch sides with the view that only humans can be moral agents in the fullest sense, and because of this only they can cause harm. This means that nature cannot offend against itself. We cannot blame nature for the apparent ugliness caused by natural disasters. In the course of constructing their fabulous homes, beavers make a mess, but although nature can be a victim of an aesthetic offense, it is otherwise innocent. As Godlovitch puts it, 'Nature is literally a party offended by certain human acts but a party without its own aesthetic view.'[18] I have to set aside the thorny question as to whether he is right about this: can nature be an aesthetic, let alone moral, agent in any sense?[19] My particular interest is in how an aesthetic offense shows a lack of aesthetic sensitivity, regardless of who or what actually experiences the offense.

What Godlovitch is getting at here is the manner or style of an action, which can be an aesthetic matter. It may take a certain kind of taste to fashion one's actions, be they delicate, careful, subtle, awkward, clumsy, bold, heavy-handed or graceless. These are aesthetic concepts, and they describe the way we do things. There are other ways of doing things, but they are more obviously in the moral domain of concepts; for example, to act considerately or thoughtlessly. Doing something in an aesthetically pleasing or unappealing way does not necessarily make the action better or worse. To do something with grace does not mean the action will be moral; one can kill with grace but the act is still wrong.

This way of construing aesthetic offenses shows that the moral and aesthetic dimensions of a single act can be distinguished. This indicates too how aesthetic concerns may have a bearing on how we lead our lives. Kant and Schiller held the view that the aesthetic sensitivity and freedom of aesthetic experience are prerequisites to moral character, but they insist that that experience is autonomous, for the conditions of the aesthetic response are otherwise unattainable. I will have more to say about this later when I discuss how aesthetics and ethics can exist in harmony.

In the arts, this manner or style is all important. I am not asserting a form/content distinction here, but rather I want to point out how, say, a character is constructed or a plot structured is essential to fashioning the content or moral story in a narrative.[20] The moral story and its representation support each other and work together for the effect they produce. But this does not entail that the two are indistinguishable, or that the failure of one must result in the failure of the other: Each *can* stand on its own.

Turning to examples of aesthetic offenses against nature, style matters. The cultivated landscapes of forest agriculture can be truly sustainable and thus ethically sound, but the way in which the trees are planted and harvested is one dimension of critically assessing this agricultural practice. The trees can be planted and harvested in ways that are either tasteful or distasteful, depending on a number of factors, such as whether the plantations fit in the context of their surroundings. The sharp, straight lines of some plantings look incongruous even in Scottish glens already modified in other ways by people living in them. Similarly, the harvesting practice of clear-cutting may be efficient, but to the eye it creates temporary devastation equivalent to letting off a small bomb. We know the site will be replanted or will regenerate; we know the site is after all an agricultural landscape rather than a more natural one. But still we feel shock. Our objection – based on witnessing an offense against nature (albeit cultivated nature) – is based on many different reasons: aesthetic, ecological, and so on.

Aesthetic offenses can take other forms besides the obvious ones Godlovitch discusses. Despite the aim of environmental art to celebrate or draw attention to nature's forms, some works may commit an aesthetic offense, or what Donald Crawford and Allen Carlson call an 'aesthetic affront' to nature.[21] Earthworks which involve moving tons of earth or rock are disruptive, as they 'forcibly assert their artefactuality over and against nature' and work aesthetically against rather than harmoniously with the aesthetic and ecological features of their sites.[22] New aesthetic qualities are created, but they often create disintegrity in the landscape.

Our attempt to establish a closer relationship to nature through aesthetic engagement can also lead to a false or sentimental understanding of it, which in turn may lead to environmental management which fails to take nature, and the particular aesthetic qualities of a place, on its own terms. Conservation practices themselves even commit aesthetic offenses. Some environmental restoration projects, for example, involve restoring aesthetic or expressive qualities in such a way as to create something more like a museum piece, where nature's aesthetic qualities become transformed solely to suit humans in inappropriate ways. Nature is then unable to tell its own story, and the preservation of aesthetic qualities through restoration can prevent the emergence of different and new qualities.[23]

All of these examples point up a problem which ought to be addressed before moving on because it points to different levels of aesthetic response. Aesthetic responses can be thin or thick.[24] Our responses are thin when we respond to surface qualities, where we focus our attention on perceptual qualities in the narrowest sense without feeding knowledge into the experience. It is just the way something looks, feels, tastes, smells, sounds, and so on, coupled with immediate thought and feeling. Thick responses, or what Godlovitch likes to call 'sub-surface aesthetic sensitivity', occur when knowledge supports in some significant way the aesthetic qualities we discover and engage with.[25] It is often with thick responses that conflict between moral and aesthetic value emerges, for these will be cases in which we cannot see or infer the harm done to a landscape through some aesthetic means. Sometimes the damage will be obvious and the knowledge comes directly, through mere perception and inference. Each type of response can be equally valuable, depending on what is being appreciated and its context. Sometimes our aesthetic experiences are more free and unhindered when less cognitive, and significant knowledge is not required for an appropriate aesthetic response.[26] Also it is likely that we *can* detect aesthetic offenses through a thin response, as demonstrated by the clear-cutting case. On the other hand, when new knowledge is fed into an aesthetic experience, it may enable us to perceive aesthetic qualities otherwise unnoticed. And detection of a moral offense often requires the knowledge characteristic of a thick aesthetic response, as demonstrated by the case of the polluted sunset. When our aim is to resolve conflict between aesthetic and moral value in the practical context of environmental decision making and to decide on the best course of action, we ought to have as much knowledge on hand as possible. When we have, a resolution comes more readily because one of the two values takes precedence – and very often it is moral value that wins out. Having knowledge of harm we cannot perceive is just what enables us to condemn the damage done by pollution and turn away from the sunset, despite the beauty we still find there.

Harmony

Moderate autonomism preserves the separation of the aesthetic and moral domains. It supports the intuition that moral concerns can be legitimately brought into aesthetic appreciation, but rejects the view that aesthetic defects follow from moral defects and that moral merits create aesthetic merits. To further defend this position, I shall sketch out points of harmony between these two domains of value. By showing just where they overlap and intersect, I hope to refine the very distinction I have put forward.

One significant reason we sometimes find it so very difficult to distinguish the aesthetic from the moral lies in the fact that there are some points of intersection between them. This can be articulated in a number of ways, but is perhaps best summed up by Marcia Eaton when she says: 'In order to understand morality and thus become a mature moral person, one's action must have both appropriate style and content, and this requires aesthetic skills.'[27] And later, 'Aesthetics can become as important as ethics not because making an ethical decision is like choosing wallpaper, but because it is like choosing one story over another.'[28] These quotations present two strands of thought about the way aesthetic skills – perceptual sensitivity, imaginative freedom, creativity, expression – help us in our moral lives; first, to make individual moral decisions, and second, in the overall formation of moral character.

Earlier I introduced Kant and Schiller as supporting the importance of aesthetics to morality. Central to Kant's notion of the aesthetic response is the idea of the free, harmonious play of two mental powers, imagination with the understanding. That is, we are not constrained by conceptual thought in our aesthetic encounters but rather, in our disinterested delight in beauty, we enjoy the free play of imagination with the perceptual qualities of the aesthetic object and revel in the immediate impact of this sort of experience. For Kant, beauty becomes a symbol of morality, that is, the activity of the aesthetic experience of beauty gives us the opportunity to experience the kind of freedom we discover in the autonomous act of moral choice.[29] The disinterested, non-utilitarian character of aesthetic experience supports the free, non-goal oriented activity of the mental powers (a feature that also enables Kant to make an analogy between moral and aesthetic experience). Compared to artistic experiences, the experience of natural beauty provides the best opportunity for this, since it is absolutely unconstrained by the artist's intentions and own desired responses from the audience. The experience of beauty and its accompanying freedom prepare us to some extent for the freedom characteristic of morality.[30] The experience of the sublime is also significant, for through it we recognize our moral independence and define ourselves in relation to the natural world.[31] Schiller took these ideas a practical step further by maintaining that the development of aesthetic skills is a prerequisite to social harmony.[32] For both Kant and Schiller, these skills are developed in the purest way through aesthetic experience, hence the importance of the autonomy of the aesthetic for unhindered practice (but this should not lead us to believe that the aesthetic services the moral).

Imagination is not the exclusive domain of aesthetics. It is an epistemological tool used in some of our most basic experience and, according to Kant, its activity is a condition of experience itself. But imagination is at its most free in aesthetic experience, and it is exercised most often there, where we are less constrained by practical concerns. Emotion, too, is hardly exclusive to aesthetics, but we take our emotions for a test drive without obligation in our responses to the fictional worlds of novels, films and other narrative arts. Indeed, according to Aristotle, this is the point of tragic drama, for it offers the opportunity to respond emotionally – even cathartically – to stories and to educate oneself about the appropriateness of those responses. Through aesthetic experience we enjoy imaginative freedom and develop the emotional sensitivity required for making sound moral decisions. Imagination enables us to empathize, envisage alternative scenarios and invent creative solutions to dilemmas. Practiced emotion prepares us for sympathy and our own emotional hardships in relation to the decisions we make.

Hume supports this view, if a little prudishly, when he says that 'a cultivated taste for the polite arts ... rather improves our sensibility for all the tender and agreeable passions; at the same time that it renders the mind incapable of the rougher and more boisterous emotions'.[33] He went further and identified taste as the common sentiment which enables us to locate 'beauty and deformity, vice and virtue'.[34] Hume's remark could be seen to undermine autonomism, but I do not think so. What he shows is that moral and aesthetic capacities may derive from common sources such as taste – a delicacy of feeling – or the others I have already mentioned. This must in some way reveal why we feel a sense of loss (moral and aesthetic) when we feel revulsion at the sight of a mountain severely 'wounded' by an enormous quarry. The source of the feeling may in fact be common (this is speculation), and the skills of one may aid the other, but the character of the types of experiences and the bases of each type of value are not shared.

The second strand of thought about the way in which aesthetics supports ethics concerns stories: how we might use aesthetic skills to construct the most ethical real life narratives. R.M. Hare suggests how this might work with the story of moral character. In deciding what kind of person one ought to be, 'it is as if a man were regarding his own life and character as a work of art, and asking how it should best be completed'.[35] Skills of art and aesthetic criticism come to mind here. We judge the style of one's actions as coarse or delicate and borrow terms from the language of criticism, such as integrity, harmony, congruity, incongruity, coherence and incoherence, to describe moral character and action. Similarly, we may judge the integrity of another person's life narrative or indeed any narratives we encounter. For example, finding integrity in a conservation narrative, say, the restoration of a particular landscape, depends upon locating congruity, no sharp breaks in the story, and respect and sensitivity to the landscape's past and future rather than falseness or sentimentality.

In relation to stories, we may also draw upon the stories we like and approve of in fiction to form our own moral character. We might emulate the qualities of a favorite fictional heroine, or widen our understanding of common dilemmas through different ways in which fictional characters have solved them, without losing touch with our own real encounters in our own real world. Literary experience does not teach us morals, but it can deepen our understanding of the way people can be, and of the sorts of choices people make and how they live with those choices. We are unlikely to grasp all of that without imaginatively engaging with the characters and their fictional lives. The views discussed here are recognized by a number of philosophers who want to give a broader picture to our moral lives than one limited to the capacity to reason.[36]

Aesthetics and Respect for Nature

I have argued that we ought to adopt moderate autonomism's approach to understanding the nature of the relationship between moral and aesthetic value. The conflicts arising between these values in decisions about conservation practices are often serious and may appear unresolvable. Philosophical reflection on this conflict enables us to identify where the real problems lie and who or what actually creates them. In the context of aesthetic value, the hope is that we acquire a better grasp of where this type of value fits into the environmental picture, and when it matters and when it does not. I should emphasize that I am not prioritizing aesthetic value by supporting an autonomist position. We can still favor moral over aesthetic value and there may be a strong moral imperative to do so. My point is that we should not mix them up.

But we have found that aesthetic and moral domains are not poles apart, for our ability to exercise aesthetic sensitivity and our ability to make right choices both draw on our capacities of imagination and feeling. If aesthetics supports ethics in some of the ways described above, could ethics actually presuppose aesthetics? In respect of the aesthetic appreciation of nature, this type of relationship has been put forward by Eugene Hargrove, John Passmore and Robert Elliot.[37] They believe that an aesthetically sensitive relationship to nature can engender a benevolent attitude toward it. In his 'Land Ethic', Aldo Leopold recognizes the strong connection between beauty, truth and goodness in our approach to the natural world. In fact, we could interpret his ideas as recognizing the distinction between aesthetic offenses and immoral actions toward nature, when he says that, in developing an ethical attitude to the environment, we need to 'Examine each question in terms of what is ethically and esthetically right.'[38] To understand what is 'esthetically right', he instructs us to develop our aesthetic sensibility for nature.

Although none of these writers has developed this sort of position far enough to judge the potential of it, it is an attractive idea. But I suggest caution. While aesthetic experience can support moral deliberation, it provides just one foothold among others. An aesthetic relationship to nature values nature disinterestedly; that is, without self-interest and on its own terms. A possible consequence of this is a more intimate engagement with nature, where we deepen and broaden our appreciation of it, but the relationship is at the same time respectful of nature's mystery, its 'otherness'.[39] The trouble is that the same people who care about the natural environment often harm it. Even if aesthetic engagement engenders a sympathetic attitude, moral constraints, such as justice, are needed to provide the solid foundation required for a practicable environmental ethic.

Notes

1   Mary Devereaux (1998), 'Beauty and Evil', in Jerrold Levinson (ed.), *Aesthetics and Ethics: Essays at the Intersection*, Cambridge: Cambridge University Press, p. 241.

2   Some of these different types of cases are outlined in James C. Anderson and Jeffrey T. Dean (1998), 'Moderate Autonomism', *British Journal of Aesthetics*, **38** (1), April, 164–6.

3   The first case is of Benvenuto Cellini's model Caterina, cited by Curtis Brown (1995), 'Art, Oppression, and the Autonomy of Aesthetics', in Alex Neill and Aaron Ridley (eds), *Arguing About Art*, New York: McGraw-Hill, pp. 298–9. There are a few examples of the second case but I have in mind the case of Brendan Lee, who was killed while filming a scene because bullets were in the gun used as a prop.

4   Most of the material written on the conflict between aesthetics and ethics is in the philosophy of art. I recognize the significant differences between artistic appreciation

and aesthetic appreciation of nature; however, in this particular context, many of the same issues apply when moving from one realm to the other. There are of course a number of considerations that arise with art but not with nature. For example, the moral responsibility of the artist has no place in discussion of nature (except in cases of environmental art). The status of nature as a moral or aesthetic agent is an issue that emerges within the environmental context, but not in the artistic context. However, for a discussion of whether artworks have rights, see Alan Tormey (1973), 'Aesthetic Rights', *Journal of Aesthetics and Art Criticism*, **32** (2), 163–70.

5   For discussion of this issue and the examples below, see Trevor Lawson, Kate Rawles and Rob Gritten (1998), 'Alien Invasion', *BBC Wildlife Magazine*, **16** (9), 38–40.

6   At one time there may have been conflicts of a different kind. Destruction of forests to make way for farming would have caused ecological damage in the name of use or economic value, and the aesthetic value of the forest would also have been sacrificed for the need or desire for cultivation. Arguably, the conflict no longer exists because we become used to the new landscape and develop a taste for it. There may be conflict for some people now – people who want to reforest Britain – although what sort of conflict there is depends on the reasons for which they want reforestation.

7   Noël Carroll (1996), 'Moderate Moralism', *British Journal of Aesthetics*, **36** (3), July, 236. A view similar to this is held by Berys Gaut (1998), 'The Ethical Criticism of Art', in Jerrold Levinson (ed.), *Aesthetics and Ethics: Essays at the Intersection*.

8   Carroll (1996, p. 233).

9   Carroll uses remarks on tragedy from Aristotle's *Poetics* to make a similar point. See Carroll (1996, p. 232).

10 Cheryl Foster (1992), 'Aesthetic Disillusionment: Environment, Ethics, Art', *Environmental Values*, **1**, 211.

11 Example from Foster (1992, p. 212).

12 Ibid., pp. 212–13.

13 Clive Bell (1914), *Art*, London: Chatto & Windus; Oscar Wilde, 'The Decay of Lying' (from *Intentions*), reprinted in Richard Ellmann (1970) (ed.), *The Artist as Critic: Critical Writings of Oscar Wilde*, London: W.H. Allen. It is unclear whether or not Wilde was actually sympathetic to radical autonomism, since much of what he says in relation to it can be construed as ironic.

14 Anderson and Dean (1998), 'Moderate Autonomism', p. 152.

15 Stan Godlovitch (1998), 'Offending Against Nature', *Environmental Values*, **7**, 130–50. Aesthetic offenses are classed as a sub-class of a general class of offenses which include breaches of etiquette, legal wrongs, pettiness and others. He does not call the general class an overarching class of moral offenses. See Godlovitch (1998, p. 132).

16 Ibid., p. 134.

17 Ibid., p. 135.

18 Ibid., p. 136.

19 I will also have to set aside the issue of who experiences the offense. It is of course an offense against nature, but who actually *feels* offended is another matter. We know that some species can suffer, and it may be the case that some species can feel an emotion not unlike the human feeling of being offended, but it is on the whole the potential appreciators of the environment who experience the feeling of being offended. Godlovitch attempts to deal with this issue by making a useful distinction between internal and external natural aesthetic offenses. See Godlovitch (1998, p. 135).

20 See David Hume's remarks on tragedy, where he emphasizes that the representational aspects of tragic drama are crucial to producing the desired effect: David Hume (1995), 'Of Tragedy', reprinted in Alex Neill and Aaron Ridley (eds) (1995), *Arguing About Art*, New York: McGraw-Hill, pp. 198–204.

21 Allen Carlson (1986), 'Is Environmental Art an Aesthetic Affront to Nature?', *The Canadian Journal of Philosophy*, **16** (4), 635–50; Donald Crawford (1983), 'Nature and Art: Some Dialectical Relationships', *Journal of Aesthetics and Art Criticism*, 49–58.

22 Crawford (1983), 'Nature and Art', pp. 56–57; Emily Brady (1998), 'Rooted Art?: Environmental Art and Our Attachment to Nature', *IO: Internet Journal of Applied Aesthetics*, **1**, Spring (*http:/www.lpt.fi/io/brady.html*).

23 For discussion of these issues, see: Ronald Hepburn (1993), '"Trivial and Serious" in Aesthetic Appreciation of Nature', in Salim Kemal and Ivan Gaskell (eds), *Landscape, Natural Beauty and the Arts*, Cambridge: Cambridge University Press; Ronald Hepburn (1998), 'Nature Humanised: Nature Respected', *Environmental Values*, **7**, 267–79; Yuriko Saito (1998), 'Appreciating Nature on its Own Terms', *Environmental Ethics*, **20**, 135–49.

24 Cheryl Foster uses this distinction in her discussion of aesthetic disillusionment (Foster, 1992). She cites Allen Carlson as originating the distinction in this context in his article (1976), 'Environmental Aesthetics and the Dilemma of Aesthetic Education', *Journal of Aesthetic Education*, **10**, 69–82.

25 Godlovitch (1998, p. 146).

26 I have argued for this claim in Emily Brady (1998), 'Imagination in the Aesthetic Appreciation of Nature', *Journal of Aesthetics and Art Criticism: Special Issue on Environmental Aesthetics*, **56** (2), 139–47.

27 Marcia Muelder Eaton (1997), 'Aesthetics: The Mother of Ethics?', *Journal of Aesthetics and Art Criticism*, **55** (4), 361.

28 Ibid., p. 362.

29 Immanuel Kant (1987), *Critique of Judgment*, trans. Werner Pluhar, Indianapolis: Hackett, s. 59.

30 Paul Guyer (1996), *Kant and the Experience of Freedom*, Cambridge: Cambridge University Press, p. 96.

31 Kant (1987, ss. 23–9.

32 Friedrich Schiller (1967), *On the Aesthetic Education of Man*, Oxford: Clarendon Press. Arnold Berleant has recently developed these ideas further to understand a social aesthetic: (1999), 'On Getting Along Beautifully: Ideas for a Social Aesthetics', in Pauline von Bonsdorff and Arto Haapala (eds), *Aesthetics in the Human Environment*, Lahti: International Institute of Applied Aesthetics Series, vol. 6, pp. 12–29.

33 Quoted in Guyer (1996, p. 126).

34 David Hume (1983), *Enquiry Concerning the Principles of Morals,* ed. J.B. Schneewind, Indianapolis: Hackett, p. 88.

35 R.M. Hare, (1965), *Freedom and Reason*, Oxford: Oxford University Press, p. 150; cited by Eaton (1997, p. 362).

36 See, for example, Martha Nussbaum's work on morality and literature, including: (1986), *The Fragility of Goodness: Luck and Ethics in Greek Tragedy and Philosophy,* Cambridge: Cambridge University Press; (1990), *Love's Knowledge: Essays on Philosophy and Literature*, Oxford: Oxford University Press; (1996), *Poetic Justice: The Literary Imagination and Public Life*, Boston: Beacon Press.

37 Eugene Hargrove (1989), *Foundations of Environmental Ethics*, Englewood Cliffs, NJ: Prentice-Hall; John Passmore (1980), *Man's Responsibility for Nature*, London: Duckworth, p. 189; Robert Elliot (1997), *Faking Nature*, London: Routledge, ch. 2.

38 Aldo Leopold (1966), 'The Land Ethic', in *A Sand County Almanac with Essays on Conservation from Round River*, New York: Oxford University Press, p. 262.

39 Stan Godlovitch explores the dynamics of different approaches like this one: Godlovitch (1994), 'Icebreakers: Environmentalism and Natural Aesthetics', *Journal of Applied Philosophy*, **11** (1), 15–30.

Chapter 10

From Beauty to Duty: Aesthetics of Nature and Environmental Ethics

Holmes Rolston, III

In both aesthetics and ethics something of value is at stake. What are the relations between these different normative modes? If beauty, then duty. If so, is the logic the same in art and in nature? If not beauty, then no duty? But not all duties are tied to beauties. Other premises might as well or better yield duties. Aesthetic imperatives are usually thought less urgent than moral imperatives. Nor is all aesthetic experience tied to beauty. Perhaps ethics is not always tied to duty either, but is logically and psychologically closer to caring. Already the analysis is proving challenging.

Right or Wrong Place to Start?

Aesthetic experience is among the most common starting points for an environmental ethic. Ask people, 'Why save the Grand Canyon or the Grand Tetons' and the ready answer will be, 'Because they are beautiful. So grand!' Eugene Hargrove claims that environmental ethics historically started this way, with scenic grandeur: 'The ultimate historical foundations of nature preservation are aesthetic.'[1] More recently, the U.S. Congress declared, in the Endangered Species Act, that such species have 'esthetic value ... to the Nation and its people' and urges 'adequate concern and conservation'.[2] In the presence of purple mountains' majesties or charismatic megafauna, there is an easy move from 'is' to 'ought'. One hardly needs commandments.

More precisely, the move seems to be from fact of the matter: 'There are the Tetons', to aesthetic value: 'Wow, they are beautiful!' to moral duty: 'One ought to save the Tetons.' *Prima facie*, one ought not to destroy anything of value, including aesthetic value. That is an unarguable beginning, even if carelessness sometimes needs repair by legislation.

Aesthetic values are often thought to be high level but low priority: jobs first, scenery second; one cannot tour the Tetons if one is broke. So this aesthetic ethic will need to be coupled with more persuasive power lest it be overridden when amenities are traded against basic needs. At this point, one can switch to resource and life support arguments. The forests turn carbon dioxide into oxygen, they supply water for drinking and irrigating; they control erosion; they serve as a baseline for scientific studies. Biodiversity has agricultural, medical and industrial uses. Couple these lines of argument: healthy ecosystems, public welfare, resource benefits and aesthetic quality of life, and the combination of heavyweight and more 'spiritual' arguments will supply ample rationale for conservation.

That is practical in everyday life: everyone needs bread and loves beauty. Further, for those interested in philosophical issues, this is the quickest way out of the postmodernist confusions. We do not need epistemological realism, which is so problematic, as every academic knows. Ordinary relativist scenic enjoyments will do, joining them to routine resource use: amenities coupled with commodities. These motivations are ready to hand. Take a drive to the mountains. Enjoy the view, look at the fields en route, and think how air, soil and water are basic human needs. Press these points – environmental security and quality of life – and you will get no argument from the postmodernists, anti-foundationalists, deconstructionists, non-realists, pragmatists, pluralists or whatever is the latest fashionable critique.

Easy though this transition from beauty to duty is, we need a closer analysis. It may turn out that the initial motivations are not the most profound. Epistemologically, yes, aesthetics is a good place to start. Metaphysically, no: the worry soon comes that this beauty is only in the mind of the beholder. The metaphysicians will ask their probing questions. Any ethic based on aesthetics is going to be quickly undermined epistemologically, and in just the ways that the postmodernists, anti-foundationalists, deconstructionists and all those other troublemakers worry about. Any aesthetic value is some kind of a construct, set up on human interaction with nature. More radical environmentalists will insist that this falls far short. One is not yet respecting what is really there.

Now we have to backtrack and start again. Aesthetics is the wrong place to begin in environmental ethics, at least to begin in principle, though perhaps not always in practice. Aesthetics is also the wrong place to center environmental ethics, in principle and in practice. Nevertheless, one ought to celebrate – and conserve – beauty in nature. Aesthetic experience is indeed a capstone value when humans enjoy nature, but that does not make it the best model for all values carried by nature. The problem is that the aesthetic model keys value to the satisfaction of human interests; indeed, it leashes value to just one particular kind of interest. But there are many non-aesthetic human interests, and these may urge compromising, even sacrificing, aesthetic values. Starting off with an aesthetically oriented approach may disorient us and leave us with too weak a locus of value to protect all the values in jeopardy.

Consider an analogy. I am asked, 'Why are you ethical toward your wife?' I reply, 'Because she is beautiful.' Certainly, beauty is a dimension of her life, but it is not the main focus of her value. I respect her integrity, rights, character, achievements, her intrinsic value, her own good. In some moods, I might say that all these features of her person are 'beautiful', whereupon her 'beauty' would have become more or less synonymous with her 'goodness' (in the traditional philosophical vocabulary) or her 'value' (in more recent vocabulary). But I would wrong her to value her only in so far as she is 'beautiful', at least in the usual aesthetic sense. Certainly, her goodness is not concentrated in her capacity to produce in me pleasurable aesthetic experiences. That might fail with age or accident. I would also fail her if I failed to enjoy her beauty. That might give me an entrance to her further merits. Mutatis mutandis, our relations with sandhill cranes and sequoia trees might be similar.

Some are already objecting that my analogy is based on a category mistake. An art object is not a woman; a woman is not an art object. My analogy is misleading. The better analogy to appreciating the Grand Tetons and the Grand Canyon would be enjoying a Bierstadt painting. That I do enjoy for the pleasure it brings. Concerned about the conservation of the painting, its aesthetic value is its only reason for being. Likewise with national park scenery.

Have I a counter-reply? Yes. We are misled rather by the art object analogy. Surely, we easily see such a mistake with animals and birds. A sandhill crane is not an art object; an art object is not a sandhill crane. An art object is an artifact; a sandhill crane is not art in fact. The crane is a wild life, on its own, with autonomous, vital integrity, as no art object is. Expanding to the landscape, the crane lives in and migrates through ecosystems, such as Yellowstone and the Tetons. Nature is a living system: animals, plants, species, ecosystems, and any analogy to art radically misunderstands wild nature. An art object is inert, it has no metabolism, no vitality, no regeneration, no trophic pyramids, no succession, no evolutionary history. One is not in community in a museum. In a landscape, one is in biotic community. Treating nature as though it were found art will misuse such nature.

Yet aesthetics does figure large in conservation. Aldo Leopold, famously, connected duty and ethics in his land ethic: 'A thing is right when it tends to preserve the integrity, the stability, and beauty of the biotic community. It is wrong when it tends otherwise.'[3] So aesthetics can give rise to duty. But it will not be by bringing into focus human pleasurable experiences à la art. Environmental value theory needs a more foundational, biologically based account. Leopold connects the 'beauty of the biotic community' with the continuing existence of its members 'as a matter of biotic right'.[4] That does join beauty with duty, but it may also bring the complaint that rights no more exist in nature than does beauty.

Respecting What is Not (Yet) There

Of the multiple forms of value that environmental ethics is concerned to protect, aesthetic value is especially paradoxical. Beauty in nature, typically the first justification given for conservation, has a seminal place in the sophisticated land ethic of Aldo Leopold. Yet aesthetic experience, at least of this kind, seems not to be present anywhere in non-human nature, considered objectively as it is in itself. Perhaps there are some precursors to aesthetic experience in animal pleasures or courting birds, but a critical appreciation of nature as worthwhile experience for its own sake arises only in human consciousness. A hiker may admire the vista as he crests the summit; the marmot, alarmed by the hiker's arrival, has not been enjoying the view.

The forest is not even green without us, much less beautiful. The fall leaf colors are lovely. They result when the chlorophyl (experienced as green) is withdrawn. What colors! Bright and deeper reds, purples, yellows, subtle shades of brown. They result from the chemicals that remain, earlier overwhelmed by the chlorophyl. The hiker's aesthetic experience increases on such days. But none of this has anything to do with what is actually going on in the forest. The chlorophyl is capturing solar energy. The residual chemicals defend the trees against insect grazing or serve other metabolic functions. Any color enjoyed by human visitors for a few hours is entirely epiphenomenal to what is really taking place.

And so with all aesthetic experiences. One enjoys the hawk flying above, poised in the wind; but the hawk is no artist, nor has it anywhere been naturally selected as an adaptive fit owing to aesthetic properties. In the cirque basin below lies a string of paternoster lakes surrounded by the headwall, a marvelous scene. But geologists never list scenic beauty as one of the geomorphological factors in landscape construction. In fact, of Leopold's three features of ecosystems that generate the land ethic, 'integrity, stability and beauty', a skeptic might well object that not one is objectively real in nature. Ecosystems are not stable but dynamically changing, often contingent and chaotic. They have little integration, more aggregated jumbles than integrated wholes. Any beauty is not actually there but in the eye of the beholder.

Well, if not exactly in the eye of the beholder, beauty in nature is always relational, arising in the interaction between humans and their world. Just as there is no creature with a philosophical world-view and an ethic before humans arrive, nothing has any developed sense of beauty. Humans ignite beauty, rather as they ignite ethics in the world. Here we may wish to give a dispositional twist to value. To say of any natural thing, n, that n is valuable means that n is able to be valued, if and when human valuers, Hs, come along. There is no actual beauty autonomous to the valued and valuable forests, cirque lakes, mountains, sequoia trees or sandhill cranes. There is aesthetic ignition when humans arrive, the aesthetics emerges relationally with the appearance of the subject-generator.

But why worry so much about what is not yet there until we come? Why not feature what is obviously there upon our arrival? When humans are valuing nature, at least in the aesthetic mode, we are joined with nature in creative dialectic. What one wishes to appreciate and conserve is not nature but the nature–human relationship. The aesthetic genius is located in the pairing. Arnold Berleant puts it this way: 'One contribution that the aesthetic makes to the cognition of landscape lies in recognizing the human contribution to the experience as well as to the knowledge of it. Environment does not stand separate and apart to be studied and known impartially and objectively. A landscape is like a suit of clothes, empty and meaningless apart from its wearer. Without a human presence, it possesses only possibilities.'[5]

Well, that is true enough in the scenic–aesthetic sense; landscapes apart from humans are empty of such experience. Humans do need to wear their landscapes to appreciate them. But perhaps this ought not to set the governing model for all valuation, totalizing any and all concepts of value. Is the landscape meaningless, without value, possessing only possibilities – so long as it is without a human presence? If and only if humans, then beauty – actual beauty at least. Possibilities are always there, but these possibilities are always and only for us, not for the hawks and marmots, who are aesthetically incapable.

Now a worry looms. Is this something to be celebrated, this human relating to nature, and any conservation that may come of it, or is this something to suspect? Aesthetics might be emptying out other dimensions of value, blinding us to what is there when we are not. What if nature is not my suit of clothes?

Aesthetic value, it seems, must be anthropogenic (generated by humans), though perhaps not anthropocentric (centered on humans), in contrast to more biocentric or ecosystemic values. An ethic based on such relational value will have both strengths and weaknesses. On the strong side, this ethic will be closely tied to positive human experiences, supplying incentive. Where there is desirable aesthetic experience, the desire to save easily follows. There is no need to command any such ethic; it is not an ethic of duty laid onto otherwise unwilling agents.

The downside is that just this environmental ethics of positive desire is more a human option, more dependent on our current aesthetic preferences, more personally idiosyncratic, more culturally relative, even contingent on our changing tastes. If our grandchildren decide that they prefer ski lifts and runs up and down the Grand Tetons, disliking mere scenery; if they should enjoy more the participatory aesthetic experience of riding high over the forests on the way up, and graceful skiing, flow experiences, on the way down, so be it. Shifting aesthetic preferences shift incentives and shift duties. Fashions change; we come to like new suits of clothes.

Do we not need to base an ethic on something that is actually there? Respect for life, for endangered species, or for intrinsic values in fauna and flora, for the welfare of biotic communities, or for the systems of life support, or for speciation and evolutionary genesis – by contrast, all seem concerned with what is there independently of human encounter. Aesthetic values, though they are important and though they readily support an ethic, can be in the end less forceful than moral duties to others.

The aesthetic ethic will be a sort of light-in-the-refrigerator ethic. The light comes on when we open the door; until then, everything is 'in the dark'. But maybe the way to think of it is that, when we open the door, we see what is already there. The cake in the refrigerator is not sweet until we eat it, nor is it beautiful until we admire it. These are always possibilities, but only possibilities without us. But then again the cake is actually there with all its properties, whether we open the door or not. The sugar in the cake was originally stored for plant metabolism. When we light up the beauty in nature, if we do it right, often we are seeing something already there. The trees are not green until we light them up; but the green, we recall, is chlorophyl, which is there without us, energizing the tree, and valuable to the tree before we came and after we leave, evidenced by those glucose sugars. Maybe the aesthetic ethic, seeing only possibilities, is overlooking deeper actualities.

Aesthetic Capacities and Aesthetic Properties

Perhaps the previous analysis makes the aesthetic response too optional. My experience that the forests of the Grand Tetons are green is not optional, even though the 'green experience' appears when I arrive. My experience of the mountains' majesty is more optional, but not entirely so. There is required of me an appropriate relation to these mountains. My experience is of beauty and grace in the running impala, and it is not an option for me to say that they are awkward and ugly. That would simply reveal my ignorance, my insensitivity, not my variant and legitimate preferences.

There are two sorts of aesthetic qualities: aesthetic capacities, capacities for experience that are only in beholders, and aesthetic properties, which lie objectively in natural things. The experience of beauty does arise in the beholder, but what is this experience of? It is of form, structure, integrity, order, competence, muscular strength, endurance, dynamic movement, symmetry, diversity, unity, spontaneity, interdependence, lives defended, coded in genomes, regenerative power, speciation, and so on. These events are there before humans arrive, the products of a creative evolutionary and ecosystemic nature; and when we humans value them aesthetically, our experience is being superposed on natural properties.

The attributes under consideration are objectively there before humans come, but the attribution of value is subjective. The natural object causally affects the human subject, who is excited by the incoming data and translates these as aesthetic value, after which the object, the tree, appears as having value, rather as it appears to have green color. Aesthetic experience of nature can be epiphenomenal and incidental to natural functions, as it is when humans arrive to enjoy fall leaf colors. But the experience can run deeper. We ought to value the processes and products of a generative nature that we are discovering, sometimes more than we are projecting our values onto nature. Nature carries its more elemental aesthetic properties objectively, and these are ignited in the subjective experience of the arriving beholder.

We do enjoy seeing impala leap; there is grace in their motions. The aesthetic experience arises in my encounter with them, but the muscular power driving their locomotion is an evolutionary achievement objectively realized in the embodied animal. My aesthetic capacities track their aesthetic properties. There is aesthetic stimulation, for instance, in the sense of abyss overlooking a canyon, staring into space; similarly, with the fury of a hurricane at sea. That experience is in the beholder, but the abyss and fury (the aesthetic properties) are not in the mind; they are in nature. Perhaps 'fury' is an anthropomorphic metaphor, but the high wind driving the wind and rain is not. Human emotions track the motions of nature.

To put this provocatively, the world is beautiful in something like the way it is mathematical. Neither aesthetic experience (in the reflective sense) nor mathematical experience exist prior to the coming of humans. Mathematics and aesthetics are human constructs; they come out of the human head and are used to map the world. But these inventions succeed in helping humans to find their way around in the world because they map form, symmetry, harmony, structural patterns, dynamic processes, causal interrelationships, order, unity, diversity, and so on, discovered to be actually there.

It is true to say that the world is objectively mathematical and at the same time to say that mathematics is a subjective creation of the human mind. Mathematical properties are really there, though mathematical experience awaits the human coming – and analogously with aesthetic properties and capacities. It is thus no accident that mathematicians are so often among those who find the world aesthetically delightful in its symmetries, curves and patterns. A crystal is not a mathematician, but packing atoms into crystals, given also their electronic bonding capacities, results in ordered patterns that express mathematics, and delight mathematicians, as with the symmetries of the thirty-two crystal classes.

If the mathematics analogy is bothersome, we can make the same point with engineering. Animals and plants are not engineers, but natural selection and the demands for function and efficiency place engineering constraints on organisms, and the results have design that can please engineers. Studies of dragonflies in the Carboniferous show that their wings 'are proving to be spectacular examples of microengineering' giving them 'the agile, versatile flight necessary to catch prey in flight'. They are 'adapted for high-performance flight'.[6] 'To execute these aerobatic maneuvers, the insects come equipped with highly engineered wings that automatically change their flight shape in response to airflow, putting the designers of the latest jet fighters to shame.'[7] Their flight, say these scientists, is 'elegant'.[8] Anyone who has watched humming birds at bergamot can appreciate something of such engineering excellence. What is philosophically significant is how this engineering for survival, the natural property, generates aesthetic experience in humans with their aesthetic capacity. Of course, such skills in flight are objectively there, whether or not witnessed by admiring engineers.

Animals and plants are not artists, but these same constraints for order result in form, symmetry, integration, sweep and curve, and these results can please aestheticians, as with dragonflies and humming birds in flight, or impala on the run. You may object that natural selection plausibly demands good engineering, but natural selection does not so plausibly demand beauty. That point is well made by those who insist on artistic standards of beauty. But gestalts begin to re-form if we let our criteria for beauty be reformed by the standards of biotic community. We are further claiming now that a biological appreciation of the world finds it beautiful, but this intensifies the importance of those properties that are really there. What we behold is as real as the eye of the beholder.

Beauty and the Beast

Suddenly those impala spook. Marvelous, see them leap! How nimble! How quick! What grace in form and motion! The herd almost flows over the veldt. Look again; they are in panic because wild dogs have appeared. Am I to see this as a kind of ballet or as a struggle for survival? Or is there a kind of beauty in the struggle for survival? Their fleet-footedness is marvelous; and, more marvelous still, it has been generated on Earth in an ambience of conflict and resolution.

In the charismatic megafauna, the observer enjoys organic form in spontaneous locomotion, on the loose, without designs on the human beholder. The animal does not care to come near, sit still, stay long, or please. It cares only about its own survival. It performs best at dawn, or twilight, or in the dark. Such wild autonomy is stimulating aesthetically. Wildflowers sway in the breeze, but they do not move; they are moved by the wind. The animal must eat and not be eaten. Unlike plants, the animal resources, though within its habitat, are at a distance and must be sought. There is a never-ceasing hunt through the environment for food, an ever-alert hiding from its predators. If, as a carnivore, one's food moves as well as oneself, so much the more excitement. Animals' motions are close-coupled to the survival game. In the higher animals, with developed nervous systems, human emotions are attracted by animal bodily motions and drawn through these into animal emotions, invited to empathize with somebody there behind the fur and feathers.

Aesthetically, there is grace in the overtones of such motion. Solving the engineering problems of animal motion (the mathematics!) routinely yields symmetrical dynamics of rhythmic beauty: the impala on the run, the eagle in flight, the streamlined fish, the nimble chipmunk. Even where this grace seems to fail – in the lumbering moose calf, or the fledgling fallen from the nest – the observer is caught up in the timeless clamoring for life. Behind the motion and sentience there is struggle. The animal freedom brings the possibility of success and failure. The scenery cannot fail, because nothing is attempted, but living things can be more and less accomplished of their kind. An adult bald eagle excites more than an immature one, a more commanding token of its type.

Here we couple aesthetics with genetics and evolutionary ecology (now transcending engineering and mathematics). The aesthetician sees that ideal toward which a wild life is striving and which is rarely reached in nature. The observer zooms in with her scope on the full-curl ram, or the artist paints warblers ornamented in their breeding prime. In the language of the geneticists, the artist portrays and the admirer enjoys that phenotype producible by the normal genotype in a congenial environment. In a distinction going back to Aristotle, the ideal is true to the poetry of a thing, though not true to its history, and yet the poetry directs its history.[9] Such an ideal is still nature's project.

Admirers of wildlife enjoy the conflict and resolution in the concrete particular expression of an individual life. How the impala do run, and run for their lives, and with such grace! The weather-beaten elk are not ugly, when one senses their competent endurance through winter. The spike ram is not displeasing, because its potential is inspiring. Warblers in spring are indeed in prime dress, but warblers in fall plumage are equally fitted to their environment, neither less ideal, less real, nor less beautiful, only requiring more subtlety to appreciate, now that the expenditure of energy and motion is not in color and reproduction but in camouflage and survival toward winter. The struggle between ideal and real adds to the aesthetic experience. There is aesthetic vitality, and respect for life is more closely coupled with the appreciation of beauty than we first thought. The Darwinian nature 'red in tooth and claw', the fittest struggling to survive, and resulting in adapted fit, also in an ecological harmony and interdependence, is a prolific world lavish in its biodiversity. Life persists with beauty in the midst of its perpetual perishing, and the struggle is integral to the beauty.

Aesthetics Gone Wild

Increasingly, we are committing ourselves to the claim that it is what is 'out there' that counts, even if it only lights up into aesthetic experience when we arrive. What counts as aesthetically positive is being instructed by objective nature as much as being projected onto nature. This is a quite different ambience from the leaf colors in the fall. Nature is phenomenal, and we are thrilled when let in on these phenomena. There is nothing epiphenomenal about that. Scenic beauty might require our framing it up and igniting it. But the wildness of a place, in which we also aesthetically delight, is not in the mind. 'Wild' means 'apart from the hand (or mind) of humans'. The sense of beauty may be in the mind, but the wildness sensed that generates the experience of beauty is not.

But now, critics will complain, we are confusing the 'wild' with the 'beautiful'. What is 'out there' is not always pretty; often it is drab, monotonous, uninspiring. Romantic admirers of wildlife overlook as much as they see. The bison are shaggy, shedding and dirty. The hawk has lost several flight feathers. Every wild life is marred by the rips and tears of time. None of the losers and seldom even the blemished show up on the covers of *National Wildlife*. Wildlife artists select the best and discard the rest. The aesthetician repairs nature before admiring it. Landscape artists and architects are like flower arrangers; nature does provide raw materials, but raw nature is quite aesthetically mixed. One hunts, and picks and chooses, to make a bouquet or a garden. Save the Tetons; but there is no reason to save the Kansas plains – not aesthetically at least. Admire the bull elk in display; but a rotting elk carcass is ugly. This led Samuel Alexander to claim here that we, not nature, are the artists:

> The nature we find beautiful is not bare nature as she exists apart from us but nature as seen by the artistic eye.... We find nature beautiful not because she is beautiful herself but because we select from nature and combine, as the artist does more plainly when he works with pigments.... Nature does live for herself without us to share her life. But she is not beautiful without us to unpiece her and repiece.... Small wonder that we do not know that we are artists unawares. For the appreciation of nature's beauty is unreflective; and even when we reflect, it is not so easy to recognize that the beauty of a sunset or a pure colour is a construction on our part and an interpretation.[10]

Sunsets and fall colors, yes. But impala on the run and life persisting in the midst of its perpetual perishing? The more we reflect, the less easy it becomes to see these deeper dimensions of aesthetic value as nothing but a reflection. Alexander is looking for found art, or flowers to arrange. We are finding beauty by coming to share the life that nature lives for herself.

Do we wish to paint nature pretty, removing the warts? Or to paint nature as it is, warthogs and all? Is the poetry an ideal never real, until we repiece nature to our liking? Or is the poetry the history of struggle to make the ideal real, nature as she is in herself, those natural processes of conflict and resolution? Half the beauty of life comes out of it, as do the wildflowers that the artist arranges, or the exquisite nautilus shell secreted against its environment. The canines of the wild dogs have carved the impala's muscles; the impala's fleet-footedness shapes a more supple dog. I recall aesthetic stimulation watching a warthog escape from lions. We admire this element of fight even in the maimed and blasted, even in the inanimate, gnarled timberline fir. The coming of Darwin is often thought to have ruined nature's harmonious architectures, to have left nature ugly, but the struggles he posits, if sometimes overwhelming, are not always unaesthetic. None of life's heroic quality is possible without this dialectical stress.

Leopold is looking over a marshland, watching sandhill cranes: 'Our ability to perceive quality in nature begins, as in art, with the pretty. It expands through successive stages of the beautiful to values as yet uncaptured by language. The quality of cranes lies, I think, in this higher gamut.'[11] Perhaps we do not so much leave aesthetics as do we transform it in successively more perceptive stages? Or perhaps we elevate aesthetics to discover values transforming into those uncaptured by the usual aesthetic language. 'Out on the bog a crane, gulping a luckless frog, springs his ungainly hulk into the air and flails the morning sun with mighty wings ... He is the symbol of our untameable past, of the incredible sweep of millennia which underlies and conditions the daily affairs of birds and men.'[12]

If we are using the 'pretty' criteria, the crane is an ungainly hulk, gulping the mangled frog, but such hulks have haunted the marshes for forty million years. We reach 'a sense of kinship with fellow-creatures; a wish to live and let live; a sense of wonder over the magnitude and duration of the biotic enterprise'.[13] Is this aesthetic? Yes and no. A sense of biotic community with ancient cranes? There is certainly nothing like that in art, and this not beauty in any wow-look-at-the-Tetons sense. The beautiful has passed over into respect for life. It can as plausibly be said that we have left the territory of aesthetics and crossed into the realms of intrinsic and ecosystemic values. Nor is one content to rest the matter in some pleasurable relationship set up between wild cranes and humans today enjoying them. The motivation for conservation demands realism about cranes out there and the integrity of their lives, in which we humans today take pleasure.

We will need some epistemological representation of the cranes as objective living beings, without which this aesthetic experience cannot be genuine. This aesthetic account is highly constrained by facts of the matter. Nature is by now certainly mattering intrinsically, for what it is in itself, and not simply instrumentally, for the pleasure it brings us. These historical properties of the crane, re-enacted in its species line, become pivotal in the aesthetic.

The claim earlier was that a landscape is an empty suit of clothes, meaningless apart from a human wearer. That hardly seems Leopold's aesthetic. True, Leopold watching the crane is aesthetically stimulated; the crane gulping down the frog is not. Leopold is not making any usual 'instrumental' uses of the crane; he is not collecting its eggs to eat or using its feathers to decorate his wife's hat. He is valuing his crane experience intrinsically; but that is as and only as he first evaluates the crane for its intrinsic worth, occupying its niche in the marshland ecosystem. Maybe this is not biotic rights exactly, but he finds the crane an object of respect in its own right. He enjoys the crane right where it is on its landscape. This is a 'marshland elegy'.[14]

Ethics with an ecosystems approach will discover how beauty is a mysterious product of generative nature, an aura of objective aesthetic properties that may require an experiencer with aesthetic capacities for its consummation, but that still more requires the forces of nature for its production. The wonderland one is appreciating is not in the eye of the beholder, even if the wonder is.

Perhaps it will now seem that we are erring in the opposite direction from that we feared at the start: we are overemphasizing the objective and underappreciating the subjective. Humans are becoming mostly observers of nature's wondrous show. So we must return to the participatory dimensions of aesthetics. Notice here, at least, for the promise of an ethic, that these are no lightweight reasons. The aesthetic cry is: 'De profundis!'

Participatory Aesthetics

Aesthetics is often thought to be characterized by disinterest, which is always to be separated from uninterest; but disinterest might still be thought an unlikely motivator for caring conservation. Care requires some kind of interest. Further, the emphasis on wild otherness, on nature as other than culture, might also contribute to the lack of care. A frequent injunction in environmental ethics is to 'let nature take its course'. Leave those cranes alone on the marsh! Leave the Tetons and the Grand Canyon wild! This 'hands off' ethic, respectful though it is, is one of non-involvement. The cranes and sequoia trees have been looking out for themselves for millions of years; the Tetons and the Canyon are places that can run themselves. Wild places and wild lives command our appreciation, but meddling is irresponsible. Wild welfare is not my duty.

So we need a course correction. Aesthetic experience of nature is in engagement as much as in detachment. Disinterest does preclude utilitarian concern, immediate self-interest or instrumental uses; but disinterest is not passive observation. There is immersion and struggle for us, as much as for the fauna and flora we observe. We initially may think of forests as scenery to be looked upon. But a forest is entered, not viewed. It is doubtful that one can experience a forest from a roadside pullover, any more than on television. The forest attacks all our senses: sight, hearing, smell, feeling, even taste. Visual experience is critical, but no forest is adequately experienced without the odor of the pines or of the wild roses.

There is the kinesthetic bodily presence, flesh and blood moving through time and space. One seeks shelter for lunch, to discover, cooling down after the brisk walk, that there is too much shade; and one moves to the sun, and enjoys the warmth. Later, the sunset is lovely, but are we prepared for the night? One is surrounded by the elements, and a total sensory participation is at once vital to aesthetic experience and vital to life. Bodily presence in the forest, the competence demanded and enjoyed there amidst its opportunities and threats, the struggle for location in and against the primordial world – this engagement enriches the aesthetic experience. Perhaps only 'spirit' can enjoy aesthetic experience; but humans are and ought to be spirit in place.

Aesthetics goes wild, out of cultivated control, out of the human orbit, we have been insisting, even though we must be there to light things up. But now we have to notice that we ourselves are as much enlightened as we light up what is otherwise in the dark. We come to care not only about our being there but about these others. We realize our differences from them; we set aside a refuge for them where we only visit. In this wildness, we are not at home and must take some care. Yet at the same time our sense of identity enlarges into local, regional, global biotic communities.

One takes pride in the national parks as the cathedrals of America; we want wilderness for our children and grandchildren, as much as for them also the opportunity to visit the Louvre or the Hermitage. One does not draw one's living from the Grand Tetons or the Grand Canyon. But there is deep engagement, a sense of embodied presence as one climbs the Teton trails or descends into the Canyon, or watches the cranes over the marsh. One is making a life with such experiences, even though one is not making a living. So now the paradox deepens: just this being drawn out of ourselves into this autonomous nature, out there independently of ourselves, commands respect and responsibility, and we find ourselves reformed, with deeper identities than we had before.

We too live in this world. In wilderness we visit, but we must return to our native dwellings on rural and urban landscapes. When nature is nearer at hand and must be managed on our inhabited landscapes, we might first say that natural beauty is an amenity – only an amenity – and injunctions to its care would seem less urgent. But this gestalt changes with the perception that the ground is under our feet and the sky over our heads, that on Earth we are at home. Disinterest is not self-interest, but the self is not disembodied. Rather the self is incarnate and emplaced. This is ecological aesthetics, and ecology is vital relationships, a self at home in its world. I identify with the landscape on which I reside, my home territory. This 'interest' does lead me to care about its integrity, stability and beauty.

To biology we must add geography and to geography add biography. We cannot know who we are, we cannot know what is going on, until we know where life is taking place. Behind ethics is ethos, in the Greek, an accustomed mode of habitation. This takes humans past resource use to residence. When we ask about well-placed goodness in communities that we inhabit, both biotic and cultural, the dimension of the aesthetic is vital. Life without it is anaesthetized. There are the Grand Tetons and the Grand Canyon; even more this is a Grand Earth. The whole Earth, not just the marsh, is a kind of wonderland, and we humans – we modern humans more than ever before – put so much of this grandeur in jeopardy. No one, well placed in the world, can be either logically or psychologically uninterested in that.

From Beauty to Duty

How to couple aesthetics and ethics? Easily, we said at the start. Logically, one ought not to destroy beauty; psychologically, one does not wish to destroy beauty. Such behavior is neither grudging nor reluctant, never constrained by disliked duties to an other; rather, this is joyful caring, pleasant duty, reliable and effective because of the positive incentive. This ethic comes automatically. Now, in conclusion, the connections have become more subtle. Duty is what is 'owing' to others in one's communities. Most immediately, this is the social community of classical ethics; and now environmental ethics includes the biotic community, a land ethic. What is 'owing' to fauna, flora, species, ecosystems, mountains and rivers, to Earth, is appropriate respect. Whether this is better termed 'caring' or 'duty' will no longer be an issue when we feature these natural properties and processes, achievements, lives defended, these generative evolutionary ecosystems, and ask what is an appropriate admiration for them. This expanded aesthetics includes duties, if you wish to phrase it that way; or this enlarging aesthetics transforms into caring, if that is your linguistic preference.

Can aesthetics be an adequate foundation for an environmental ethic? This depends on how deep your aesthetics goes. No, where most aestheticians begin, rather shallowly (even though they may be aesthetically rather sophisticated). Yes, increasingly, where aesthetics itself comes to find and to be founded on natural history, with humans emplacing themselves appropriately on such landscapes. Does environmental ethics need such aesthetics to be adequately founded? Yes, indeed.

Notes

1   Eugene Hargrove (1989), *Foundations of Environmental Ethics*, Englewood Cliffs, NJ: Prentice-Hall, p. 168.
2   U.S. Congress (1973), *Endangered Species Act of 1973* (Public Law 93–205), sec. 2a.
3   Aldo Leopold (1968), *A Sand County Almanac*, New York: Oxford University Press, pp. 224–5.
4   Ibid., pp. 211, 204.
5   Arnold Berleant (1997), *Living in the Landscape*, Lawrence, KS: University Press of Kansas, p. 18.
6   R.J. Wootton, J. Kuikalová, D.J.S. Newman and J. Muzón (1998), 'Smart engineering in the mid-Carboniferous: how well could palaeozoic dragonflies fly?', *Science*, **282**, 749–51.
7   Gretchen Vogel (1998), 'Insect wings point to early sophistication', *Science*, **282**, 599–601.
8   Wootton *et al.* (1998), 'Smart engineering in the mid-Carboniferous: how well could palaeozoic dragonflies fly?'
9   Aristotle, *Poetics*, 1451.
10 Samuel Alexander (1933, 1968), *Beauty and Other Forms of Value*, New York: Thomas Y. Crowell, pp. 30–31.

11 Leopold (1968), *A Sand County Almanac*, p. 96.
12 Ibid.
13 Ibid., p. 109.
14 Ibid., p. 95.

Further References

Brady, Emily (2000), 'The aesthetics of the natural environment', in Vernon Pratt (ed.), *Environment and Philosophy*, London: Routledge, pp. 142–63.

Cooper, David E. (1998), 'Aestheticism and environmentalism', in David E. Cooper and Joy A. Palmer (eds), *Spirit of the Environment: Religion, Value and Environmental Concern*, London: Routledge, pp. 100–112.

Godlovitch, Stan (1998), 'Offending against nature', *Environmental Values*, **7**, 131–50.

Hepburn, Ronald (1998), 'Nature humanised: nature respected', *Environmental Values*, **7**, 267–79.

Lee, Keekok (1995), 'Beauty for ever?', *Environmental Values*, **4**, 213–25.

Seel, Martin (1998), 'Aesthetics of nature and ethics', in Michael Kelly (ed.), *Encyclopedia of Aesthetics*, vol. 3, New York: Oxford University Press, pp. 341–3.

Chapter 11

Embodied Music

Arnold Berleant

Art bids us touch and taste and hear and see the world, and shrinks from what Blake calls mathematic form, from every abstract thing, from all that is of the brain only, from all that is not a fountain jetting from the entire hopes, memories, and sensations of the body.[1]

Critique of 'Body'

Western philosophy has long been dominated by a tradition of subjectivism that finds expression ('expression' is itself a sign of that tendency) in a whole vocabulary of mentalistic terms and their cognates, terms such as 'meaning', 'feeling" intention', 'self', 'consciousness' and, of course, 'mind'. For many, this tradition is the whole of philosophy. It has become more rather than less widespread in philosophical practice as the material world – as this is understood by science, technology and economics equally – has come to dominate social and political life.

This is not to dismiss such concepts and interests, for they represent many important issues that need to be considered. I want, however, to challenge the larger context in which they occur. It is my view that subjective or mentalistic presuppositions cannot help but deeply color both the direction and outcome of query. Philosophical idealism has been a powerful force and it has dominated much of philosophy in the West, as well as in the East. What is most important in philosophical inquiry, however, is to plant both our feet on foundation stones that rest on the firmest ground, that make the fewest assumptions, and that are embedded in the clearest and strongest evidence available.

A counter-tendency has arisen in our day that leads away from largely mentalistic philosophy and the powerful influence of subjectivistic doctrines to philosophical discussion that gravitates toward its opposite pole. Instead of being preoccupied with nuances of thought, meaning, feeling and the intricate byways of consciousness, many philosophers now talk of body and, under the influence of Merleau-Ponty, of the flesh. More recently, Wolfgang Welsch has found in our bodies a condition for every operation. Philosophically, the body acts as a counter-balance against the immaterial influences of the electronic media, and he cites Lyotard, Dreyfus, Virilio and Baudrillard, who find in the body a similar salubrious force. But for Welsch the body is more than this. Our bodies possess a certain sovereignty, an obstinacy in the face of the pervasive influences of the media. They offer a point of stability against the subtle power over us of the electronic worlds.[2]

This turn toward the body is welcome. It works as a corrective to both philosophical and cultural immaterialism. Perhaps it is also part of the obsession of both our commercial culture and the counter-culture with cultivating the body as an object, especially an erotic object. From a philosophical perspective, a philosophy of the body may be a historical emergent, provoked by some of the social developments of our time: postmodernism's challenge to the canon of received truths, feminism's confrontation with patriarchal power and the pieties that both mask and enforce that power, and the materialism both of scientific research and of the consumer economy.

This focus on the body is a positive development. 'Body' draws our attention to things that have traditionally been overlooked in philosophy. Yet to speak of 'body' is as one-sided as it is to speak of 'mind'. What would we think of a journal called *Body*? By the same token, what *should* we think of a journal called *Mind*, as if you could understand body without mind or mind without body? Indeed, what are both of these but historically grounded fictional constructs that reflect and encourage conceptual divisiveness, a persistent Cartesianism that, in dividing the question, settles nothing, but rather originates problems of its own?

I am afraid, however, that much of Western philosophy remains mired in the dualistic premises of seventeenth and eighteenth-century science and that it has failed to reconstruct itself in the mode of twentieth-century physics and biology. Cartesian dualism is itself one of the consequences of idealism. It flourishes everywhere, despite significant alternatives that have appeared over the past century and a half, from Marx to Merleau-Ponty to Justus Buchler. Indeed, that recent intellectual oddity, the philosophy of mind, rests firmly on this idealistic tradition.

Can we even speak of either mind or body without the one entailing the other?[3] They are, at the very least, complementary terms. What is meant, for example, by speaking of 'my body'? Who or what is this 'my', the owner of this body? And what is the difference between speaking of 'my body' and speaking of 'my hand', 'my leg', 'my head'? Who is the 'I' that is the personal referent in all of these instances, the 'I' who possesses the arm, the foot, the body? Is the owner of the arm or foot different from the owner of the body? The 'owner'? Perhaps 'body' is less a material or ontological entity than what anthropologists call a folk category dressed in academic robes, like many other philosophically sanctioned concepts.[4]

Some Philosophical Extensions of the Traditional Notion of Body

In attempting to free ourselves from what may be false problems, it will help to consider some rather different extensions of the traditional notion of body as a material object. The first of these is the Japanese philosopher Kitarō Nishida's concept of the historical body. The use of tools under historical (that is, cultural) conditions demonstrates the primary union of subject and object that is basic to Nishida's philosophy. *Technē*, the act of making things with tools, does not confine itself to the subject. It consists in penetrating into things and in the function of things becoming ours. 'Taking tools in hand, the human being finds himself already in the world of historical life.'[5] As we make things with tools, we act in the historical world. Action presupposes desire, which comes from our body, but at the same time it is influenced by historical conditions. Making things, then, is acting bodily, and this Nishida regards as a subjective–objective historical fact. 'Our bodies are historical in two senses. First, they intervene historically in the world, and make things; at the same time, they are historical because they are already formed through history.'[6]

Merleau-Ponty develops a similar reciprocity in exploring the subtle insinuation between seeing and the visible and between touching and the touched.[7] He finds in the reversibility of each of these pairs 'the claim that the flesh of the world perceives itself through our flesh which is one with it'. In a telling metaphor, he calls the body 'a charged field'.[8] 'Charged field' is a pregnant phrase. It suggests energy that reaches out, not 'out', for that implies its complement 'in'. Rather it envisions the pervasiveness of energy. The body is a concentration of forces that is part of a larger field. In this reciprocity of perceiving–perceived, which Merleau-Ponty associates with *Einfühlung*, we are *in* the object we are describing, we are *of* it. 'My body is made of the same flesh as the world'[9] Yet at the same time as he asserts a continuity between my flesh and the flesh of the world, he reverts to subjectivism when he takes the body as the *Nullpunkt*, the point from which the world is measured.[10]

Then there are the ways in which the body speaks to things and things speak to the body. Some writers refer to bodily intentionality, found not only through movement but from the thought of movement, as well.[11] The notion of bodily intentionality nicely fuses thought, action and object. Coming at this mutual magnetism of body, thought and object, the psychologist J.J. Gibson speaks of the 'affordances' of things for behavior. 'To perceive is to be aware of the surfaces of the environment and of oneself in it. The interchange between hidden and unhidden surfaces is essential to this awareness.'[12]

Body and Environment

Perhaps the idea of environment most fully encompasses the rich contextual field of human experience. Not only does the concept of body need to be reconfigured; its very boundaries must be redrawn. Our concept of body is changing and we can no longer easily demarcate its borders. Biological ecology has grown into cultural ecology, as we continue to enlarge the complex interlocking dimensions of the human context. Environment embraces the recognition that body is contextual in still more ways: organically, conceptually and ontologically. Not only is body known in its setting but it finds its existence, its meaning and its being in and through its context. No body stands alone.

Most important for humans is the cultural environment. Awareness is growing that no body exists without culture and that culture shapes the body in specific ways. Moreover, we cannot speak of the body as such but only of particular bodies that constitute different ways of being in the world: in different physical environments, in different social environments and in different historical cultures. The cultural environment profoundly influences body size, facial expression, deportment and movement – such as a person's walk – and affects such features as hair style and dress. Dress, for example, is not just the body's image but a part of body, not its external skin but the outermost layer of all that lies beneath it: size, height, bulk, feelings and ideas about one's bodily self. Food is a central part of psychosocial life, an active synthesis of body, belief, feeling and attitude. Grasping the idea that body is environmental, then, sets us in a different direction. It takes the body as thoroughly contextual.[13]

With all this, what can we make of an aesthetics of the body? If we cannot speak of the body as such, what then can we say about an aesthetics of the body? To hold that beauty can be located in the body is no less absurd than to pontificate that it lies in the beholder's mind. Is there a non-dualistic alternative? Can there be an aesthetics of the person? *This* may be a more interesting question. Perhaps in exploring the engagement of the whole person in the world we can begin to illuminate an integrated, holistic human aesthetic. In the discussion that follows, reference to 'body' is entirely metaphorical. More specifically, 'body' is used synecdochically, as a part that is indissolubly bound to an integral whole, the human person.

One way to speak of the body from this environmental standpoint is to forgo the word 'body' altogether and talk only of 'embodiment'. 'Embodiment' is preferable to 'body' because it incorporates, literally 'brings the body into', the context of his or her cultural, social, historical and personal experience, experience that holds as many dimensions of consciousness as it does of materiality.

Music as Embodied

Let me give this general picture a particular setting, an artistic one. When I experience any art appreciatively, what occurs is not a wholly personal, subjective, unique and esoteric event but a fulfillment of the rich and complex capacities I possess as a human person situated at a particular time, place and circumstance. In this sense all art is situated and embodied as a transactional process involving the whole person.

To think of art, however, as an object – a painting, a piece of music, a poem – fragments what is an integral process. From whatever place in the aesthetic field we start, whether it be the artist, object, appreciator or performer, the other factors have a quiet presence. Thus the active, physical process of producing living art is embedded in the work, and the traces of that activity become part of the experience of appreciation. The brush strokes in a painting are not merely surface irregularities but the markings of the brush, the hand that held it and the artist who guided it. Color tonalities are not just surface qualities but were chosen, just as Roger Fry pointed out that a line is the record of a gesture. In a similar way, musical sounds are more than auditory sensations; they are produced in some way: executed by the bow of a stringed instrument, by breathing into a woodwind or brass instrument, by the movement of fingers on piano keys or hands and feet on the organ. The singing voice is part of a person, and a social presence underlies call-and-response singing and work songs, just as spatial distance is inherent in the sound of antiphonal music.

Dance quite literally embodies music. Most dance is done to music or other sound, perhaps in part a consequence of its somatic effects. Ethnic dancing, for example, is inseparable from cultural styles in music and musical instruments. National dance traditions in Europe, such as the Balkan, Scandinavian, Turkish and English, are distinctive and strikingly different from one another. The same can be said of African, Asian and Native American dancing. Even when diverse traditions are combined, as in Candomblé, a syncretic ecstatic religion in Brazil, the music, chanting and dance become yet another singular amalgam.[14] In the West, music written to be danced to, from the minuet to the waltz, to disco, may find its way into other musical traditions, from Bach's instrumental and orchestral suites to Ravel's *Valses nobles et sentimentales* and Bartók's *Dance Suite*. Lastly, music not written for dancing may be translated into bodily movement, as in Balanchine's *Double Concerto* to Bach's *Concerto* for two violins and his *Duo Concertante* to Mozart's work of that name for violin and viola. Even 'quiet' listening engages the body subliminally. These are only some of the many ways in which our bodies engage in the practice of music.

But music in dance not only enters and activates our bodies. Its scope is more diffuse still, for music spreads out to engulf the space in which it occurs. We can think of the space defined by the dominating presence of sound as 'sound space'. Thus musical listening is bodily engagement with sound in a setting. What we have in embodied music, then, is actually environmental: body–sound–space.

Music does not exist unless it is embodied. The ear is always involved: the ear of the listener guided by the ear of the performer which, in turn, is guided by the ear of the composer, much as, in painting, the eye of the artist is invariably present in the painting. Because music always occurs as an event and usually first as a performance, bodily involvement is necessary. Even in electronic music, the composer actively fashions the sounds in a way comparable to a performer in a recording session. Further, the actual performance of music demands far more than fingers, arms, lips or tongue: playing an instrument engages the entire body. One feels the sound entering one's body, the sound vibrations going through to the feet. Madeline Bruser emphasizes that the performer 'become(s) saturated with [the vibrations], achieving direct contact with the living texture of music. The mind of the composer lives in [the performer's] body.'[15] (Shades of dualism!)

Sudnow's account of Jimmy Rowles's jazz piano playing bears out this same bodily engagement in music: 'I watched him ... move from chord to chord with a broadly swaying participation of his shoulders and entire torso, watched him delineate waves of movement, some broadly encircling, others subdividing the broadly undulating strokes with finer rotational movements, so that as his arm reached out to get from one chord to another it was as if some spot on his back, for example, circumscribed a small circle at the same time.'[16] The pianist and scholar Charles Rosen writes of how the entire body of the pianist engages in producing every crescendo and decrescendo. The very physical instrument exerts an attraction on the pianist, who feels a physical need for contact with the keyboard. Moreover, the sonorities and other traits of the instrument influence and affect the composer and the listener, as well.[17] Our auditory imagination becomes actively involved, supplementing the decaying sound of a piano tone, contributing to the sounds that are actually heard, and hearing the inaudible by sometimes supplying notes that are unheard. In his late writings, Barthes speaks of the listener as a reader performing the music, indeed, composing it a second time. Rosen makes a similar point: 'The listener must constantly alter, purify, and supplement what he hears in the interests of musical intelligibility and expressiveness, taking his cue from what is implied by the performer.'[18] In a live performance, the body is engaged with focused intensity.

The Western obsession with objects – objects that subjects use, control or possess – extends to art. We easily identify art with visual objects such as paintings and sculptures, and with literary ones such as novels and poems. Doing this in the performing arts may seem somewhat more difficult but it does not deter the theoretical imagination. Thus dance becomes ballets, and theater, plays. Locating the musical object may seem more awkward still. The problem seems to trouble some philosophers but does not deter audiences, who find it entertaining to focus their attention on the gyrations of conductors and the gestures of soloists. The object-centered focus of art has a powerful grip on our understanding and an exclusive hold on our attention.

I have tried to show that such a focus is partial and quite misleading. Argument may not be powerful enough to dislodge the rigid grip of convention. I should like to turn, therefore, to two examples, a literary one that both states the multidimensional character of music directly and exemplifies it in practice, and a musical one that exemplifies musical embodiment on many levels and with unusual richness.

Wallace Stevens's, 'Peter Quince at the Clavier'

The poetry of Wallace Stevens reflects the subtle joinings of an unusual poetic sensibility with a powerful intelligence that extend to embrace a metaphysical domain. Stevens exhibits these characteristics through the musical theme of 'Peter Quince at the Clavier'.[19] The poem shifts repeatedly in denotation and metaphor from spirit to body to flesh. At first this might seem to be inadvertent ambiguity or abject confusion. That, I believe, is quite mistaken. The poem embodies not confusion but rather a fusion, the deliberate recognition of their continuity and inseparability: Music as heard, felt and then remembered joins spirit and body in an indissoluble unity.

Analyzing the poem from this standpoint shows that fusion clearly. In the following text, the terms in **bold face** denote references to music, the terms underscored are references to the body, and those in *italics* may be understood as manifestations of consciousness. Here poetry synthesizes with understated eloquence what philosophers have struggled unsuccessfully to separate.

Peter Quince at the Clavier

I

Just as my <u>fingers</u> on these **keys**
Make **music**, so the selfsame **sounds**
On *my spirit* make a **music**, too.

Music is <u>feeling</u>, then, not **sound**;
And thus it is that what I <u>feel</u>,
Here in this room, <u>desiring</u> you,

Thinking of <u>your blue-shadowed silk</u>,
Is **music**. It is like the **strain**
<u>Waked</u> in the elders by Susanna.

Of a green evening, clear and warm,
She <u>bathed</u> in her still garden, while
The <u>red-eyed elders watching</u>, <u>felt</u>

The **basses** of their <u>beings</u> <u>throb</u>
In witching **chords**, and their thin <u>blood</u>
Pulse pizzicati of <u>Hosanna</u>.

II

In the green water, clear and warm,
Susanna <u>lay</u>.

She <u>searched</u>
The <u>touch</u> of springs,
And found
Concealed *imaginings*.
She <u>sighed,</u>
For so much **melody**.

Upon the bank, she <u>stood</u>
In the cool
Of spent <u>emotions</u>.
She <u>felt</u>, among the leaves,
The dew
Of old **devotions**.

She <u>walked</u> upon the grass,
Still **quaver**ing.
The <u>winds</u> were like her <u>maids</u>,
On timid <u>feet</u>,
<u>Fetching</u> her woven scarves,
Yet <u>wavering</u>.

A <u>breath</u> upon her <u>hand</u>
Muted the night.
She <u>turned</u>–
A **cymbal crashed**,
And **roaring horns**.

III

Soon, with a **noise** like **tambourines**,
Came her attendant <u>Byzantines</u>.

They *wondered* why Susanna <u>cried</u>
<u>Against</u> the <u>elders</u> by her <u>side</u>;

And as they <u>whispered</u>, the **refrain**
Was like a willow swept by rain.

Anon, their lamps' uplifted flame
Revealed Susanna and her *shame*.
And then, the <u>simpering</u> Byzantines
<u>Fled</u>, with a **noise** like **tambourines**.

IV

Beauty is momentary in the *mind* –
The fitful <u>tracing</u> of a portal;
But in the <u>flesh</u> it is immortal.

The <u>body</u> <u>dies</u>; the <u>body's</u> beauty <u>lives</u>.
So evenings <u>die</u>, in their green <u>going,</u>
A wave, interminably flowing.
So gardens <u>die</u>, their meek <u>breath</u> <u>scenting</u>

The cowl of winter, done *repenting*.
So <u>maidens</u> <u>die</u>, to the auroral
Celebration of a maiden's **choral**.

Susanna's **music** <u>touched</u> the <u>bawdy</u> **strings**
Of those white <u>elders</u>; but escaping,
Left only Death's ironic **scraping**.
Now, in its immortality, it **plays**
On the clear **viol** of her *memory*,
And makes a constant *sacrament* of **praise**.

Debussy's 'La Cathédrale engloutie'

Stevens's musical trope displays body and consciousness as an unbroken whole. It is a brilliant recognition of the remarkable force with which music is able to engage us as integral human beings. What this poem of music exhibits in the evocative medium of language, music itself does directly and immediately. Although I believe this is true of all music, irrespective of genre, a particularly eloquent illustration of the rich complexity of musical embodiment, joining together many facets of human being in a seamless flow of sound, is Claude Debussy's evocative *Prelude No. X* for piano, *La Cathédrale engloutie* (or *The Sunken Cathedral*), whose title appears retrospectively only at the end of the printed score.

For the sake of clarity, I have grouped my comments on this work around several different centers: cultural association, sound, performance and musical knowledge, although in the live act of listening they are fused together. Cultural association begins the discussion because, in this particular piece, it pervades many of the other factors. While it comes first here, in the performance of the piece, it is actually last, for the title of the prelude, explicitly relating the piano's chords to the muffled bells of a cathedral, appears at the end of the printed score rather than at the beginning. The explanation usually given is that Debussy did not want the audience to listen to the music as an illustration of the scene but rather to grasp it directly by ear. It is interesting that, in describing how this occurs, we are led to make use of bodily referents and metaphors.

Certain sounds are characteristic of impressionist music, a stylistic movement centered in France at the end of the nineteenth century and the early decades of the twentieth. Among them are the whole tone scale and parallel chords, which include parallel intervals of a fifth, something carefully avoided in earlier periods. These sounds are especially pronounced in the music of Debussy and nowhere more so than in this prelude. Debussy builds the piece on octaves, on fifths, on fourths, their inversion, and on seconds and ninths, which result from the superposition of fifths. Combining these intervals produces harmonic sequences that are distinctively impressionistic in tonal quality. At the same time they recall the early development of Western ecclesiastical music known as organum (ca. 800–1250), which moved away from monody and toward harmony by adding parallel octaves and fifths.

Octaves, fifths and fourths, moreover, are the pitches most pronounced in the overtone series. Indeed, the first fifteen bars of this prelude are built entirely on the first three overtones, sounds that lie above the fundamental or principal note but are much weaker: the octave, fifth, and fourth (for example, G, g, d, g^1). Most of us are oblivious to these faint pitches, but we do hear the richness and resonance they contribute to the note that is directly sounded. These overtones are especially pronounced in church bells, whose distinctive ringing reverberation comes from the unusually powerful overtones that are produced when a bell is struck forcefully. Joining the hollow resonance of these harmonic structures with melodic materials that make extensive use of octaves, fifths, fourths, seconds and ninths, intervals commonly found where multiple bells are used, vividly evokes the distinctive sound of cathedral bells.

Still another, subtle evocation of a cathedral has its basis in memory. Many short phrases are repeated exactly or approximately, and there are several phrases that are symmetrical, like a palindrome that reads the same backward as it does forward, which in music theory is called *cancrizans* or crab. These have the effect of a kind of echo that, together with the impressionistic use of the damper pedal, which allows successive chords to run together, helps create the auditory atmosphere of a cathedral's great resonating space.

Most directly apparent of all is the way in which the body enters into the performance of this and any musical work. Not only the hands but the torso, the legs and the feet are involved. The performer feels the physical vibrations of the sound from direct contact with the instrument as well as through the ears, and of course is deeply absorbed in listening as part of the process of guiding the body in producing these sounds on the piano. The sounds spread throughout the space that embraces the pianist and the piano, and engulf the audience in a continuity of space, sound and bodily presence.

Knowledge is probably the most variable of the factors in musical experience because its influence results not only from the cultural conditioning of the participant, whether performer or listener, but also from the education, training, past exposure and other such differences in personal history. Yet knowledge is nonetheless a forceful influence. It functions as a filter through which our perception and engagement in the entire musical situation take place. Not just national traditions but historical styles of composition, performance and appreciation affect the experience of music, and all of these may be mediated by cognitive structures.

Conclusion

The experience of music offers powerful proof of human embodiment. It is environmental engagement at its highest pitch and offers an eloquent argument for the full fusion of human being, a kind of reasoning I call the argument from experience. When Walter Pater observed that 'All art constantly aspires towards the condition of music',[20] he may have been extolling music at the expense of the other arts. But perhaps he recognized that music evokes the experience of embodiment with unusual forcefulness, directness and immediacy. Yet every art, or rather every appreciative engagement with art, does something of the same thing, each in its own characteristic perceptual way. Art thus offers us what philosophy has no language to express directly: the unity of human being and the continuity of our multiple dimensions. By making this aesthetic fusion explicit in aesthetic experience, we can begin to reveal art's ways, which are perhaps the closest we can come to presenting the unsayable.[21]

Notes

1   William Butler Yeats (1952), 'The Cutting of an Agate', in B. Ghiselin (ed.), *The Creative Process*, New York: New American Library, pp. 106–7.
2   Wolfgang Welsch (1997), 'Artificial Paradises? Considering the World of Electronic Media – and Other Worlds', in *Undoing Aesthetics*, trans. Andrew Inkpin, London: Sage, pp. 183–4.
3   Berel Lang (1995), *Mind's Bodies*, Albany: State University of New York Press, is an imaginative effort to overcome their separation.
4   It is useful to distinguish between 'body' and 'the body'. 'The body' designates an object and is a clinical term. 'Body', in contrast, is personal, not objective. 'Body' always possesses a generalized eroticism, in some fashion, an eroticism that includes among its qualities touch, presence, aura and movement.

     The anthropological term 'folk category', in spite of its potential significance, is little known in philosophical discourse. It refers to the claim that every society operates with conceptual models. 'A society's culture consists of whatever it is one has to know or believe in order to operate in a manner acceptable to its members, and to do so in any role that they accept for any one of themselves ... It is the forms of things that people have in mind, their models for perceiving, relating, and otherwise interpreting them' (Ward H. Goodenough, (1968), 'Cultural Anthropology and Linguistics', *Report of the 7th Annual Round Table Meeting on Linguistics and Language Study*, ed. Paul L. Garvin, Monograph Series on Languages and Linguistics no. 9, Institute of Languages and Linguistics, Washington: Georgetown University, pp. 167–8), quoted in Robert A. Manners and David Kaplan (eds.) (1968), *Theory in Anthropology, A Sourcebook*, Chicago: Aldine, p. 476. See also Ward H. Goodenough (1970), *Description and Comparison in Cultural Anthropology*, Chicago: Aldine, p. 104.
5   'There do not exist such independent entities as subject and object .... The opposition of subject–object is rather thought of because we see the things by our acts. The things oppose themselves thoroughly against us, and I called technē the act that we make things with tools. Technē does not simply belong to the subject. It consists in penetrating into things, and in the function of things becoming ours. Taking tools in hand, the human being finds himself already in the world of historical life' (Kitarō (1936), 'Logic and Life', *Nishida Kitarō zenshū (Works)*, Tokyo: Iwanami, 1965–88, vol. 8, p. 297). Quoted in Ken-ichi Sasaki (1998), *Aesthetics on Non-Western Principles*, Version 0.5, Maastricht: Jan van Eyck Akademie, p. 37.
6   'Being an operating element in the historical world, we make things with tools. To make things ... means to act bodily. And so it must not be simply subjective but [a]

subjective–objective historical fact. That we act presupposes that we desire. From where does a desire come? A desire ... must be aroused from the bosom of our body. So the body must be formed historically too. We should notice that the body is not a simple biological body: the human body must be a historical body' (K. Nishida (1936), pp. 344–5), quoted in K. Sasaki (1998, p. 38).

7   Maurice Merleau-Ponty (1968), *The Visible and the Invisible*, Evanston: Northwestern University Press, esp. pp. 142, 272. See also Arjas Inari (1998), 'Poetics of the Substantial: Transcendence in the Context of Environmental Aesthetics', unpublished MA thesis, Department of Literature, Theater and Aesthetics, University of Helsinki, pp. 26, 29.

8   M. Merleau-Ponty (1968, p. 267).

9   'It is by the flesh of the world that in the last analysis one can understand the lived body (*corps propre*) – The flesh of the world is of the Being-seen, i.e. is a Being that is *eminently percipi*, and it is by it that we can understand the *percipere*: this perceived that we call my body applying itself to the rest of the perceived, i.e. treating itself as a perceived by itself and hence as a perceiving, all this is finally possible and means something only because *there is* Being, not Being in itself, identical to itself, in the night, but the Being that also contains its negation, its *percipi*' (Ibid., pp. 250–51).

10   '*Flesh of the world*, described (apropos of time, space, movement) as segregation, dimensionality, continuation, latency, encroachment – Then interrogate once again these phenomena-questions: they refer us to the perceiving–perceived *Einfühlung*, for they mean that we are already *in* the being thus described, that we *are of it*, that between it and us there is *Einfühlung*. That means that my body is made of the same flesh as the world (it is a perceived), and moreover that this flesh of my body is shared by the world, the world *reflects* it, encroaches upon it and it encroaches upon the world (the felt *senti* at the same time the culmination of subjectivity and the culmination of materiality), they are in a relation of transgression or of overlapping – This also means: my body is not only one perceived among others, it is the measurant (*mesurant*) of all, *Nullpunkt* of all the dimensions of the world.' 'The *touching itself, seeing itself* of the body is itself to be understood in terms of what we said of the seeing and the visible, the touching and the touchable. I.e. it is not an act, it is a being at (*être à*). To touch *oneself*, to see *oneself*, accordingly, is not to apprehend oneself as an object, it is to be open to oneself, destined to oneself (narcissism)' (Ibid., pp. 248–9).

11   Inari Arjas (1998, p. 26).

12   J.J. Gibson (1979), *The Ecological Approach to Visual Perception*, Boston: Houghton Mifflin, p. 255.

13   One can identify a series of body–environment connections, from the body in (the) environment to the bodily environment, the environmental body, body–environment and, finally, the human environment (as bodily).

14   Candomblé is strongly African, especially influenced by the Yoruba, but joined with Native American and European elements. In this religion the members seek spirit possession by their gods through chanting and drumming.

15   'Hearing does not stop inside your ears; it takes place in the whole body. Even deaf people can dance to music because they feel the vibrations in their bodies' (Madeline Bruser (1997), *The Art of Practicing*, New York: Bell Tower, p. 171; see also chs 6, 10, 12 and *passim*).

16   David Sudnow (1978), *Ways of the Hand: The Organization of Improvised Conduct*, Cambridge, MA: Harvard University Press, p. 82; see also pp. 83, 146 and *passim*.

17   Charles Rosen (1999), 'On Playing the Piano', *The New York Review of Books*, 21 October, pp. 49–52, 54.

18   Charles Rosen (1995), *The Romantic Generation*, Cambridge, MA: Harvard University Press, p. 3. Rosen demonstrates this by analyzing examples from Beethoven and Schumann. Also 'The romantic "heart", an excorated metaphor, is a powerful organ, extreme point of the interior body where, simultaneously and as though contradictorily,

desire and tenderness, the claims of love and the summons of pleasure, violently merge: something raises my body, swells it, stretches it, bears it to the verge of explosion, and immediately, mysteriously, depresses it, weakens it. This movement must be perceived *beneath* the melodic line; this line is pure and, even at the climax of melancholy, always utters the euphoria of the unified body; but it is caught up in a phonic volume which often complicates and contradicts it' (Roland Barthes (1985), 'The Romantic Song', *The Responsibility of Forms*, New York: Hill and Wang, p. 289).

19 Wallace Stevens (1915), 'Peter Quince at The Clavier', in William Stanley Braithwaite (ed.), *Anthology of Magazine Verse for 1915 and Year Book of American Poetry*, New York: Gomme and Marshall, pp. 15–17, reprinted in Wallace Stevens (1923, 1931, 1947), *Harmonium*, New York: A.A. Knopf, pp. 153–7.

20 Walter Pater (1873), 'The School of Giorgione', *The Renaissance: Studies in Art and Poetry*, 2nd edn (1877) and subsequent editions.

21 I have explored the notions of aesthetic engagement and fusion in many different contexts and directions, including A. Berleant (1970), *The Aesthetic Field: A Phenomenology of Aesthetic Experience*, Springfield, IL: C.C. Thomas; A. Berleant (1991), *Art and Engagement*, Philadelphia: Temple University Press; A. Berleant (1992), *The Aesthetics of Environment*, Philadelphia: Temple University Press; A. Berleant (1997), *Living in the Landscape: Toward an Aesthetics of Environment*, Lawrence, KS: University Press of Kansas, and many recent papers.

Chapter 12

Dot.com Dot.edu: Technology and Environmental Aesthetics in Japan

Barbara Sandrisser

In a brief, delightful essay, Bran Ferren predicts that, within the next two hundred and fifty years, computer technology along with lawyers and taxicab drivers will long be obsolete, considered solely as historical curiosities. Great discoveries and inventions, including designing new, hybrid electronic/ biological life forms that are far more intelligent than we humans are, will undoubtedly cause us to re-evaluate what makes the human life form so special. Ferren suggests that art, story telling and humor 'will be the only surviving vocations left from those we know today'.[1] It is the invented life forms that will do our reasoning. Human artists, he says, will become the most valued and irreplaceable professionals. Finally, human creativity will be valued, and thus aesthetic intercourse will become commonplace. Ferren concludes by hoping that our art will keep us human and our humor keep us sane. He urges the first space aliens to immediately visit the National Gallery of Art because, he dryly asserts, 'I want our art to explain who and what we are before our leaders do.'[2]

I must admit that I like this scenario. Not only will new rules of etiquette and conduct need to be forged, but an exhilarating, new aesthetic awareness will emerge. The age of manipulating existing information instead of pursuing and exchanging original ideas will be behind us and we can direct our attention to creating and appreciating new forms of art and wit, while simultaneously valuing past achievements. Instead of feeling intimidated or threatened by technology, humans will finally understand that what is important is not how clever we and our machines are but how insightful our hearts and minds become. Yet I cannot help wondering whether we will ever grasp the notion that the surface of the earth on which we stand, walk and ride, and over which we float or fly, is an intimate part of our spirit, particularly since current planetary exploration suggests that, in the future, humans and other life forms may opt for another place in space to enjoy their existence.

It seems that, as we speed into the future, the promise of technology seems more enticing by the millisecond. However, not all technology is greeted with open arms. In the mid-nineteenth century, still photography was derided as superficial and soulless, devoid of any aesthetic merit.

Indeed, the camera and occasionally the photographer were frequently
accused of stealing the souls of their subjects. In the late nineteenth and
early twentieth centuries, moving images were criticized as being mere
entertainment for the masses. Of course, now that we live in the twenty-first
century, we understand the value of film as an art form. Today, many of us
feel threatened by what is, arguably, the most intriguing technology of the
late twentieth century: the computer and its increasing power to change our
view of this planet and the universe. At best, we seem ambivalent and even a
bit wary about the future of aesthetic awareness and understanding, in much
the same way as our ancestors were when first looking at photographs and
moving images. In short, in spite of sophisticated technological advances
encompassing virtually every aspect of our daily lives, we are not yet
'dot.calm'.

Ferren's suggestion that technology will continue to leap ahead to first
mimic many complex aspects of the human brain and then far exceed it is,
of course, already happening. In 1993 in Japan, the Real-World Computing
Project was established to develop software that would help computers
'intuit' their environment. Headquartered in Tsukuba, commonly referred to
as Japan's 'science city', with research centers throughout the world (except
the United States, where government lawyers feared losing trade secrets),
the goal of the ten-year project is to develop computers that learn by example,
not by receiving explicit commands or by having all the relevant facts at
their disposal. One practical outcome of the research, according to Irisawa
Hajime, executive director, might be to train robots to perform delicate
farming tasks, such as removing stems from strawberries.[3] Mundane as this
sounds, it has profound implications for migrant farm workers, as well as
for computer artists, architects, choreographers, composers and artists in
forms yet to be created.

Yet, still lurking in the back of many minds is the fear that computers will
subsume us: that human life forms and computers will somehow merge into
one entity, resulting in the irretrievable loss of those special qualities that
make us human. Leaving aside pacemakers and the fictional 'six million
dollar man', whose various computerized body parts enabled him to perform
heroic feats of speed and strength, the underlying fear remains that we will
become 'dot. compost', that is, increasingly disembodied. The body/
computer-mind alienation certainly exists, but our bodies and, presumably,
our minds are only obsolete when we are dead. To paraphrase the American
humorist Steven Wright, we need our bodies to carry our brains from place
to place. Wright clearly values his body as more than a moving storage
cabinet and, thus, he wants us to understand the ultimate folly of constant
disembodied experience.

One way of exploring the notions of technology and aesthetics together is
by fast forwarding, rewinding and logging on to some futuristic environmental
and architectural projects, real and imagined. I will focus on a few recently
realized projects, mostly in Japan, and on a few imagined ones which exist

as conceptual places in film and in architectural drawings. Although many examples of technology (and aesthetics) gone awry endure, I think that, generally, technology and aesthetics continue to complement each other. In the ancient past, the two seemed quite compatible, judging from what little remains today on the ground, in visual arts and in descriptive writing. Even the words 'technology' and 'aesthetics', both derived from the classical Greek, suggest that fabricators, weavers (teksôn), and carpenters/builders (tektôn) need technical and artistic skill (tekhnē), acute sense perception (aīsthetikos) and feeling (aīsthanesthai) in order to create harmonious and sensuous surroundings.

Since more and more of us perceive the world abstractly through our computers, I suggest that we scroll forward to the mid-twenty-first century. In the continuing conflict between humans and machines, here is a glimpse of our fears of the electronic future. The architect's role is severely diminished, since anyone can design preliminary schematics and control the detail drawings via computer, while simultaneously distancing oneself from the earth's (or any planet's) surface and from the community context. Or, perhaps, one can simply download, free, anyone's design for one's own use, after a few technical refinements, in effect obliterating the design's uniqueness and devaluing the original designer's creative wisdom, experience and knowledge. The old idea of architect/artist – that is, an architect who can draw – is long gone. The computer is now the expert, not human beings searching for design solutions. 'Smart' houses already exist; that is, houses that are programmed via computerized sensors to observe and 'memorize' our movements, while simultaneously performing chores like turning on the outside sprinkler to water the flowers, turning lights on and off to the desired brightness, regulating heat and water according to our changing preferences, and even announcing to us that a visitor or burglar is in a specific room inside the house. No matter how technologically efficient in predicting our changing needs, big computer brother watching us can be unsettling, especially since our tactile control is limited. Indeed, there appears to be a poltergeist in our smart house. In the past, art and architecture helped us to understand life, to shape it and to find aesthetic fulfillment. Now the rules have changed, values have altered, and time-honored assumptions are dismissed. Our notions of craft, skill and their aesthetic impact are changing. In short, it is easy to design a house by mouse, perhaps unwittingly programming one's personal poltergeist into the finished product. It seems that excessive technology can sometimes provoke us into destroying our environment rather than existing within it.

If this view seems slightly out of sync, consider the Luddites as we scroll back to the nineteenth century. Between 1811 and 1816, groups of British workers rioted because the knitting machine, power looms and wool-shearing machines had taken away their jobs. The workers repeatedly tried to destroy the machines they felt were destroying their lives. The British elite called them Luddites, after a mythical, many say real, person named Ned Ludd, who, in 1779, gleefully smashed machines designed to knit hosiery. The word 'Luddites' recently returned to late twentieth-century language via cyberspace. According to one of Bill Gates's Microsoft lawyers, Luddites today wish 'to arrest the march of progress driven by science and technology'.[4] Ironically, should we yearn for more information regarding Luddites and their rejection of technology, we can log on to the Internet and call up *www.nmc.edu/~kovacsj/luddit~1.htm.*

Smashing machines or totally rejecting technology does not encourage us to experience our earth any better. Fear coupled with anger only encourages more aggressive behavior. Even restraining technological advances can be problematic. (Note the current debate on the pros and cons of cloning.) However, in Japan, giving up guns and returning to swords (1543–79) is a good example, perhaps the only one in history, where a sophisticated culture deliberately reverted to a less advanced technology for complex and insightful reasons.[5] Simply stated, guns did not fit in comfortably with Japanese culture, specifically samurai culture, which valued sword etiquette. As guns increased in early sixteenth-century Japan, soldiers no longer felt the need to exchange courtesies before the battle (nor was it safe). Dying began to lose its honor and dignity.

Today in some academic and government circles it is considered politically incorrect to suggest that cultural sensibility and aesthetics play important roles in how we experience environment, yet we all know this to be true. To explore the interplay between the aesthetics of a culture and environment, let me take you along a complex path that includes tunnels, bridges, low and high tech vernacular, and natural day lighting, culminating in the union of modern technology and aesthetics in the form of the Miho Museum, designed by I.M. Pei.

The Anaesthetics of Tunnels

While in Japan in the late 1980s, I traveled by ferry from Aomori to Hakodate and back. Despite the cold December weather, I stood outside on the upper deck as the ferry pulled away from the dock. The skyline of Aomori, a small city located on the northern tip of Honshu, slowly receded into the distance. As the ferry slipped past Mutsu Bay into the Tsugaru Strait, it fought against the high, gray–green waves that were slowing its progress. Below deck, families with *obentos*, beer, green tea and other treats, sat on tatami mats eating, talking and laughing. Children played and ran around and old people slept. I sat on a bench next to the window, looking at the rough water and at the coastline, whenever it appeared, listening to the sounds around me, smelling the salty air and the food. I knew that the opportunity to travel back and forth from Aomori to Hakodate on an old-fashioned ferry boat would soon end. The Japanese government had almost completed a state-of-the-art tunnel linking the main island with its northern neighbor. As I dug into my *obento* and drank my hot tea, I pondered the notion of how modern architectural and engineering technology frequently deprives us of our ability to experience the sensuous and sensual qualities of environment. I imagined myself one year later inside the new tunnel, more or less confined to my train seat, seeing nothing but darkness outside my window and experiencing very little of interest inside. I imagined feeling buried inside the tunnel; I missed unanticipated, sensuous pleasures. All my senses seemed muffled. I and others sat like quiet little robots, immersed in our laptop computers or sleeping.

It seems that how we perceive and feel environment has a direct impact on how we design it. Environment, in the broadest sense, includes all aspects of life inside and outside our bodies. We live and environment lives; we die and our environment dies with us, since, presumably, the dead no longer experience sensuous and sensual pleasure, unless we believe in those wonderful Japanese ghosts, who somehow materialize, albeit temporarily, to drink sake and, on occasion, make love with lonely widows. Today, our ability to fast forward and rewind film, to scroll forward or backward on our computers, or to enter a virtual reality can be almost as intoxicating as the real experience, displacing ordinary reality and human sensations, although efforts are currently under way to provide us with those experiences as well.

Twentieth-century visionary writers, such as Aldous Huxley, George Orwell and Michael Crichton, and mid-nineteenth-century ones like Jules Verne, managed to link environment and technology with imagination, creating literature that explored future technologies and their impact on human sensibilities. In a recently discovered manuscript called 'Paris in the 20th Century', Verne predicted the first primitive computer, describing it as a huge calculator resembling a piano used by brokerage houses. He also discussed facsimile machines, elevated trains, teaming road traffic in gas-powered vehicles, and the most grisly technology of all, the electric chair, which was soon after designed and subsequently introduced in the United States. Still, Verne's view of Paris is tinged with gloom, for despite technological advances, or perhaps because of them, individual aesthetic sensibilities seem obliterated by a government interested in profit and in keeping the masses in check by placating them with technological trinkets.

Let us for a moment scroll backward in time. In 1924, German film maker Fritz Lang conceived the idea for his famous futuristic silent film, *Metropolis* while aboard a ship sailing to the United States. As the ocean liner entered New York's harbor, he stood on deck watching the tall, narrow buildings emerge into view. As the ship drifted toward the pier, Lang, like many before and after him, thought he felt the buildings scrape the sky. Their scale and beauty fascinated him, yet in his mind's eye they all seemed like one giant machine devoid of any heart or soul.

Lang's film can best be described as an essay on the misguided and overwhelming power of technology – a technology that subsumes all traces of those qualities which make our lives worth living. The story focuses on a large twenty-first-century city where a Platonic division of society has occurred. The wealthy live and work above ground; they reap the benefits of direct access to the sun, Plato's metaphor for the 'highest' form of knowledge. Thus they bask in the comfortable environment that technology produced for them to enjoy. The poor workers live underground, the Platonic cave, where the sun never shines, and service the machines. Neither has contact with the other except through controlled administrative channels. The city is owned and ruled by a wealthy industrialist who is a technocrat, that is, seduced by the promises of technology. Naturally, the city is completely urban, a technological dream, completely structured and controlled by humans. No animals or birds, no trees and no flowers exist in Metropolis, except one small, carefully designed garden. No wilderness exists above or below ground.

Lang's architectural background and classical education clearly influenced the movie sets. His father had been an architect and Lang briefly studied engineering. In the film, what is above ground appears magical and fantastic, even to us viewing it today. A landing platform for airplanes tops a giant, 150-story tower. Delicate bridges supported by faceted truss 'legs' span the spaces between the lower buildings. The technological maze below ground consists of many levels, most far deeper and more complex than the New York City subway system that was constructed at the end of the nineteenth century and which Lang undoubtedly rode during his visit. Workers spent their lives consumed by technological maintenance, never experiencing the surface of the earth, the sky, the sun, stars and moon, or the seasons. The largest underground chamber housed the enormous power center called *die Herzmaschine* (the heart machine), which permitted everything above ground to function properly and efficiently. Most people living above ground took these benefits for granted, not realizing that, if the heart (machine) stopped, everything would stop. The heroine of the film appears as a female human and also as a robot modeled after her physical appearance. Although the human character is responsible for inciting the workers to riot and demolish the machinery, in the end it is the robot that is destroyed by the technocrats, not the human heroine. Lang deliberately choreographed the masses of people above and below ground in such a way that the audience could immediately grasp the nightmarish plot without necessarily reading the captions.

Fritz Lang's wife, Thea von Harbou, wrote the script. Both clearly foresaw the kinds of ethical and aesthetic values that might perish in a world too narrowly focused on technological victories. They warned of the perils of existing in an urban area replete with technological triumphs yet devoid of any sense of personal place or environmental interaction. Leaving aside the issues of social justice for the workers underground, the film's more subtle message suggests that the power of architecture affects our very being. It also suggests that those assigned underground can still initiate changes that incorporate a more balanced relationship between above ground and below ground, between technocrats and artists, between the built environment and the natural environment, and between the past and the future.

While Fritz Lang walked along New York's narrow streets in 1924, taking in the variety of immense structures looming overhead, French painter Fernand Léger, who had studied architecture as a young man, made a short film about technology, called *Ballet Mécanique*. A reluctant soldier during the First World War, Léger had experienced the full force of newly designed war machines, such as tanks and artillery. These, coupled with his attraction to industrial machine forms found in urban environments, influenced all his creative work. Whether painting, film making, designing theater sets and murals, or photographing urban landscapes, Léger pictured the future as driven by technology. His abstracted machines were always dynamic and forceful, yet his people seemed strangely silent, lacking emotion, even childlike – in a word, robotic. Their message was, perhaps, that the future was already with us.

And so it is, but the future did not necessarily follow Léger's sociopolitical path. One year after Léger's death in 1955, Dutch artist Constant Niemvenhuys (who uses only his first name) began an eight-year visionary project entitled 'New Babylon', an imaginary city in which technology takes over the mundane tasks, leaving the inhabitants free to recapture their lost sensibilities by enabling everyone to enjoy creative amusements, along with more sybaritic ones. Rather than living preoccupied with technology, Constant's New Babylon encourages us to become more self-indulgent, more hedonistic and, most striking perhaps, more childlike, despite his rejection of a mechanistic way of life.

Today, research in the various sciences confirms that environment, technology and behavior are intertwined, a seemingly obvious conclusion. What may be less apparent is why this is so. Sherry Turkle suggests that, when a new technology permeates society, we tend to view it selfishly, asking what can it do for me? 'Only with some time and distance do people tend to turn to its subjective effects, what it does to us as people,' Turkle notes. She feels that we are just at that point now with the computer. 'We make our technologies and our technologies shape us in turn.'[6]

Technology Gone Awry

At the same time, through technology we unburden ourselves. Computers enable us to come to design conclusions quickly and accurately. Despite their speed and efficiency, however, human design skills and ingenuity sometimes get displaced or even lost in the process, as in the following example of real, not imaginary, architecture. A few years ago, just as the economic bubble was about to be burst in Japan, the Makuhari Business Park emerged, soon to be part of a new urban project called Makuhari, situated on reclaimed land on Tokyo Bay. Located near Funabashi, midway between

Tokyo and Chiba City, Makuhari was one of a number of satellite centers
under construction along Tokyo Bay. The Chiba Prefectural Government
funded the project, in part because of its optimum location right next to the
expressway leading to Narita airport. Some sections near the outskirts of the
site were still under construction. Patios II, a group of low and mid-rise
housing units designed by the New York firm, Steven Holl Architects, was
not yet on the ground.

A number of architects were invited and many more competed to create a
new urban environment with state-of-the-art structures that would pave the
way into the twenty-first century. I used the double meaning of the word
'pave' deliberately, since, as far as I could see, the ground was paved. The
centerpiece of the new development is Maki Fumihio's elegant convention
center, which swooped along the skyline. It is surrounded by office buildings,
a hotel and parking areas, forming a heavy, vertical counterpoint to Maki's
light, airy and curvy structure. Large-scale footbridges crisscrossed the
expressway. Outdoor escalators moved efficiently between different levels.
A different architect using sophisticated technology conceived each building.
All were impressive and imposing. Potted plants, some unintentionally
whimsical, were strategically placed along circulation routes. A carefully
contained, rectilinear mini-park was bisected by a narrow, shallow artificial
waterway that led into a circular pool. Soldier-like trees, evenly planted,
stood at attention flanking the waterway. Finally, a massive red-painted steel
and concrete portico, large enough to drive a small truck through, provided
an overwhelming clue for the entryway to the convention center. Oversized,
bright-red steel, parasol-like flowers on the soffit endeavored to lessen its
formidable scale.

Technically, this imposing, almost stately environment functions
beautifully. Most of the site, including the rigid, unyielding mini-park, was
computer-generated. Everything stands in static monumentality within its
pre-assigned place. Makuhari fulfilled the role of icon to economic wealth,
political prestige, late twentieth-century technology, and even to architectural
machismo. Did it seem too orderly, too designed, too domineering because
it was fairly new? Tajima Noriyuki and Catherine Powell call it 'a sanitized
pastiche of a western urban model' and note that 'the drawbacks of the
"prefabricate-and-lower-into-place" style of city building were apparent'.[7]
One is reminded of the grim, oppressive images in *Metropolis*. Overlooking
the initial sense of distance one frequently feels when examining modern
large-scale architectural projects, Makuhari seemed to rebuff the very people
it was attempting to entice. The visitor is encircled by what I call 'dour
space', that is, surroundings devoid of any sensuousness, humor, wit or
weeds.

Bridges as Public Art

During the late twentieth century, Japanese architects and engineers nevertheless produced some of the best projects in the world, projects that express grandeur without pretentiousness, stateliness without ostentation, wit that avoids absurdity and, frequently, both overt and covert sensuousness and sensuality. Bridges in Japan exemplify these ideas. They tend to dominate the surrounding land and seascape, and the aesthetic and sophisticated clarity of their structure is exposed for all to see and experience. Between Honshu and Shikoku, seven of ten planned bridges incorporating three different routes are now complete. The most recent bridge, and at present the longest suspension bridge in the world, the Akashi Kaikyo, which connects Awaji Island to Kobe, opened in April 1998. The Seto Ohashi, which opened in 1988, consists of six individually designed bridges which hop from island to island in the Inland Sea, beginning in Sakaide and ending overland in Honshu as an elevated expressway near Kurashiki. Consisting of five different kinds of suspension bridges and one truss bridge, each reflects the specific geography and the ecological conditions found along the route.

Jiro Tajima and Kazuo Sugiyama note that, in Japan, aesthetic considerations play a large part in contemporary bridge design. Moreover, they suggest that in the future, as in the distant past, bridges will exceed their primary function of transporting traffic. Throughout history, bridges in Japan were meeting places for people, including fishermen and young couples, who frequently pledged their undying love for each other while standing on a bridge overlooking the water. During the Meiji era in Japan, young women were photographed on bridges that were engulfed by wisteria blossoms, indicating their availability for marriage. Future bridge designs will likely include more possibilities for people to participate actively in the bridge experience. Tajima and Sugiyama remind us that bridges are a measure of civilization and thus 'bridge engineers will be required to design and construct bridges with high enough aesthetic values to satisfy the aesthetic requirements of society'.[8]

Technology and Aesthetics as Companions

Every island along the Japanese archipelago hosts superb examples of the successful merger between technology and aesthetics. In Okinawa, the University of the Ryukyus currently sits on a new campus rather than on the site of the old Shuri Castle, which was completely destroyed during the last months of the Second World War and has only recently been reconstructed. One of the university's new buildings houses computer technology facilities for faculty and students. The structure is beautifully sited on a wooded bluff overlooking the river. Its round design, seemingly simple, incorporates its hidden technology, while the rough texture and color of the facade suggest traditional Okinawan tiles. The building does not scream TECHNOLOGY! Yet that is its purpose.

Another building that does not scream TECHNOLOGY! is located near the small, remote city of Muraoka in Hyogo Prefecture. On the surface, Ando Tadao's wood museum appears almost vernacular. Upon closer inspection one can only admire the sophisticated role of technology. I call the museum Ando Tadao's 'tree stump' building, because from afar it appears to be an enormous decapitated tree. There is little architectural competition, since the building is surrounded by nature. Most of the trees on the site were saved and more trees and other plantings were added to enhance the relationship between the museum and the forest. The forest emerges inside the building, itself, in the form of a complicated support system deliberately designed to look like tree trunks and branches.

Low Tech and the Aesthetics of the Vernacular

From the mid-1980s onward, the Japanese economic boom encouraged considerable museum construction throughout Japan. It seemed that virtually every city, small or large, reaped the benefits. Many were dedicated to one local artist or collector. In Sapporo, for example, a crisply designed, modest white brick building houses the paintings completed by Kotaro Migishi, before he died at 31. This museum building successfully mixes 1970s passive solar ideas with late 1980s low-key technology. Generous amounts of natural daylight penetrate selected areas of the museum, a sensible idea, since in winter Sapporo's days are short. The large glass portions of the museum reflect the surrounding trees, making the museum an intimate part of the natural environment in all seasons. The interior spaces are spare yet welcoming, and the state-of-the-art ambient lighting, which is more intense during the cold winter months, is uplifting to visitors, especially during the many gray, snowy days. Here the architect combined low-tech with high-tech, resulting in a structure sensitive to its particular place.

I mention these examples not only because they seem to blend low-tech and high-tech efficiently and effortlessly, but because they exhibit elegant craftsmanship. Clearly, they are not commonplace technotrash conceived and constructed by dolt.coms. The beauty of the architecture emerged as a consequence of the variety of technical tools used, including human drawing skills joined with human ingenuity and experience.

Still, combining low-tech with high-tech can present some amusing problems, especially when designing a traditional movie set that encompasses many hectares, such as the one located in Kyoto, which actually looks like one of Japan's many outdoor museums. It is difficult to make samurai films by shooting only on location, thus an elaborate outdoor vernacular-style town containing all aspects of urban life, including brothels and decapitated head displays, was carefully constructed to 8/10mm scale (or 80% of normal size). The buildings having been made a bit smaller, the actors appear larger on screen. Artificial lighting, indoors or outdoors, is carefully hidden. Virtually all building materials are genuine, not synthetic imitations, which results in considerable maintenance, on the one hand, and natural aging on the other. The contrived outdoor studio/museum succeeds in evoking a sense of a busy town, rewound back in time. The set, which includes falling leaves, dirt and roof tiles needing repair, looks quite real.

The Miho Museum

Thus far, this chapter has explored multilayered paths in time and space in much the same way as the photos, architectural drawings of imaginary places, and films created during the nineteenth and twentieth centuries. The early twentieth century brought us Einstein's relativity theory, a brilliant theory that rewrote our notions of time and space. A few years later, in a different yet equally extraordinary way, Marcel Proust in his book, *Remembrance of Things Past*, helped us to understand the interdependence of time, space, place and memory and how this affects our sensibilities. In the twenty-first century, computer technology, even when combined with national and private wealth, need not trample the aesthetic and sensuous sensibilities of those who design and those who live with these designs. Elegance appears in many guises. The Miho Museum, designed by the Chinese–American architect I. M. Pei, incorporates all the technological and aesthetic ideas noted throughout this chapter: the tunnel, the bridge, the vernacular, natural lighting, visionary thinking. Most important, it exemplifies how dynamic and fluid time, space and place were, are and will continue to be, and how this affects our aesthetic awareness. Through this architectural, engineering and environmental undertaking, Pei created a stunning testament to the value of design inspiration and intuition (some call this previsualization: the ability to visualize from the outset the complexity of the design in one's mind), combining his personal vision with extraordinary technological innovations.

In order to reach the museum, located just outside Shigaraki, in Shiga Prefecture, one must first leave all public and private transport behind.[9] From the small entrance pavilion, visitors first walk up a wide path lined with cherry trees, and then into a tunnel, leaving the outside world behind while simultaneously anticipating what lies ahead. Walking through this 200 meter long tunnel can be compared to cleansing one's palate before tasting a good wine. The light at the end of the tunnel reveals an elegant, asymmetrical suspension bridge and, beyond that, what initially appears to be a low-key traditional Japanese style structure with *irimoya* hipped glass roofs. After crossing the bridge, three flights of stairs flanked by modern Japanese lanterns await the visitor.

This anticipatory walk engages all our senses, much like the long walk and ascent required to reach Shinto shrines and Buddhist temples. We are drawn to both the landscape and the deceptively modest building, more than 80 per cent of which is hidden underground, because tunnel, bridge and museum, together with the bell tower in the distance, merge with their environment. The fact that the museum is imbedded in a mountain that is part of a nature preserve raised enormous technical, logistical and ecological problems. Since no access road existed, a temporary one was discreetly laid out through the forest to bring in construction materials, which were then placed on specially designed platforms so as to preserve the forest floor. Landscaping was equally daunting. All the trees that had been removed in order to blast into the mountainsides for the tunnel and the museum needed to be replaced with the same species, so that the side of the mountain looked as it did before construction. The official count is 7000 replaced trees, plus hundreds of new ones.

The museum itself is a technological masterpiece. State-of-the-art earthquake precautions were incorporated into the design, including sophisticated technology to 'isolate' selected artworks. The glass hip roofs are actually skylights fitted with adjustable sunshades to control light and glare. Traditional wood slats were not a viable option here, so to create a warm, more traditional, interior atmosphere, thin aluminum pipes covered with digitized film lamination simulating hinoki wood were designed. Looking outside, first at the old pines, then at the forested mountains beyond, one is immediately propelled into the future while simultaneously experiencing the past. Current, even 'futuristic' technology is so important that the project clearly could never have been completed without it. When we experience the site, we experience the technology. It is not hidden; rather, it is more like a quiet, yet strong partner.

At this point, the inevitable questions arise. Will all these low-tech, high-tech, futuristic museums and other kinds of environmental designs that engage our sensibilities eventually be replaced by the 'art click', or even more seductively, the 'aesthetic click'? Probably not, although we are already in the midst of a new digital aesthetics that promises to make virtual vulgarians of us all. Will our rural landscape eventually become nothing more than a media-scape? Again, probably not, although many of our dense urban environments, such as Tokyo and New York, have been described as media-scapes for years. In much the same way that we accepted photography and the moving image in the nineteenth and twentieth centuries, it may be appropriate at the beginning of the twenty-first century to look at future technologies as a partnership between human beings, computers, humanized robots and as yet unknown machines, all working together to create new aesthetic environments on this planet and elsewhere.

Welcome to aesthetics dot.com. Technology is now an intimate part of most of our waking moments and some of our sleeping ones as well. Perhaps the next few hundred years will bring us continued aesthetic curiosity and enriched aesthetic diversity, along with more wit and humor. I hope that we can survive in both an illusionary world and in a virtual world, one being the world we create, the other the one we log on to. Still, occasionally I may need reassurance that I actually exist, that I am a part of physical reality and that all my sensibilities are still actively engaged in a material world. Like Steven Wright, I want to be sure that my body is carrying my brain around and that the two are enjoying the journey together.

Notes

1   Bran Ferren (1999), 'The Creators', *New York Times Magazine*, 19 September, section 6, p. 54.
2   Ibid.
3   Kyodo News Service (1993), 'Computer project to mimic the brain', *The Japan Times Weekly*, international edn, 1–7 February, p. 16.
4   William Safire (1998), 'The Return of the Luddites', *New York Times Magazine*, 6 December, p. 34.
5   Noel Perrin (1979), *Giving Up the Gun*, Boston: David R. Godine.
6   Quoted in Katie Hafner (1998), 'At Heart of a Cyberstudy, the Human Essence', *New York Times*, 18 June, p. G9. Sherry Turkle is Professor of the Sociology of Science at MIT.
7   Tajima Noriyuki and Katherine Powell (1977), *Tokyo: Labyrinth City*, London: Ellipsis London Limited, p. 28.
8   Jiro Tajima and Kazuo Sugiyama (1995), 'Historical Transition of Suspension Bridge Tower Forms in Japan', *Bridge Aesthetics*, Washington, DC: Transportation Research Board, National Research Council, pp. 133–4.
9   A small electric car exists to help those who prefer not to walk or who are unable to walk.

Chapter 13

Environmental Directions for Aesthetics and the Arts

Yuriko Saito

Environmental Aesthetics as a Challenge to Art-based Aesthetics

Among today's aestheticians it appears to be a general consensus that aesthetic objects do not refer to a set of special objects but rather are determined by our attitudes and experiences. This suggests that there is no theoretical limit with regard to what can be an aesthetic object.[1] However, it is noteworthy that the actual discussion in contemporary Western aesthetics centers almost exclusively on traditionally defined fine arts, such as painting, sculpture, music and literature, while examining the definition of art, expression in art, artist's intention, art and reality, art and ethics and the issues specific to each artistic medium. Indeed, sometimes aesthetics is identified with the philosophy of the arts. An aesthetic object consequently comes to be characterized by those features typically found in art objects: determinate spatial and temporal boundaries, relative stability and permanence, unified and coherent design, intentional creation primarily for the aesthetic expression of an idea, and certain conventional agreements governing our experience and appreciation.

Some present-day aestheticians do point out this curious discrepancy between art-centered aesthetics and the acknowledged prevalence of aesthetic objects. For example, one aesthetician discusses how the notion of disinterestedness was originally proposed by the eighteenth century British aestheticians, founders of modern Western aesthetics, as a way of defining aesthetic experience in general, but observes that 'this catholicity in the denotation of "aesthetic object"... has gone strangely unremarked'.[2] Another observes, 'although many aestheticians insist that aesthetic qualities are not limited to the arts, even those thinkers generally take the arts as the primary focus of their discussion'.[3]

Finding problems and limitations with this art-centered aesthetics, some modern aestheticians have posed challenges and provided alternatives. One is the investigation of popular arts and crafts. Another concerns everyday objects and activities, such as food and sport. One more area of recent exploration concerns the environment, both natural and human-made, the subject of the present discussion. Though the environment is unlike works of art in many

171

respects, the emerging discipline of environmental aesthetics shows how misleading it is to regard the environment as a 'wannabe' art, falling short of what is expected in a work of art. This hierarchical scheme of the art-centered aesthetics does not do justice to the environment's own rich set of aesthetic values. In his seminal work, which first called attention to the problem of neglecting the aesthetics of nature, Ronald Hepburn argues that:

certain important differences between natural objects and art-objects should not be seen as entailing the aesthetic unimportance of the former, that (on the contrary) several of these differences furnish grounds for distinctive and valuable types of aesthetic experience of nature.[4]

He warns that, by limiting our inquiry to art-centered aesthetics, we will fail to ask ourselves 'whether there might be other tactics, other attitudes and expectations more proper and more fruitful for the aesthetic appreciation of nature'.[5]

The environment is also a recent focus of the art world. Dissatisfied with some of the presuppositions and constraints embedded in the Western art world, some contemporary artists started working with or in reference to the environment, widening the scope of art objects. Their challenge to the established art world parallels environmental aesthetics' challenge to the art-based aesthetics. In what follows I will discuss those dimensions of our aesthetic experience of the environment not recognized by art-centered aesthetics, which in turn characterize important aspects of contemporary artworks.

The Frameless Character of the Environment

The environment as an aesthetic object differs from a paradigmatic art object because of its frameless character. A painting, for example, is literally framed, demarcating the aesthetically relevant items from the irrelevant ones (such as the surrounding wallpaper). Furthermore, even within a frame, we ignore irrelevant elements (such as the back of a canvas or the smell of fresh paint) according to conventional agreements. A symphony consists of the sound created by the orchestra conforming to the composer's score, excluding the outside traffic noise, coughing of the audience, cool breeze coming from the air conditioner, and the texture of the carpet.

Determining what is and is not a part of a work of art is not always free from controversy. For example, art restorers have to decide whether cracks and darkened colors on the paint surface are part of an old painting and should be preserved. Likewise, we cannot always dismiss the visual effect of the printed page of a poem. However, even in these and similar cases, we decide what elements constitute a work of art by consulting the conventional agreement of the artistic medium, the artist's intention, the historical/cultural practice and the technique used for creation. These considerations generally override the overall aesthetic effects; that is, even if we see an amusing contrast between the painting and the surrounding wallpaper, we intentionally disregard it, unless the work is an installation piece that may render their contrast artistically significant.

On the other hand, when we sometimes experience environment as a framed object, except in the case of some architectural pieces, the frame is primarily determined by aesthetic considerations, without reference to historical factors relevant in the case of art. For example, when we look at a scenic vista, we sometimes use our aesthetic sensibility and imagination to construct an imaginary frame to organize internal unity and coherence, as if we are looking at a photograph through a camera lens or at a landscape painting reflected in a Claude glass.

More often than not, however, we experience and appreciate environment as surrounding and enveloping us, with indefinite elements and indeterminate boundaries. My office environment is defined by my spatial orientation relative to the structure of this room, various objects cluttering the space, the lighting, the feel of warmth coming from the radiator, the intermittent traffic noise, and much more. And when I walk along a street lined by trees and houses, are the rain and cold wind part of that environment? What about the falling leaves? The sound of a flock of geese in the sky? The noise of the traffic? The smell of burning leaves? The feeling of wet feet as I step in the puddle? Can I distinguish between aesthetically relevant elements from those which are irrelevant? And how?

'Framing' an environment as an 'object' appropriate for art-based aesthetics, even if possible, compromises those features of the environment characterized by its very nature of enveloping our entire body.[6] The environment is not a neatly-packaged and self-contained bundle prepared by someone for our aesthetic pleasure, nor is it accompanied by conventional agreements for selecting relevant materials for our aesthetic experience. On the one hand, this frameless character of the environment may appear to be an aesthetic disadvantage, because coherence, unity and harmony, normally considered aesthetic merits, presuppose a determinate design within a clear boundary. On the other hand, this relative lack of a clearly defined design can be an asset, because our imagination and creativity become engaged in providing aesthetic experience for ourselves. Speaking of the natural environment, Ronald Hepburn comments:

> where there is no frame, and where nature is our aesthetic object, a sound or visible intrusion from beyond the original boundaries of our attention can challenge us to integrate it in our overall experience, to modify that experience so as to make room for it. This of course, *need* not occur; we may shut it out by effort of will, if it seems quite unassimilable. At any rate, our creativity is challenged, set a task; and when things go well with us, we experience a sudden expansion of imagination that can be memorable in its own right.[7]

This framelessness of the environment also characterizes recent artworks. Sometimes it is presented as a denial of solid objecthood, as in Robert Morris' *Steam* (1974), which consists of 'a hot, amorphous cloud seeping from the ground, billowing skyward and dissipating'.[8] But the most prominent examples are so-called land art or earthworks, which emerged in the United States in the late 1960s. By taking their art projects outdoors and working directly in, on or with the land, many land artists challenged, among other things, one important assumption of Western paradigmatic art: the spatial determinacy and self-contained identity of the art object. Robert Smithson's *Spiral Jetty* (1972) cannot be confined to the spiral structure on the lake shore designed by the artist. Neither can Christo's works be identified simply with the orange curtain (*Valley Curtain*, 1970–72), white fence-like fabric (*Running Fence*, 1972–6), pink plastic (*Surrounded Islands*, 1980–81), or yellow and blue umbrellas (*The Umbrellas, Japan–USA*, 1984–91). The environment surrounding and accentuated by each constructed object is equally part of these artworks. Two commentators on earthworks remark:

> As manipulations of three-dimensional materials in physical space, many of the first projects are sculptures. Yet, executed and sited in a specific location on which they depend for their power, they have the ability to melt and spread beyond the limits of their individual materiality, confusing the traditional sculptural scheme in which the experience begins and ends with the object.[9]

Through these and similar works, earthwork artists not only challenged the museum and gallery system entrenched in the Western art world, which treats art objects as commodities subject to buying and selling; they also offered an alternative model for art by inviting us to exercise our imagination and creativity in constructing our own conceptual framework for aesthetic appreciation. The same commentators on earthworks continue: 'resituating the site of the aesthetic epiphany from the object to the beholder and the surroundings in which the object was perceived... relocate(s) the artist and viewer from observer of nature to participant in it'.[10]

Our participation in creating an aesthetic experience of the environment and environmental art is not limited to exercising imagination and creativity. It includes our literal participation through bodily engagement, which is minimized in art-based aesthetics.[11] We typically experience Western paradigmatic art through the so-called 'higher senses', vision and sound, in addition to the intellectual faculty. Furthermore, the preferred mode for having an aesthetic experience is to be detached and distanced. Bodily engagement with the object is generally discouraged beyond walking around a piece of sculpture and walking closer to scrutinize the paint surface. We refrain from touching and smelling a visual art object, as well as from making sounds, moving about, or participating in a classical music concert, ballet performance or theater production.

I can offer several reasons for this preferred mode of experience. For one, controlling the sensations gained through the so-called 'lower senses' (of taste, touch and smell) is unwieldy. The first two require the recipients' active involvement, while providing smell to everyone in a uniform fashion is difficult. Furthermore, while perceptions through the higher senses are amenable to conceptual, sometimes even mathematical, analysis, those of the lower senses are at least thought to be not intelligible enough for such interpretation. In general, according to Western dualism, our response to a certain texture, smell and taste reminds us of the animalistic – meaning bodily – functions, not noble or sophisticated enough to grace our aesthetic experience.

We can, and sometimes do, remain uninvolved beholders when aesthetically appreciating the environment, as in looking at a vista or an architectural edifice from afar. However, more typically we are involved and interact with the environment. We experience the indoor environment by living in it, using it, moving about in it, and so on. Our appreciation of the outdoor environment cannot be separated from the feel of temperature, precipitation and wind against our skin, in addition to the distinct smell (and sometimes taste) defining the sense of place, such as the saltiness of the ocean, musty smell of decaying leaves in the forest, and burnt chestnuts and pretzels on a New York City street in winter. Similarly, how can we exclude from our experience of a snow-covered field the fun of making footprints and a snowman, or the sensation of sand and waves against our feet while walking barefoot on the beach? Experiencing and appreciating these environments fully *as environment*, I believe, involves our entire body and senses, which will be compromised if we, as detached spectators, behold them as if they were works of art. Paul Ziff, an aesthetician, reminds us that different works of art require different 'aspections', the ways of looking determined by the specific activities on our part to appreciate their aesthetic values appropriately and maximally. For example, 'I survey a Tintoretto, while I scan an H. Bosch,' because 'a different act of aspection is performed in connection with works belonging to different schools of art, which is why the classification of style is of the essence.'[12] This notion of aspection can be extended to apply to different kinds of aesthetic objects, such as art and the environment. What may be the most appropriate and rewarding way of experiencing one object may not be so with respect to another.

Some environmentally oriented modern artworks are designed to engage the viewer's entire body, including the lower senses. Meg Webster's works with living plants, such as *Glen* (1985), are often described as inviting touch and exuding scent. So is Walter de Maria's *New York Earth Room* (1977) with its striking smell of earth and peat in the middle of a gallery space. Some works by Carl Andre and Mary Miss require the viewers to walk along, walk through or crawl into them. Sometimes the creation of works also requires the bodily engagement of the artists themselves, as best exemplified by Richard Long, whose works consist primarily of his walking.

Andy Goldsworthy's exclusive use of his body as a tool for his creative activities, such as licking flower petals to glue them together, is guided by his desire to have intimate bodily contact, including taste, with the material. Thus, in both creating and appreciating, the environment offers rich possibilities for aesthetic experience through its open-ended designation, a departure from the restrictions governing traditional aesthetics and art making.

The Temporal Character of the Environment

Another noteworthy contrast between the environment and Western paradigmatic art concerns their respective temporal modes of existence. An art object is presumed to be stable and permanent, while the environment is more characteristically in flux and impermanent. Determining the identity of an art object, of course, is not simple. For example, as material objects, paintings and sculptures do age, despite our best effort to arrest this process. As for literature and music, although the words and notes themselves stay the same, their interpretation and performance practices change. However, in general, we believe that the identity of a work of art does and should remain recognizable. Thus not only do we refrain from changing the object but also we try our best to 'preserve' the object in its original condition and to 'restore' it if the aging effect becomes obtrusive.

In comparison, except for some specific environments, such as a famous work of architecture or a scenic site, we do not expect the environment to be, nor do we try to preserve it as, permanently 'frozen' in one particular state. A building is transformed by addition or modification, and a townscape altered by the construction of a new highway and bridge, while a coastal scape becomes transformed by beach erosion after a massive hurricane, and a volcano looks entirely different after an eruption. Even without such dramatic changes, gradual and steady transformation takes place due to weathering and aging, seasonal change and natural growth cycles. The environment also changes in a relatively short period of time, according to the time of the day, the changing weather conditions, traffic and pedestrian flow, and the use of space at a particular moment. As one writer points out in his discussion of domestic aesthetics, 'unlike paradigmatic art forms like painting or poetry, interiors do not just sit around after their completion unaltered for the centuries. They are lived in, worked in, and worked on and so they are also transformed, if only by being worn upon daily.'[13]

This lack of stability and permanence of the environment may at first appear to be aesthetically disadvantageous. Immanuel Kant would have believed so, as he claims that constantly changing objects, such as 'the sight of the changing shapes of a fire on the hearth or of a rippling brook', do not have beauty, although 'they bring with them a charm for the imagination'.[14] The indeterminate design of constantly changing objects makes it impossible to analyze their structure the way we can with stable and clearly constructed objects, as in the traditional fine arts.

However, it is only in reference to an art-centered aesthetics that impermanence and flux are considered aesthetically negative. To the contrary, transience and mutability can be, and have been considered to be, aesthetic merits.[15] For one thing, perpetual movement, surprising change or eventual extinction can relieve the fatigue factor and render our experience exciting and challenging by stimulating our imagination. This is why Joseph Addison includes 'the novel' or 'the uncommon', such as perpetually shifting or unusual objects, as one source of the pleasures of the imagination. According to him, 'we are … so often conversant with one set of objects and tired out with so many repeated shows of the same things that whatever is new or uncommon contributes a little to vary human life and to divert our minds, for a while, with the strangeness of its appearance'.[16] How many of us are not struck by the overnight transformation of our yard into a white, snowy wonderland? Or by the contrast between a skyscraper glittering in the morning sun with the same building disappearing into a thick fog in the evening? Or by the way the addition of a new piece of furniture changes the feel of the entire living room?

The impermanence of an object also lends a sense of uniqueness, urgency and pathos to our experience. This is the aesthetics of the Japanese tea ceremony, which elevates and celebrates the once-in-a-lifetime experience constituted by various non-repeatable factors, such as the particular season, the weather condition, the time of the day, the flight of birds, as well as the make-up of guests and the host's preparation. Rather than dismissing or lamenting those factors, which simply emerge beyond anyone's control, the aesthetics of *ichigo ichie* (one time, one meeting) incorporates them into the overall aesthetic whole. This aesthetic acceptance of chance, accidents and transience also underlies the creation and appreciation of Japanese pottery. While the potter is required to yield to the often unplanned and unexpected result of the firing process, the users are also encouraged to accept and cherish cracks and chips resulting from long use.

This aesthetics provides a counterpoint to the long-held assumption in Western aesthetics that the artist exerts control over every aspect of his or her creation, directing the content of the viewer's experience, and that the finished work is sacrosanct, to be maintained and protected from any alterations. While the aesthetic celebration of spontaneous occurrence has been a long tradition in Japan, in Western art history it is only during the last half-century that such spontaneity, chance and change have become accepted as viable aesthetic values. Chance music, happenings, action painting and auto-destructive art immediately come to mind.[17]

Environmentally oriented or situated art also embraces this aesthetics. Sometimes impermanence is pre-programmed, as in the temporary installation works by Christo. But a more frequently-held strategy, starting with earthworks, is for the artists to relinquish a total control over the objects and instead submit them to nature's process. Such was the notion of 'entropy' embraced by Robert Smithson: 'the process of transformation which works undergo when abandoned to the forces of nature'.[18] His works, such as *Partially Buried Woodshed* (1970), *Spiral Hill* (1971) and *Spiral Jetty* (1972) embody this notion by including decay and deterioration as their integral part. His contemporary, the earth artist Michael Heizer, also denies permanent objecthood in his work: 'what art now has in its hands is mutable stuff which need not arrive at a point of being finalized with respect to time or space. The notion that work is an irreversible process ending in a static icon-object no longer has much relevance'.[19] Accordingly, he took 'pleasure in publishing photographs of the deterioration of pieces years after they were made'.[20] Similarly working from observing nature, Hans Haacke tries to 'make something which experiences, reacts to its environment, changes, is nonstable' and to 'make something sensitive to light and temperature changes, that is subject to air currents'.[21]

Some other modern artworks situated outdoors are notably fragile, affected by nature's elements within a short period of time. Michael Singer's earlier works, such as *The Ritual Series* (1970s and 1980s), feature delicately balanced tree branches and twigs placed in ponds, and are characterized by their ephemerality. Singer explains that, 'in order to experience and learn from the natural environment ... I felt the need to yield to it, respect it, to observe, learn, and then work with it'.[22] Transience also figures prominently in Andy Goldsworthy's outdoor works, from early stick throws to later arrangements of leaves, petals and pine needles, culminating in works with snow, all requiring photographic documentation. Regarding the snowball pieces, Goldsworthy remarks: 'A snowball made in a day when the snow was good, fresh, not thawing, sunny and calm has to differ from one made in the wind, rain and dark with wet thawing snow. Each snowball is an expression of the time it was made.'[23] He sums up his art-making activity as his 'way of trying to come to terms with the transience of life and not trying to fight that by making always permanent things: to accept and enjoy it'.[24]

Modern environmentally oriented art's submission to nature's process is not limited to aging, disintegration and disappearance. Some artists harness nature's growth and maturing process in their works. David Nash's *Ash Dome* (1997–present) relies on the trees' natural growth for its completion, while Agnes Denes's *Wheatfield – A Confrontation* (1982) includes harvesting of the wheat nurtured by the artist and her assistants. Mel Chin's *Revival Field* (1990–93) also consists of various toxin-absorbing plants' growth.

In all of these works, as one commentator observes, the artists are 'more concerned with process than with product'.[25] While not proposed as a conscious agenda by these artists, their emphasis on the process implicitly challenges the classical Western ontology which privileges Being over Becoming and rather shares an affinity with Taoism and Buddhism. Furthermore, the attitude of relinquishing total management over their creation and accepting and yielding to forces beyond their control leads to a different conception of the roles of artists and art objects. Instead of a pre-designed object expressive of a specific idea appreciated purely for, by and in itself, an art object comes to function rather as an environment and clue to facilitate our experience of something beyond itself, such as natural or planetary phenomena.

Consider, for example, James Turrell's *Roden Crater* (1977–present). Its focus is not really the volcanic structure featuring underground chambers; rather, it is the experience of the celestial phenomena made possible by looking out from the chambers over the volcano's rim. The same can be said of Nancy Holt's *Sun Tunnels* (1973–6). Walter de Maria's *Lightning Field* (1980) is about the awesome display of lightning made possible by numerous metal poles. The constructed objects of these works are vehicles to make our experience of nature's phenomena, their main attraction, possible.

In this sense, these artworks function very much like our environment in so far as they facilitate a certain designated or desired experience. The aesthetic appreciation of the environment, therefore, concerns the quality of our experience made possible by its sensuous surface. In one sense, the human-made environment is successful to the degree to which we are not aware of it, being thoroughly absorbed in the experience at hand. This difference in the role of art and the environment leads Victor Papanek, himself a designer, to criticize the tendency in present-day American architectural practice to confuse the function of architecture with that of art. He claims that 'we designers and architects are encouraged to think of ourselves as artists, with the result that a good deal of design and architecture seems to be created for the personal glory of its creator'.[26] In contrast, the environmental direction in modern aesthetics and art suggests the rich sources of positive aesthetic experience, accessible only when we free ourselves from the assumption that the aesthetic object has to be fully designed and completed through the creator's control and manipulation of the material.

The Pragmatic Dimension of the Environment

Another important difference between traditional art and the environment lies in the way they affect our lives. Although art makes us think and feel, provokes novel perceptions and ideas, and sometimes even suggests a course of action, very few works of art directly change or determine our everyday affairs. At the same time, we are encouraged to put aside any personal or pragmatic concerns for the moment when attending to a work of art. The environment, on the other hand, has direct impact on our daily life. A well-designed environment makes living easy, comfortable and safe. Some environments and environmental phenomena, such as 'sick' buildings, polluted rivers and natural catastrophes like typhoons and tornados, literally threaten our health and life.

These practical aspects of the environment may appear to impede our aesthetic experience, distracting us from its sensuous surface, the focus of aesthetic experience. Those who advocate art-based aesthetics would remind us that distancing ourselves from everyday practical concerns by adopting a disinterested attitude is necessary for attending to the aesthetic aspects of the environment. Regarding art, proponents of aesthetic formalism or modernism held that 'the amount of pure pleasure provided by a work of art was ... measured by how effectively that work separated itself from everyday time and space to provide an imaginary oasis of ideal reflection'.[27]

While practical considerations often tend to lead us away from the object itself, they can also modify, transform, enhance or sometimes determine its sensuous surface. Consider, for example, the description of the fog at sea by Edward Bullough, an account of aesthetic distancing which has become a classic. In it he claims that a distancing attitude is necessary for boat passengers to experience the thick fog at sea aesthetically, so that they will not be preoccupied with the danger of being shipwrecked. However, he does not limit the source of our aesthetic experience of the fog at sea to its 'opaqueness as of transparent milk, blurring the outline of things and distorting their shapes into weird grotesqueness'. Rather, the intensity of the experience is derived from 'the uncanny mingling of repose and terror' brought about by the seemingly peaceful appearance of the phenomenon 'hypocritically denying as it were any suggestion of danger' and which 'contrast[s] sharply with the blind and distempered anxiety of its other aspect'.[28] Distancing, therefore, according to Bullough, is not detracting the imminent sense of danger and terror from our awareness; it is rather experiencing the phenomenon accompanied by all its practical significance with the 'unconcern of a mere spectator'.[29]

The fog example is also instructive for another reason. This experience is very personal in the sense that it is circumstance- and person-dependent. The sense of danger caused by the thick fog, an integral aspect of the boat passenger's aesthetic experience, will also be shared when on an airplane or driving a car, but not when walking along the beach, or looking at the blurred outline of a distant mountain. The fog in these cases will enhance the sense of quietude and solitude without a tinge of anxiety or uneasiness. Unlike our typical experience of an art object, therefore, the aesthetic appreciation of the environment can be modified or intensified by integrating our pragmatic concern at the moment. Ignoring or minimizing the practical aspects of the environment, therefore, unduly restricts the richness and depth of its aesthetic value.

The aesthetic experience of a human-made environment also cannot and should not be divorced from its practical dimension. All the aspects of the sensuous surface, such as the spatial configuration, color and texture of the materials, the lighting, the sound-carrying capacity and the ease of movement, cannot be appreciated (or depreciated) unless we know whether the function of the particular environment is to provide a public meeting place, a hospital for terminally ill patients or a playground for children. Spatial design that engenders insecure and anxious feelings may be appropriate in a certain theme park, while it is not appreciated in a hospital or a school.

Some recent artworks appropriate this inseparability of the aesthetic and the practical that characterize our environmental appreciation. Various artistic projects to reclaim devastated land constitute one kind. Pioneered by land artists of the 1960s, such as Robert Smithson, Michael Heizer and Robert Morris, land reclamation continues to be practiced by more contemporary ecologically minded artists such as Nancy Holt, Agnes Denes, Mel Chin, Patricia Johanson, and Helen Meyer Harrison and Newton Harrison. Whether dealing with a toxic landfill or contaminated wetland, these artists' projects integrate their artistic design with the actual clean-up of the site, as well as the restoration of native plants, providing habitat for indigenous animals and other living creatures. Accordingly, our appreciation of their works cannot be directed solely at their design on the land, nor should it be based strictly on their practical value of clean-up and rehabilitation of the site. Rather, it should be directed at the way these two values merge in the sensuous surface, such as the way in which the walkway structure echoes the root structure of the indigenous water plants in Patricia Johanson's *Fair Park Lagoon* (1981–6), or the way in which the cross shape of Mel Chin's *Revival Field* provides distinct sections for testing different plants' ability to absorb toxins from the soil.

Some artists engage in activism. One of the initiators of this form of art is Joseph Beuys, whose artworks include the project to plant 7000 oak trees in Germany (1982). Mierle Laderman Ukeles's performance pieces and installation, *Flow City* (1983–90), aim at raising public awareness regarding garbage. Betty Beaumont helped create a successful marine eco-system on the Atlantic ocean floor (*Ocean Landmark Project*, 1978–80), while Lynne Hull's sculptural pieces provide perching places and water holes for birds in the prairie and desert. The power of the environment to affect our daily life directly is here appropriated in those artworks where the aesthetic values cannot be separated from their effects on real life, blurring the distinction between art and life.

Do We Need Environmental Aesthetics?

The preceding discussion has shown important parallels between many present-day art objects and environmental aesthetics, both of these challenges to the traditional, Western, mainstream ways of creating art and thinking about aesthetics. However, if traditional art-based aesthetic theory is expanded to accommodate those new forms of art, which are very much like the environment, do we need a separate environmental aesthetic theory? That is, do we need an alternative to the traditional art-based aesthetic theory or rather its modification and expansion?

There are some reasons for not proposing a new environmental aesthetics. For one, we could adopt the strategy of parsimony by making use of Occam's razor. Second, we may agree with Oscar Wilde that nature imitates art rather than the reverse;[30] hence our aesthetic experience of the environment is indebted to the environmentally oriented contemporary art. Both of these considerations suggest that modification and expansion of traditional art-based aesthetics can account not only for recent environmentally oriented art but also for our aesthetic experience of the environment.

However, there are important differences between the environment and art, even environmentally directed ones, that should not be ignored. One is that, except for some works of architecture that are very much like works of art designed with a specific artistic intent,[31] the environment as an aesthetic object is not situated in the art world. Environment can be expressive of various qualities, but it does not make an artistic statement the way works of art do. In contrast, even environmentally directed art such as earthworks are located in an art-historical context and cannot but participate in the art world, even if their point is to challenge or escape from the art world. Only by reference to the art-historical context can their artistic gestures be interpreted as being subversive, novel and refreshing. Agnes Denes's *Wheatfield* is entirely different from the equivalent wheatfield cultivated by a Midwestern farmer. Though both engage in farming practice and provide an agricultural landscape, the latter does not carry the artistic meaning necessarily attributed to the former. So even when the artwork shares a number of important aesthetic characteristics with the environment, an equally significant distinction keeps them separate.

Second, although some environments are remotely located and regarded as precious objects much like works of art, such as the crown jewels of our national parks, our everyday environment is always with us; we must always be in some kind of environment. In contrast, the experience of art is generally limited to specific occasions. Perhaps this makes art objects' impact on us more prominent and noticeable and that of the environment subterranean and unnoticeable, seldom articulated or reflected upon. However, the inseparability of the environment from our lives makes it in a way a more powerful force in shaping and affecting our lives, its impact wide-ranging and profound.

This ubiquity of experiencing the environment suggests the final problem of absorbing environmental aesthetics under art-based aesthetics. While Wilde may be correct that most of us have learned how to appreciate fog after the introduction of Turner and the impressionists, who constitutes 'us' here? Those of us steeped in the Western artistic tradition with access, both cultural and economic, to the art world. I believe that the mission of environmental aesthetics is not simply to enlarge the domain of traditional Western art-centered aesthetics but, more important, to acknowledge the rich and diverse aesthetic experiences felt by those who do not share our familiarity with and membership of the art world. A Midwestern farmer may not have knowledge of, access to or interest in the contemporary art world. But I do not think there is any denying that he may have a rich aesthetic life, living in, on and with his environment. By the same token, those cultural traditions without an institutionalized art world like ours do not lack aesthetic resources. On the contrary, some of them are richly endowed with aesthetic sensibility in every aspect of their lives. As Arnold Berleant remarks, 'the custom of selecting an art object and isolating it from its surrounding ... has been ... most pronounced since the eighteenth century, with its aesthetic of disinterestedness. Yet it is at variance with the ubiquity of the aesthetic recognized at other times in the West and commonly in non-Western cultures'.[32] Among others, we can point to the Balinese culture, the Inuit tradition and traditional Japanese aesthetics as examples of cultural practices in which aesthetic concerns permeate every aspect of daily life, obliterating any distinction between art and non-art, artist and non-artist.

For these reasons, I think it is better for environmental aesthetics to maintain independence from art-based aesthetics. Although some important issues are common to both approaches in so far as they concern our aesthetic life, the celebration of diverse aesthetic objects, aesthetic experiences and aesthetic theories is more constructive and enriching than trying to come up with a mono-theory about all kinds of aesthetic manifestations. Just as Paul Ziff reminds us about the different 'aspections' required for various works of art, I believe that plurality of aesthetic objects in general requires diversity of analyses and approaches. I end with Berleant's view which best illuminates this point:

> humans along with all other things inhabit a single intraconnected realm, and...we must realize that our ultimate freedom lies not in diminishing or denying certain regions of our world in order to favor others but in acknowledging and understanding them all. This does not confer equal value on all. It admits rather that all activities, processes, and participants that together constitute nature have an equal claim to be taken seriously.[33]

Notes

1   The following two passages are representative of this view: 'Anything at all, whether sensed or perceived, whether it is the product of imagination or conceptual thought, can become the object of aesthetic attention'; 'Anything that can be viewed is a fit object for aesthetic attention' and 'one can view things in the world aesthetically without being concerned with or inhibited by their lack of status as artefacts.' The first passage is from Jerome Stolnitz (1969), 'The Aesthetic Attitude', in John Hospers (ed.), *Introductory Readings in Aesthetics*, New York: Free Press, p. 27. The second is from Paul Ziff, (1977), 'Anything Viewed', in Susan Feagin and Patrick Maynard (eds), *Oxford Readers: Aesthetics*, New York: Oxford University Press, pp. 29, 24.

2   Jerome Stolnitz (1977), 'Of the Origin of "Aesthetic Disinterestedness"', in George Dickie (ed.), *Aesthetics: A Critical Anthology*, New York: St Martin's Press, p. 624.

3   Thomas Leddy (1995), 'Everyday Surface Aesthetic Qualities: "Neat," "Messy," "Clean," "Dirty"', *The Journal of Aesthetics and Art Criticism*, **53**, 259.

4   Ronald Hepburn (1984), 'Contemporary Aesthetics and the Neglect of Natural Beauty', in *'Wonder' and Other Essays: Eight Studies in Aesthetics and Neighboring Fields*, Edinburgh: The University Press at Edinburgh, p. 16.

5   Ibid.

6   The problems of experiencing and appreciating the natural environment as an art object, such as a piece of sculpture, and as a two-dimensional landscape are explored in Allen Carlson (1979), 'Appreciation and the Natural Environment', *The Journal of Aesthetics and Art Criticism*, **37**, 267–75.

7   Hepburn (1984, p. 14).

8   Jeffrey Kastner and Brian Wallis (1998), *Land and Environmental Art*, London: Phaidon Press, p. 102.

9   Ibid., p. 16.

10 Ibid.

11 For the notion of 'engagement', I am indebted to the works of Arnold Berleant, such as (1991), *Art and Engagement*, Philadelphia: Temple University Press; (1992), *The Aesthetics of Environment*, Philadelphia: Temple University Press; and (1997), *Living in the Landscape: Toward an Aesthetics of Environment*, Lawrence, KS: University Press of Kansas. While he stresses the importance of engagement in our experience of art as well as of the environment, I am stressing more the literal bodily engagement required in experiencing the environment.

12 Paul Ziff (1958), 'Reasons in Art Criticism', in Israel Sheffler (ed.), *Philosophy and Education*, Boston: Allyn and Bacon, p. 235.

13 Kevin Melchionne (1998), 'Living in Glass House: Domesticity, Interior Decoration, and Environmental Aesthetics', *The Journal of Aesthetics and Art Criticism*, **56**, 199.

14 Immanuel Kant (1974 [1790]), *Critique of Judgment*, trans. J.H. Bernard, New York: Hafner Press, p. 199.

15 For this often neglected subject of our aesthetic appreciation of the effect of aging, see David Lowenthal (1990), 'The Look of Age', in his *The Past is a Foreign Country*, Cambridge: Cambridge University Press.

16 Joseph Addison (1975 [1712]), 'The Pleasures of the Imagination', in John Loftis (ed.), *Essays in Criticism and Literary Theory*, Northbrook: AHM Publishing Corporation, pp. 142–3.

17 For some examples of auto-destructive art, see Lowenthal, 'The Look of Age', pp. 172–3.

18 Kastner and Wallis (1998, p. 99).

19 Cited in Kastner and Wallis (1998, p. 24).

20 Kastner and Wallis (1998, p. 29).

21 Cited in Kastner and Wallis (1998, p. 33).

22 Cited in John Beardsley (1998), *Earthworks and Beyond*, New York: Abbeville Press, p. 165.

23 Andy Goldsworthy (1993), *Hand to Earth: Andy Goldsworthy Sculpture 1976–1990*, New York: Harry N. Abrams, p. 117.

24 Recorded in a film directed by C. Guichard (1991), *Nature and Nature: Andy Goldsworthy*, Peasmarsh: The Roland Collection.

25 Beardsley (1998, p. 192).

26 Victor Papanek (1995), *Green Imperative: Natural Design for the Real World*, New York: Thames & Hudson, p. 203.

27 Kastner and Wallis (1998, p. 25).

28 Edward Bullough (1912–13), '"Psychical Distance" as a Factor in Art and an Aesthetic Principle', *The British Journal of Psychology*, **5**, 88–9.

29 Ibid., p. 88.

30 This is the view Wilde develops in *The Decay of Lying* (originally published in 1889) in which he claims: 'Nature is no great mother who has borne us. She is our creation ...

At present, people see fogs, not because there are fogs, but because poets and painters have taught them the mysterious loveliness of such effects' Hazard Adams (ed.)(1971), *Critical Theory Since Plato*, New York: Harcourt Brace Jovanovich, p. 683).

31   Examples I have in mind here include Frank Lloyd Wright's Guggenheim Museum in New York City, Frank Gehry's Guggenheim in Bilboa, and Philip Johnson's Getty Museum with an accompanying garden by Robert Irwin.

32   Berleant (1992), *The Aesthetics of Environment*, p. 157.

33   Ibid., p. 9.

Index

Addison, Joseph 177, 184
aesthetic
    appreciation 2, 3, 5, 12, 14, 15, 18,
        26, 29, 30, 33–6, 61–73, 100,
        114, 116, 118, 120, 121, 124–6,
        172, 174, 177, 179, 180, 184
    awareness 34, 157, 158, 167
    capacities 122, 132, 133, 138
    culture 39, 41, 43, 45
    disinterestedness 14, 183
    engagement 1, 12, 120, 124, 153,
        155
    environment 13
    homogeneity 104
    offence 119, 120
    senses 7
    theory 2–5, 17, 23, 25, 37, 84, 181
    value 9, 10, 13, 15–18, 91, 95, 110,
        113–15, 117, 118, 120, 123–5,
        127–9, 131, 132, 136, 180
aesthetics of nature 6, 14, 17, 62, 127,
    141, 172
affordances 96, 97
Africa 10
America 10
American landscape gardening 111
Americanization 106
amphitheaters 16
animal husbandry 106
anthropologists 20, 144
anthropology 4, 144, 153
antiphonal music 147
anti-suburban barbs 104
applied aesthetics 14, 100, 120, 122, 126
archetypal
    activity 84
    metaphor 76, 78, 86
architectural poverty 104
architecture 1, 2, 4, 12, 14, 39, 44, 45,
    47, 72, 74, 79, 84, 85, 87, 89–91,

95–101, 115, 159, 162, 163, 166,
    176, 179, 182
Aristotle 47, 80, 122, 135, 140
Arjas, Inari 154
art
    culture 42
    education 44
    institution 44, 45
    theory 4
    world 24, 40, 42, 45, 46
art and nature 3, 47, 48, 50
autonomism 115, 117, 118, 121, 122,
    125

Bali 10
Balmori, D. 111
Barthes, Roland 155
basic aesthetic values 24
Baxandall, R. 111
beauty 3, 5, 7, 15, 16, 20, 21, 26, 30,
    33, 41, 43, 46, 65, 73, 89, 91, 95,
    98–100, 105, 110, 116, 117, 120–
    122, 124, 126–32, 134–7, 139–41,
    146, 150, 161, 166, 176
being 1, 4, 6, 16, 18, 20, 27, 29, 31,
    33–7, 40, 44, 45, 48, 51, 55–9, 63,
    67, 70, 76, 79–83, 85, 92–4, 99,
    119, 121, 125, 129, 132, 135, 139,
    143, 145, 146, 151, 153, 154, 158,
    162, 169, 176, 178–80, 182, 183
Bell, Clive 118, 125
Benjamin, Walter 100
Ben-Joseph, E. 111
Berleant, Arnold 26, 37, 46, 55, 59, 140
Binford, H. C. 111
biodiversity 128, 135
biology 4, 65, 139, 144
body 7, 8, 10, 12, 15, 20, 68, 75–7,
    79–82, 84–6, 95, 100, 143–55,
    158, 169, 173, 175, 176

Bormann, F. H. 111
Brady, Emily 37, 120, 121, 126, 141
Brennan, M. 53, 59
bridges in Japan 165, 167
Brooklyn 104, 109
Bruser, Madeline 154
Bullough, Edward 180, 184

Candomblé 147, 154
Carlson, Allen 19, 21, 62, 64, 65, 72,
    73, 100, 120, 125, 173, 184
Cartesianism 144
ceramics 15, 84, 85
charged field 145
Chemetov, Paul 100
China 10
Christo 5, 69–71, 177
city development 111
Close Encounters of the Third Kind 69,
    71
color 7, 8, 10, 11, 71, 75, 110, 130,
    132, 135, 143, 147, 165, 180
common sense 7, 48, 49, 65
composition 11, 105, 108, 152
conflict and resolution 134–6
connections 7, 31, 51, 82, 140, 146,
    154
consciousness 7, 8, 12, 25, 27, 36, 130,
    143, 146, 149, 151
conservation 45, 101, 114, 120, 123,
    124, 126–31, 137, 138
contact receptors 7, 8
continuities 7
contour 8
convention 148, 164
Craig, David 54, 59
cranes 129, 130, 137–9
Crawford, Donald 120, 125
criticism 2, 4, 8, 13, 19, 21, 23, 29, 43,
    62, 65, 66, 71, 73, 79, 91, 100,
    111, 114, 115, 118, 120, 121, 123,
    125, 126, 173, 176, 177, 184
cultural
    aesthetic 9, 20
    environment 2, 9, 20, 146
    philosophy 43
    theory 103, 111
culture 1, 2, 3, 4, 5–11, 15, 17, 18, 20,
    31, 39, 41–5, 50, 51, 54–7, 68, 69,

72, 76–9, 82–4, 86, 87, 89–96, 98,
    99, 103–105, 110, 111, 114, 120,
    126, 138, 139, 144–7, 151–3, 160,
    173, 182, 183

Dada 1
dance 1, 2, 5, 12, 16, 17, 147, 148, 154
Debussy, Claude 151
depth 8, 9, 12, 93, 96, 180
design 12, 14, 15, 44, 46, 84, 91, 95,
    97, 100, 105–107, 109, 111, 115,
    116, 133, 159, 161, 163, 165, 167,
    168, 173, 176, 179, 181, 184
Devereaux, Mary 113, 124
Devils Tower 67–71
Dickie, George 46, 183
Diffey, T.J. 46
digitized film lamination 168
directional motion 9
disengagement 26, 30
disinterested contemplation 3, 5
disinterestedness 14, 15, 26, 37, 183
distance 7, 8, 30, 37, 43, 134, 147, 160,
    163, 164, 168, 180, 184
distance receptors 7
diversity 25, 33, 44, 89, 91–5, 97, 99,
    108, 132, 133, 169, 183
Doordan, Dennis P. 46
dress 135, 146
Dreyfus, Hubert 55, 56, 59
dualistic premises 144
duty 127–9, 131, 138, 140

ear 147, 151
earthworks 120, 174, 177, 178, 182,
    184
Eaton, Marcia M. 121, 126
ecological
    harm 114
    responsibilities 33
ecology 44–6, 65, 100, 101, 114, 135,
    139, 146
Einfühlung 145, 154
electronic future 159
electronic media 5, 143, 144, 153
Elliot, Robert 100, 124, 126
embodied metaphor v
embodiment 81, 83, 86, 143–55
emotion 119, 122, 125, 163

engineering 133–5, 140, 161, 162, 167
English garden 105–107
enticement 96, 97
environmental
  aesthetics 3, 4, 9, 10, 12–15, 19, 20,
    46, 121, 126, 145, 154, 157,
    172, 181–3
  art 39, 44, 114, 120, 125, 126, 174,
    184
  culture 41, 42, 44
  education 39, 44, 45
  ethics 16, 20, 21, 46, 65, 73, 120,
    124, 126–9, 131, 138, 140
  experience 7, 8, 11–13, 75, 76, 86, 90
  world 40, 42
environments 2, 6, 12, 16, 18, 62–72,
    78, 89–92, 96–8, 115, 146, 163,
    168, 175, 176, 179, 182
epistemology 4
ethics v, 1, 4, 14–16, 19–21, 24, 37, 46,
    65, 73, 100, 113–16, 119–21,
    123–31, 137–41
experience v, 1–3, 5, 7–13, 18–20, 23,
    25–7, 29–36, 39, 41, 49, 52–4, 62,
    63, 73, 75–83, 85, 86, 90, 91, 95,
    100, 110, 113, 117, 119–28,
    130–39, 145–7, 152, 153, 155,
    158–61, 165, 166, 168, 172–80,
    182, 184
expression 23, 25, 30, 37, 48, 58, 60,
    81, 97, 98, 104, 121, 135, 146, 178

feeling 1, 24, 61, 75, 81, 90, 91, 97, 99,
    101, 113, 114, 117, 119, 120,
    123–5, 138, 143, 146, 149, 157,
    159, 161, 173
Ferren, Bran 157, 169
ferry 160
fiction 2, 48–50, 54, 57, 58, 69, 113,
    123
film 11, 21, 49, 69, 71, 113, 116, 158,
    159, 161–3, 168, 178, 184
Findlay, J.N. 37
flesh 75, 80, 138, 143, 145, 149, 150,
    154
folk category 144
food 7, 18, 20, 30, 96, 134, 146, 160
formalism 65, 180
Foster, Cheryl 116, 125

framing 95, 135

gardens 12, 13, 85, 105, 150
Geballe, G.T. 111
generosity 96, 97, 99
geographers 20
Gesamtkunstwerk 12
Gibson, J.J. 20, 154
Godlovitch, Stan 118, 125, 141
Goldsworthy, Andy 178, 184
Goodman, Nelson 49, 59
Grampp, C. 111
great analogy v, 39, 43
Greek chorus 11
Guernica 66, 68, 73
Guyer, Paul 122, 126

habitability 90, 97
habitat 89–91, 95–7, 100, 101, 134, 181
habitation 89, 90, 93, 139
Hare, R.M. 123, 126
harmony 51, 83, 86, 95, 96, 100, 111,
    114, 116, 119, 121–3, 133, 135,
    152, 173
hearing 7, 11, 138, 148
Heidegger, Martin 54, 55, 58–60, 101
Hepburn, Ronald 55, 59, 120, 126, 141,
    172, 184
Herzmaschine 162
high-tech 166, 168
Hildebrand, Grant 101
Hillman, James 46
historic structures 15
history
  of ideas 4
  of production 66–8, 71, 73
homogeneity 82, 103, 104, 108, 110
Honshu 160, 165
human
  environment 9, 122, 126, 146, 154
  values 18, 99
humans and nature 51–4
Hume, David 119, 122, 125, 126
humidity 8
hybridization 106

imagination 12, 26, 31, 33, 37, 75, 79,
    81, 85, 86, 91, 95, 121–4, 126,
    148, 161, 173, 174, 176, 177, 183

impala 132–6
impressionist music 151
Inland Sea 165
institutional theory
    of art 45
    of environment 45
intention 81, 110, 143, 172
interpenetration of body and place 8
Irisawa Hajime 158
isolation 3, 15, 31, 84

Japan ix, 10, 69, 157, 158, 160, 163,
    165, 166, 169, 174, 177

Kant, Immanuel 100, 122, 126, 176, 184
kinesthetic sense 8, 10
Kivi, Aleksis 51, 59
knowledge 11, 12, 29, 30, 33, 35, 44,
    62, 65–73, 81, 82, 90, 95, 100,
    105, 107, 114, 120, 121, 123, 126,
    131, 151, 152, 159, 162, 183
Kotaro Migishi 166
Kuhns, Richard 24, 37
Kyoto 166

La Cathédrale engloutie 151
land reclamation 181
landscape 6, 7, 9, 10, 12, 13, 15–17, 19,
    20, 30–34, 37, 41, 43–7, 53, 54,
    59, 61, 62, 64, 65, 73, 78–80, 82,
    90, 98, 104, 106–8, 110, 111, 114,
    115, 120, 123, 125, 126, 129–31,
    136, 137, 139, 140, 153, 155, 168,
    173, 174, 182, 184
    design 12
    preservation 15
Lang, Berel 153
Lawson, Trevor 114, 125
Leopold, Aldo 101, 124, 126, 140
life space 20
life world 36, 50–53, 55–8
light and shadow 9, 11
line 11, 49, 59, 62, 66, 72, 73, 80, 81,
    85, 137, 147, 148, 155
lines of force 9
lived space 20
lived time 20
Long Island 103
low tech 166

lower senses 175
Luddites 159, 160, 169

Makuhari 163, 164
marshes 33, 137
mass 8, 12, 105, 106
mathematics and aesthetics 133
meaning 6, 8, 9, 14, 20, 25, 40, 62,
    75–8, 81, 83–7, 143, 146, 164,
    175, 182
Meiji era 165
Meinig, D.W. 20
Melchionne, Kevin 111
Merleau-Ponty, Maurice 154
metaphysics 4, 35
Miho Museum 160, 167
mind 7, 9, 24, 32–4, 37, 48, 49, 58, 71,
    72, 80, 87, 90, 97, 113, 122–4,
    128, 133, 136, 144, 146, 148, 150,
    153, 158, 167, 177, 182, 185
Momaday, N.S. 68, 73
moon 31, 162
moral value 18, 115–18, 121
moralism 115, 116
Mount Rushmore 67, 69–71
movement 7–12, 20, 26, 27, 29, 32, 34,
    44, 65, 66, 78–83, 86, 93, 96, 132,
    144–8, 151, 153–5, 177, 180
movie set 166
Mumford, Lewis 111
music 1, 2, 5, 11–13, 16, 17, 25, 27, 47,
    52, 89, 113, 143, 146–9, 151–4,
    174, 176, 177

National Gallery of Art 157
native North America 10
natural
    beauty 3, 15, 21, 30, 41, 65, 73, 120,
        122, 126, 139
    environment v, 2, 64–70, 76, 77, 79,
        99, 113, 114, 117, 124, 141,
        163, 166, 173, 178, 184
nature v, 3–6, 12–14, 17–19, 21, 23, 25,
    27, 29–37, 39–41, 43, 45–8, 50–
    59, 61–8, 70, 72–9, 82, 83, 86, 89,
    92, 94, 98, 100, 105, 114, 116,
    118–120, 123–33, 135–9, 141,
    166, 168, 172–4, 178, 182–4
Nevada 44

New Babylon 163
New York City 66, 103, 162, 175, 182, 185
Nicolson, M. H. 61
North by Northwest 69, 71
Noyes, R. 59

Okinawa 165
olfactory sense 8
order 1, 7–9, 16, 29, 47, 55, 62, 64, 70, 75, 76, 78, 79, 92, 96–8, 105, 110, 114, 115, 121, 132–4, 144, 153, 159, 167, 168, 178, 183
organ 106, 147, 148, 154
organum 152

pachysandra 103, 107
pain 1, 8
painting 1, 4, 5, 11, 13, 17, 23, 27, 34, 39, 47, 54, 64, 84, 129, 147, 148, 163, 172, 173, 176, 177
Papanek, Victor 179, 184
parks 10, 13, 64, 105, 106, 139, 182
Passmore, John 124, 126
pastoral 105–7
Pater, Walter 155
pattern 7, 9, 10, 25, 81
perceiver 7, 14, 95, 96
perceptual
  system 9, 20
  world 8, 13
Philadelphia 19, 21, 26, 37, 55, 59, 105, 153, 155, 174, 184
physical landscape 20
piano 147, 148, 151, 152, 154, 161
picket fence 109
Pietà 68, 73
Plato 47, 83, 115, 182, 185
pluralist view of nature appreciation 72
poetry 2, 13, 17, 25, 47, 51, 53, 54, 59, 61, 63, 73, 115, 135, 136, 149, 155, 176
political science 4
popular arts 15
pressure 8, 105, 107
previsualization 167
Prospect Park 106
psychology 4, 24, 37, 180, 184
public spaces 106

question of aesthetic relevance v, 61–3, 72, 73

Rawles, Kate 114, 125
ready made 41
regional planning 4, 15
relationships 1, 7, 18, 25, 27, 57, 93, 139
Relph, Edward 101
representation 47, 48, 50, 58, 95, 116, 119, 137
representation in architecture 95
resource protection 15
respect for nature 123
rhododendron ponticum 114
rhythm 7, 44
Richardson, David B. 46
robots 158, 161, 168
Rosen, Charles 154
Rowe, P. 111

Sapporo 166
Sarajas, Annamari 53, 59
Sasaki, Ken-ichi 153
scenic beauty 130, 135
Schiller, Friedrich 26, 37, 122, 126
sculpture 1, 4–6, 16, 67, 173, 174, 178, 184
self 5, 7, 9, 23, 27, 29, 30, 34, 41, 45, 54–6, 80, 81, 95, 109, 124, 138, 139, 146, 163, 173, 174
sensation 8, 9, 11, 20, 175
senses 7, 8, 10, 11, 20, 101, 135, 138, 145, 161, 168, 174, 175
sensory channels 8, 11
Sepänmaa, Yrjö 46
sequence 7
shape 7–10, 62, 64, 65, 72, 133, 159, 163, 181
Shikoku 165
Shuri Castle 165
sight 7, 11, 26, 30, 123, 138, 176
sight and hearing 7
significant form 64
Sillanpää, F.E. 52, 59
sounds 2, 7, 8, 10, 12, 13, 16, 25, 32, 98, 116, 120, 147–9, 151, 152, 158, 160, 174
Southworth, M. 111

space 6–9, 12, 20, 29, 31, 45, 69–71,
    76, 79–81, 84, 87, 89, 90, 92, 93,
    96, 97, 104, 111, 133, 138, 145,
    147, 152, 154, 157, 164, 167,
    173–6, 178, 180
space aliens 157
Stevens, Wallace 149, 155
Stolnitz, Jerome 62, 73
subcutaneous perception 8
subjective 17, 18, 75, 86, 132, 133,
    138, 143, 145, 146, 153, 154, 163
subjectivism 143, 145
sublime 6, 53, 55, 59, 95, 100, 122
suburbanization 104, 106, 108, 111
suburbia 103, 104, 111
Sudnow, David 154
Sugiyama Kazuo 165
synaesthesia 8

tactile experience 8
Tajima, Jiro 165
Tajima Noriyuki 164
taste 8, 20, 24, 26, 37, 96, 114, 119,
    122, 125, 138, 143, 175, 176
tea ceremony 177
Technē 145, 153
technological innovations 167
technology 2, 85, 98, 100, 143, 157–68
technotrash 166
temperature 8, 9, 58, 93, 100, 175, 178
texture 8, 9, 75, 82, 148, 165, 172, 175,
    180
Teyssot, G. 111
'the' environment 6, 7, 9
theater 1, 2, 5, 6, 16, 45, 145, 148, 154,
    163, 174
theory of culture 4
timbre 7, 11
time 1, 7–9, 11, 13, 18–20, 23, 27,
    29–31, 33, 43, 44, 50, 51, 53,
    55–9, 61–3, 67, 69, 75, 76, 78–83,
    90–92, 94–7, 108, 109, 114, 122,

    124, 125, 133, 136, 138, 139, 144,
    145, 147, 148, 151, 154, 159, 161,
    163, 167, 176–80
Tokyo Bay 163, 164
Toledo, Ohio 106
tool 55, 56, 122, 176
tract housing 104
traditional aesthetic theory 2, 5
tunnel 160, 161, 167, 168

University of the Ryukyus 165
urban environment 2, 92, 93, 164
urban planning 12
urbanism 103

Valley Curtain 71, 174
value, aesthetic 16
vernacular-style town 166
Versailles 105
vestibular system 8
video art 5
virtual reality 5, 161
visceral sensation 8
visual sensory dimension 11
volume 8, 9, 21, 24, 37, 46, 85, 148, 155

Walton, Kendall 49, 59
Washington, DC 120, 126
Western philosophy 143, 144
Wilde, Oscar 48, 58, 118, 125
wilderness 14, 16, 19, 51, 53, 55, 111,
    139, 162
wildlife 114, 125, 135, 136
wildness 51, 135, 136, 139
Wittgenstein, L. 24, 32, 37, 38
wonder 26, 28, 36, 136–8
wood museum 166
Wordsworth, William 53, 59

Yeats, William Butler 153

Ziff, Paul 175, 183, 184